WOMEN, GENDER, AND HEALTH

Susan L. Smith and Nancy Tomes, Series Editors

DYING TO BE BEAUTIFUL

The Fight for Safe Cosmetics

Gwen Kay

THE OHIO STATE UNIVERSITY PRESS • COLUMBUS

Library of Congress Cataloging-in-Publication Data

Kay, Gwen.
Dying to be beautiful : the fight for safe cosmetics / Gwen Kay.
 p. ; cm.—(Women and health)
Includes bibliographical references and index.
ISBN 0–8142–0990–4 (cloth : alk. paper)—ISBN 0–8142–5138–2 (pbk. : alk. paper)—
ISBN 0–8142–9066–3 (cd) 1. Cosmetics—Law and legislation—United States—History.
2. Cosmetics industry—United States—History. 3. Cosmetics—Health aspects—United
States—History. I. Title. II. Women & health (Columbus, Ohio)
KF3896.K39 2005
346.7304′23—dc22
          2004021551

Cover design by Janna Thompson-Chordas.
Text design by Jennifer Forsythe.
Type set in Palatino.
Printed by Thompson-Shore, Inc.

The paper used in this publication meets the minimum requirements of the American
National Standard for Information Sciences—Permanence of Paper for Printed Library
Materials. ANSI Z39.48–1992.

9 8 7 6 5 4 3 2 1

"A POSITIVE ATTITUDE, COUPLED WITH A SUNNY DISPOSITION, GAVE ONE SUFFICIENT BEAUTY"

For Janice and Edwin Kay

contents

list of illustrations

acknowledgments

IN COSMETIC TERMS, the real "foundation" of this book was a graduate seminar I took at Yale University. When I first proposed looking at skin and beauty as representations of health, Frederic Holmes hid his doubts and allowed me to hop continents, oceans, and centuries to pursue this; James Hanley, Sarah Lewis, and Louise Palmer gracefully and helpfully read and commented on this in its earliest incarnation. Without Larry's encouragement, I do not think I would have pursued this topic for so long. I, as are many others, am indebted to him. John Warner guided, prodded, and asked me the right kinds of questions at the right times. I am also indebted to Rima Apple, Andrea Balis, Eileen Cheng, Naomi Rogers, Cynthia Russett, Nancy Tomes, and Elizabeth Toon for encouragement, questions, and, on occasion, answers. As (now-former) editors of the series, Rima Apple and Janet Golden have been very supportive and encouraging. James Harvey Young has been a superb, careful, and helpful reader. My work is better for his comments.

In working on this manuscript, I have been particularly grateful for grants for collection visits and for time to research. Two Sigerist Grants from Yale University provided funding for travel to locations and archives that might have otherwise been inaccessible. Thanks to Thomas LaPorte, Special Collections, Duke University; to Duke University for a collections grant enabling me to use Duke's Hartmann Center for Sales, Advertising, and Marketing History; to the J. Walter Thompson Archives; and to Anne Goldstein for hospitality in North Carolina. Grants from the American Institute for the History of Pharmacy enabled me to spend a summer at the National Archives, College Park and Washington, D.C.; the Library of Congress; and the libraries and special collections of the American Association of Family and Consumer Sciences (formerly the American Home Economics Association) and the General Federation of Women's Clubs. A travel grant to the Franklin and Eleanor Roosevelt Library in Hyde Park showed me a different side of the personalities I had seen only through newspaper accounts, official agency letters, and congressional hearings. FDA historians Suzanne White Junod and John Swann have been particularly helpful, suggesting new avenues to pursue and sources I had been unaware of and patiently and quickly answering my endless queries. A grant from the Hagley Museum and Center for Business History provided me with my first glimpse at previously hidden company records, thanks to Katina Manko's persistence and persuasion with Avon.

I thank the American section of the Société de Chimie Industrielle for awarding me their first summer research grant through the Chemical Heritage Foundation (CHF). The time, as well as the travel to collections to use the papers of Hazel Bishop and Madam C. J. Walker, helped me stretch this in new directions. I am particularly thankful to Leo Slater and CHF staff for suggesting certain collections and facilitating my access to unprocessed collections elsewhere. I also enjoyed conversations with members of the Société on topics ranging from Clairol's acquisition in the 1950s to new anecdotes about Hazel Bishop. I am also very thankful to Ned LeBeau and Wulf Kansteiner for the gift of time in the guise of a fellowship at the Mershon Center, The Ohio State University. An office, books delivered to my door, and efficient secretarial help all made my stay there very congenial and productive. As an added benefit, I presented a new chapter to a group interested in history of medicine at Ohio State, organized by John Burnham; I am indebted for their critical comments.

Friends and family have helped me far more than words can express. I am particularly thankful to D. George Joseph and Jef Sneider for carefully reading the entire manuscript in different versions. I am still indebted to Natalia and Janice Kay for acting as able research assistants, helping me to copy, collate, and listen to me make sense of various articles and pieces of a life. Twice my parents have left the country for extended periods of time at critical writing junctures; each time their departure added to my work load. I can now safely predict when they will travel to Africa, based on future scholarship plans. From my parents I learned to love reading, I was encouraged to pursue what mattered to me, and to try new things. And so I dedicate this book, with love, to my parents, who remain convinced I still look better without anything on my face.

introduction

HOW CAN ONE story have so many different versions, so many different "lives," and so many different impacts? The combination of professional attention and a young girl's letter to a highly popular president contribute to the answer. The perseverance and personal interest of a certain FDA employee fostered a relationship that might otherwise have never occurred. On the professional, or medical, side, there was a case report, one of many, documenting and warning others about Lash Lure, an eyelash and eyebrow dye. As described by Drs. McCally, Farmer, and Loomis, in 1933 a woman about to be honored by the local PTA went to her local beauty shop to "get done." Her blind devotion to the pursuit of beauty cost her dearly: five days after her eyebrows and eyelashes were "touched up," ulcers formed in both her right and left corneas. She lost vision in both eyes. "She is entering into a number of her usual social and household activities," her physicians reported, describing her recovery. "She is especially interested in doing all in her power to stop the use of harmful cosmetics and in preventing similar and other injuries happening to other women from the same cause."[1] This case report, not the first on Lash Lure's ill effects, was one of four published in the November 11, 1933, issue of *Journal of the American Medical Association* (*JAMA*).[2] There had been similar cases before, and cases continued to appear after the report. While tragic, it appeared as if the patient was remaining optimistic in the face of darkness. And she had not died, as others had.

The second time this case appeared was in a letter written to President Franklin D. Roosevelt. The writing of this letter was not atypical. Many regarded the president and first lady as accessible, personable, approachable, and responsive, and many took pen to paper to express themselves to these national figures.[3]

1

Dear President Roosevelt,

My mother has been trying to put a new law so that no more poison will
be put in this dye. The dye is made by Lash Lure Co., in California. My
mother is totally blind and we want you to please help us get the law
across.

 I am ten years old and in the fifth grade. My dog was killed lately but
I still have my cat. I will close now, and I hope you will help my mother.

Sincerely yours,
Hazel Fay Musser[4]

What happened to this woman and her daughter? Did they truly have
no protection from Lash Lure and other cosmetics? Was President Roosevelt Hazel Fay's only recourse? And, was the cosmetic section of
department stores, salons, and boutiques rife with potential dangers
such as those detailed by this ten-year-old observer?

 In 1933, Lash Lure induced severe allergic reactions in women sus-
ceptible to paraphenylenediamine (PPD). Without any federal laws regulating cosmetics, or, more specifically, their ingredients, consumers had
little reassurance that many of their daily purchases and habits were
safe. In 2005, temporary tattoos and henna/mehndi products contain
PPD, despite laws specifically delineating acceptable PPD use. Has anything changed in the intervening seventy years to create a safer environment for consumers?

 Recent scholarship on cosmetics has largely ignored the devastating
effect of serious accidents.[5] When problems are mentioned, the public
response is not, in part because it is difficult to gauge individual
response and purchasing habits. I would argue, however, that one can
gain a sense of public discomfort and distrust about unregulated cosmetics, not only through decreasing sales following well-publicized
local or national accidents, but through activism—new or renewed—for
greater consumer protection following each incident. When, in a 1933
Paramount newsreel, a government official mentioned (not by brand
name) that a mascara had blinded women, all mascara sales immediately fell precipitously. Sales did soon rebound, but attention to and lobbying for regulation of cosmetics, part of a larger 1930s consumer movement, gained renewed vigor. The anonymous woman blinded by an
unnamed but popular cosmetic served to remind others why this perhaps trivial issue—cosmetics—was important enough to be a part of a
fight to strengthen extant food and drug laws.

The leading proponents for inclusion of cosmetics in a new law, as Hazel Fay Musser had implored the president to do, were mostly women's organizations and consumer groups. As their grandmothers had been before them, women in the Progressive Era expanded their domestic sphere of influence to the communal level, arguing that such activism was justifiable.[6] Some of the causes embraced by these women were immediate and local, such as prostitution, while others had broader social implications, such as temperance.[7]

By the time the Socialist tract on life in Packingtown, Upton Sinclair's *The Jungle*, disgusted and galvanized the public in 1905, the Women's Christian Temperance Union (WCTU) and the General Federation of Women's Clubs (GFWC) had been at work for more than a decade, promoting laws to protect consumers. The organizational structure of the WCTU and the GFWC, similar to many women's organizations of this time, relied on activism on the local level: a national committee or department might suggest certain issues for consideration by all local chapters, but local conditions and social problems always took precedence.

The lack of universal consumer protection for products ingested into or put on the body was recognized by women activists, government officials, and others long before the 1933 mascara incident. Consumer protection had been a critical part of the Progressive agenda, so much so that many women's organizations devoted considerable energy to these varied efforts. One law clearly benefited from women's groups' campaigning and grassroots activism. The 1906 Pure Food and Drugs Act, the first successful national attempt at comprehensive food and drug regulation, was a testament to the tireless work of a generation of women activists. Within a decade, however, new and old industries exploited loopholes, and many activists had turned their attention elsewhere, believing that all problems had been solved.[8]

One of the groups most dissatisfied with the law was the very agency charged with enforcement, the Bureau of Chemistry. In annual reports as early as 1918, the bureau bemoaned both a lack of funding and a lack of true protection for consumers. Many consumers assumed protection where none existed, unconsciously expanding the power of the law and the enforcement ability of the bureau to protect them. As bureau chief Harvey Wiley and his successors were quick to point out, the 1906 Pure Food and Drugs Act offered only limited food and drug protection. As the market for medical devices and cosmetics and advertising grew, the absence of laws regulating these products became more noticeable. Until some dramatic events occurred, and a clever FDA-sponsored propaganda campaign began, few people knew which products escaped FDA purview, and even fewer consumer activists did anything about it.

Mrs. Musser offered one approach to this problem of dangerous and unprotected products (see figure 1). Women's and consumer groups in the 1920s and early 1930s exemplify the grassroots activism necessary to create a groundswell of support to convince legislators of the importance of these issues. In the case of consumer protection issues—the focus of this book—this activism is even more important, because laws that protect and benefit consumers often come at the expense of large and powerful industries better equipped to lobby legislators. This, then, is a tale of consumer activism from the vantage point of organizations and agencies who sought to improve the 1906 law by guaranteeing women protection at their dressing and dinner tables.

I argue that some well-publicized incidents caused by unregulated products, particularly cosmetics, spurred consumer activism in the years from 1900 to 1945. These dramatic incidents were caused by seemingly innocuous products used by millions of women on a daily basis. If a simple mascara product caused some women to lose movement, sight, or even life, how could one know with assurance which products were safe and which were not? An even more immediate question for mascara wearers was: what made one product harmful and another harmless? How could women know which products contained what ingredients? Some women consumers became increasingly alarmed with the limits of oversight and protection offered by the government. Activist consumers ran the gamut from Alice Lakey, who in concert with FDA Chief Walter Campbell revived the moribund Pure Food League to work for revision of the 1906 Pure Food and Drugs Act, to Ruth deForest Lamb, an advertising copywriter turned FDA information officer; from Duke University law professor David Cavers, who helped craft the first version of the revision, to Royal Copeland, a homeopathic physician turned senator who touted the benefits of Fleischmann's yeast even as he sponsored legislation to overhaul the 1906 Pure Food and Drugs Act.

Newly styled consumer activists pressed for enhanced legislation and protection in the 1920s and 1930s even as government officials were pressing consumers to assume more responsibility for their own health. Consumers advocated change, just as public health officials were doing the same thing. In several cities—notably San Francisco and New York City—vigilant public health officials outlawed specific ingredients or products to protect their citizens, well ahead of federal law or, industry charged, without sufficient scientific proof of danger. What occurred on

FIGURE 1. Mrs. Musser demonstrating the ill effects of Lash Lure. (Courtesy of FDA History Office.)

the local level was often mirrored, later, on the national level. In virtually every instance of food and drug law change on any level, a serious incident provoked some segment of the population to demand increased protection. Starting on a local level, or focusing on one particular product, yielded big dividends for those determined to protect consumers. It was grassroots political activism, combined with the power of personal tragic stories, I argue, that ultimately challenged, and changed, national law culminating in the 1938 Food, Drug, and Cosmetic Act.

We see this pattern today: a sudden tragic event or a growing number of problems suddenly grab the headlines and force the government to make new policy. But it is never that sudden or that unexpected; instead, groups have been lobbying Congress and government agencies for stricter laws, greater enforcement, and more protection. The most recent examples—mad cow disease and ephedra—only underscore my contention. In less than a week, the USDA changed policy on which cows were and were not acceptable, increased testing for disease, and restricted what parts of cattle would end up in the human or animal food chains. And the USDA was criticized for doing too little, too late, to protect the American public. After all, our European counterparts have had similar laws in place for several years, but their regulatory agencies do not also promote the beef industry, a group with far more lobbying power, access, and clout than the scattered but concerned populace. The recent ban of ephedra by the FDA has led to sharp criticism of that agency for allowing this product to be on the market. Most Americans are still unaware of the FDA's limited regulatory powers on minerals, supplements, and vitamins, a limitation due to the successful lobbying of the health food industry. The federal changes that recently occurred, which serve to benefit and improve our health, were laws and policies that have been suggested and lobbied for by small grassroots organizations for years. They patiently laid the groundwork, thus setting the stage for a quick policy change.

The first chapter of this book examines some of the women's organizations and individuals active in and critical to the passage of the 1906 Pure Food and Drugs Act. Recent scholarship on the 1906 law has shed new light on the depth and commitment of women's organizations to this cause, particularly the WCTU and the GFWC. According to Lorine Goodwin, the local chapters maintained their vigilance following passage of the 1906 law to ensure adequate, prompt, and vigorous enforcement. These women fixed their attention on the now-regulated food and drugs, even as they continued to use other, nonregulated, products. Of particular concern to me is the growth of the cosmetics industry concurrent with this push for governmental oversight in the form of regulations. Just as more people were buying mass-produced food, drink, and drugs rather than making their own, some beauty products, starting with soaps and creams, were also being commercially produced. Yet cosmetics, with their potentially dangerous ingredients, were free of government scrutiny.

In the second chapter, I discuss the growth of the cosmetic market through the early 1930s. In 1900, the cosmetics industry was small, almost negligible, with sales less than $100,000. An emphasis on youth, particularly after World War I, and an increasing homogeneity of culture fostered by mass-circulation magazines and the golden years of advertising helped spur sales of cosmetics. Wholesale figures gathered by the Commerce Department suggest that young women were not the only ones making up their faces, with sales hitting an estimated $125,000,000 retail in the mid-1920s. All the cosmetics made, sold, and applied created a new job niche. The women (and men) creating cosmetics, the advertising employed to stimulate sales, and the legions of women who found their calling in beauty salons are the focus of this chapter.

The third chapter returns to the theme of activism from a multiplicity of perspectives. The women's organizations that had worked so hard for protection by and passage of the 1906 Pure Food and Drugs Act gradually turned their attention elsewhere. The formation of consumer groups, particularly Consumers' Research, in the late 1920s helped to fill this gap. Although not specifically concerned with cosmetics, Consumers' Research advocated safety and value for one's dollar, themes that echoed the sentiments of an earlier generation of women activists. Physicians, particularly those who saw the effects of "cosmetics gone bad"—often allergic reactions—were concerned about these unregulated products that could cause such discomfort, distress, and, in some cases, disfigurement.

The fourth chapter analyzes the impact of "guinea pig" books and five years of congressional debate and discussion surrounding possible revision of the 1906 act. Questions about revision of the law—how much, to what extent, what products—extended beyond concerned legislators and industries. Consumer organizations and women's groups testified at congressional hearings, made revision of the law a priority for their legislative agendas, and followed the permutations of the proposed law through Senate and House committees. For various reasons, however, most consumers remained almost wholly ignorant of this possible legislation. Unlike other, more visible, pieces of New Deal legislation such as the Agricultural Adjustment Act or the Tennessee Valley Authority, this legislation promised immediate protection and benefits for all citizens regardless of geographic location, occupation, economic status, race, or sex. Despite years of careful lobbying, it took an accident—a toxic combination of drugs resulting in the deaths of 114 people—to force the hand of legislators to end an interagency dispute and *do* something.

The fifth chapter assesses the immediate impact and aftermath of the 1938 law. As had happened in 1906, consumer groups relied on the FDA to do its job and began to turn their attention elsewhere. Consumer confidence in the agency seems to have been borne out, thanks to the aggressive seizure policies endorsed by FDA Chief Walter Campbell. Almost as soon as the law was signed by President Franklin Roosevelt in June 1938, the agency seized a product—Lash Lure—in violation of the just-passed law. A second large and well-publicized seizure of a French lipstick reinforced public perceptions of enforcement and reassured both the complacent public and skeptical activists that the agency was "on the job." Just as the attention of women's and consumer organizations turned to the war effort in 1940 and 1941, new problems with cosmetics emerged, provoked in part by war-induced chemical shortages. But the FDA, aided by alert physicians, nipped problems in the bud.

The epilogue briefly touches on more recent examples of consumer activism with regard to the food and drug supply. Individuals continue to have the greatest impact, from Frances Kelsey and her role in keeping thalidomide off the market in the United States, to the hundreds of thousands of health food customers who besieged Congress in the 1970s and 1990s to prevent FDA regulation of vitamins and nutritional supplements. As it had prior to the 1938 Food, Drug, and Cosmetic Act, the beauty industry has continued to grow in unexpected ways, from targeting men to (semi)permanent solutions, including plastic surgery and Botox injections.

This book adds to our body of knowledge in understanding the 1938 law, but more importantly it demonstrates how everyday people on a local level contributed to a national policy shift. In the process of debating this law, the vocal and visible presence of educated and activist consumers persuaded manufacturers of the need for stricter rules: not only would fly-by-night operators and disreputable manufacturers be drummed out of business, but reputable manufacturers stood to gain public approbation for their willingness, nay desire, to be regulated by an outside agency rather than internal, informal policy. Because ultimately, although consumers can impact regulation and legislation on multiple levels, their real power is in the marketplace, determining the success or failure of a product.

chapter one

"A victory of the women of this country"

THE TRADITIONAL role of women encompasses everything related to the care and maintenance of a home, from the physical structure and comforts to the well-being of its inhabitants. This entailed that women meet the clothing, health, and food needs of their families either through personal production or through commercial purchase. As consumers, women have a vested interest in getting good, quality products. As the locus of production shifted out of the home throughout the nineteenth century, and women bought rather than made some items for home consumption, tainted or adulterated food became an issue. No housewife wanted to feed her family substandard food, nor did she want to make unwise economic decisions and squander money on poor products. And, she wanted to look good, either through her own exertions or through powders, creams, and the like.

● ● ●

In 1820, chemist Frederick Accum published a volume of chemical analyses of foodstuffs to determine true product composition.[1] His work revealed what some consumers had begun to assume: the foods they purchased had been adulterated in some fashion, for better looks and higher profit.[2] One concern for many women was the complete absence of standards for food and drug products. Women, the chief purchasing agents for each family, had no way of knowing how "good" a product might actually be, thus possibly impairing the family's health, and squandering the budget on worthless products. "Applesauce" could contain vastly different percentages of apples, water, sugar or even corn syrup. Milk thinned out with water, milk doctored with chemicals to restore the white color, and milk completely untainted could all be sold as "milk." Drugs and patent medicines with dangerous or useless ingredients could claim any manner of cure, without fear of reprisal. Foods with fill and other substances, and drugs that delayed rather than advanced medical treatment, took their toll on consumer health and wealth. The situation needed to be remedied. The 1848 Drug Importation Act, signed into law by President James Polk, prohibited importing adulterated drugs. By 1880, however, this law was rarely enforced.

During the 46th Congress (1879–1881), four bills regarding adulteration were introduced. In every subsequent congressional session, at least one bill to rein in food, drink, or drug production was introduced. The products regulated, however, were commercially produced items; anything produced in the home was exempted, including some common remedies and cosmetics. Not only was it buyer beware, but also user beware. This implies, wrongly, that home-produced goods were as safe as, if not safer than, commercially made ones.

Each of the proposed bills in Congress reflected mass-produced items. Those items made within the home, such as cosmetics, could be equally, or more, dangerous than manufactured items, but were excluded. The abundance of recipes for salves, lotions, rouges, dentifrices, hair compounds, and the like in household cookbooks, domestic manuals, and cosmetic books attested to woman's ingenuity. These various books were written in the tradition of domestic medical manuals, offering not a "guide for right living," as Charles Rosenberg contends William Buchan's *Domestic Medicine* did, but rather as a guide for right skin.[3] Espousing the qualities of cleanliness and health, these late-nineteenth-century volumes catered to a self-conscious middle order able to afford the time and ingredients necessary to formulate the lotions and creams. The items for home manufacture were arranged by product. Most if not all of the ingredients for the various powders and emulsions could be purchased from the local pharmacist. Ingredients in hand, women could concoct their own products, tailoring color or fragrance to their own needs and desires. Because this was done ad hoc, it is difficult to know how many women wore how much of anything; the existence of these receipt books, however, does strongly suggest that women were, indeed, making their own products. The recipes were often variants on a theme; soap, lotion, and cold cream, for example, have the same key ingredients but assume a different chemical form.[4] Most recipes were proscriptive: a lotion for smooth skin, a perfume for the hair. Occasionally, the books offered prophylactic measures: sunburn remedies for those in need, freckle removers for those so afflicted. The constituents of these homemade beautifiers, however, often made them dangerous to one's skin and one's health.

The ingredients in the recipes ranged from the mundane—potash, spermaceti—to the aromatic—rose water, lavender oil—to the possibly dangerous—lead, mercury, copper, tin, arsenic, bismuth. Most, if not all, of these ingredients, safe or not, were available from the local pharmacist. The dangers inherent in other products, particularly homemade and commercial cosmetics—creams, blushes, and lotions—had not gone unnoticed. Recipe books called for bismuth, lead, and mercury even as they warned of their dangers. An 1866 treatise prefaced the recipe for an arsenical lotion with a warning that arsenic was "always an objectionable compound, on account of involving the use of a dangerous and insidious poison."[5] Several pages of the same manual warned of the dangers of rouge and carmine made with bismuth, lead, or mercury. About the last ingredient, the author was not so sanguine: "[T]heir constant use imparts to the skin a sallow hue and a leathery appearance, which is far from pleasing, whilst spasmodic tremblings of the muscles of the face, ending in partial or complete paralysis, have been known to be . . . produced by them. [They] act as slow, it may be very slow, poisons, by [gradually] being taken up by the absorbents of the skin, the one gradually producing all the symptoms of 'lead poisoning,' the other of 'mercurial poisoning,' including salivation."[6] The combination of the frank acknowledgment of adverse health consequences and the seemingly ubiquitous nature of these books suggests the widespread presence and discreet use of cosmetics on many a dressing table.

Making one's own cosmetics, as with any homemade product, had both its advantages and its disadvantages. Women had a great deal of control over the final product, from quantity to quality, depending on what one could afford. Because men either did not realize or did not know that women were applying quite so many things to their visages, many women applied their toilette with a light hand, the better to go unnoticed (and yet more beautiful). Simple recipes can create problems; many women must have discovered that they were allergic to something in their powders, particularly their face powders, as rice is a frequent allergen. One disadvantage of making one's own beauty products is that the results were not consistent from batch to batch; ingredients were not always available; and it was time consuming.

One beauty item, however, was firmly moved out of the home and into the realm of mass manufacture (and advertising)—soap. Soap was intended to clean, and to alter the appearance, if one believed the advertising surrounding these products; in this latter definition, it also met the definition of cosmetics, which was a product patted, rubbed, or otherwise put on the body to beautify, improve, or otherwise alter one's appearance. The mass manufacture of soap reflected a confluence of circumstances: a surplus of fat rendering from Cincinnati's hog slaughterhouses, a wave of industrialization, and savvy candle makers.[7] In addition, national periodicals, enabled by increased rates of literacy and better transportation to get magazines (and goods) distributed nationally, helped "sell" products. Advertisements for soaps of various manufactures played on Victorian sensibilities of cleanliness, and newly emerging middle-class ideals of bathing and proper behavior.[8] Soap as a cleansing agent, and a method of avoiding germs and disease, is a good selling point; as a beautifier, however, it poses some problems, not the least of which is soap manufacturers did not want to be categorized as beauty aids, but as toiletries.

A few commercial firms manufacturing cosmetics sprang up alongside soap companies and proprietary medicine houses. Creams and powders were time consuming to make. Some women who used these items did not object to buying rather than concocting their own products, as long as they could do so discretely. One such company, Harriet Hubbard Ayer, commenced production of Récamier Cream in 1886 and continued to play a significant role in cosmetic manufacturing circles through the 1940s. The cream itself was unexceptional, a fairly standard and generic recipe. However, it was packaged and advertised well: promotional literature hinted at a royal pedigree of French ancestry, and printed letters of endorsement from prominent society women and fashionable entertainers, including "Jersey" Lily Langtry, Sarah Bernhardt, and Lillian Russell.

Just as the beauty standard changed, so too did cosmetic items. Although actresses wore what could be termed "full makeup," most women limited their toilette to rouge, powder, and lotion, falling far short of the more dramatic—and blatant—mascara and eyeshadow. And since commercial production reflected taste and usage (as those desiring more could make it themselves), most cosmetic companies manufactured only face powders and lotions in the 1880s and 1890s.[9] Despite public perceptions to the contrary, there was a demand for these cosmetic items.

Like other woman entrepreneurs, particularly in the cosmetics industry, Harriet Hubbard Ayer created and sold cosmetics to support her family. After she moved her daughters from Chicago to New York City in the mid-1880s, she asked her husband for a divorce.[10] Initially,

Ayer worked in a furnishings shop but soon tried to sell a French facial cream to her clientele instead. Realizing that she needed outside financial backing for her new venture, she persuaded a former furnishings client (and her daughter's future father-in-law), Jim Seymour, to lend her $50,000. In exchange, she gave him stock as collateral, to be returned as she repaid the loan. This aid had tragic consequences, as no legal documents were signed or exchanged regarding the particulars of this agreement.[11] As the company became more successful, Ayer fought Seymour for control of her company and eventually became enmeshed in a convoluted lawsuit in 1889. Days after the suit ended in 1893, she was committed, either voluntarily or involuntarily, to a mental asylum. While incarcerated, she lost control of her company.

After her release in 1894, Ayer wrote a women's column for Joseph Pulitzer's *New York World* focusing on beauty and appearance, diet, exercise, and mental well-being. She also wrote a book on this topic.[12] At her death in 1902, she was unconnected with the company that bore her name. She had, however, pioneered many innovative strategies in the beauty business, including using her own name on products, celebrity endorsements, and creating or inventing long and illustrious lineages for her products.

The essential issue in what to produce commercially is: how many people will use this product? Soap was a universal product, used by everyone; its increasing availability led to increased use. Cosmetics, however, were a different story. Visibly worn, cosmetics adorned the faces of prostitutes and actresses, the latter as part of the costume.[13] The boundary between prostitution and trading favors was a slippery one, but clearly no "good woman" wore cosmetics.[14] Actresses arguably wore cosmetics as part of their costume, but again, good women did not pursue this calling (instead, they chose the sensible path of marriage). Other women did in fact wear cosmetics, applied with such a light hand as to render its presence almost invisible. The most common item worn was face powder to even out the complexion or make it fairer. Particularly in the summer months, and in the South, this was part of the way to prove one's status; women who were afforded a life of leisure would possess fair skin, while those forced to work, often outdoors, would have a tan, burn, or even freckles. Sun exposure also hastens aging and wrinkles, all counter to the ideal smooth, lineless face. Other items may have included discrete use of face and lip rouge. Hand and face creams were considered necessities more than cosmetics, a way to combat the realities of manual labor and add to the illusion of class. According to manufacturing census data on toilet items, with which cosmetics were included before gaining enough market share to become their own category, sales of cosmetics in 1900 stood at about $100,000.[15]

●   ●   ●

Given the many products available, from soap to soup, how was one to know what was safe? Who could be relied on to perform this service? Chemical analysis was the best method to determine purity of a food, drink, or drug. Late-nineteenth-century public health departments and personnel reflected Progressive ideas about the possibilities, responsibilities, and limits of the government.[16] As historian Judith Walzer Leavitt has suggested, municipal and state public health officials assumed increasing responsibility in those public health arenas when conditions were propitious.[17] These public health activities of the late 1800s included cleaning municipal water supplies, installing sewage and sanitation systems, regulating regional food production, and monitoring milk production facilities and slaughterhouses.[18] Those laws regulating food and beverages on the municipal and state levels existed to improve the health and well-being of its residents. The laws at the local level often reflected effective lobbying and organizing by women's organizations using their claim of maternal commonwealth as justification for political activism.

Clearly, then, change was in the air. Congress debated food and drug adulteration; public health officials and interested citizens in New York, New Jersey, Massachusetts, and elsewhere lobbied for and enforced laws investigating factories and other sites of food production.[19] Persons concerned about public health issues, including physicians, lawyers, and social workers, sought positions in which they could effectively carry forward their agenda. Harvey Washington Wiley, a chemist at the new Purdue University, became chief chemist for the state of Indiana, and subsequently assumed the position of head of the Bureau of Chemistry in the U.S. Department of Agriculture in 1883.[20] Like other public health officials, Wiley's personal politics influenced and shaped his political agenda. Initially concerned with glucose adulteration, Wiley considered adulteration on a wider scale, studying butter, milk, and oleomargarine in 1887. The Department of Agriculture's *Bulletin #13*, a ten-part series assessing food adulterants, developed over a sixteen-year period and ran to more than 1,400 pages.[21]

Home economists, concerned with the negative effects of product adulteration on consumer health, also used laboratory science to their advantage. A new branch of social science particularly appealing to women, home economics combined physiology, chemistry, economics, social work, and education with Progressive ideals.[22] One goal of this new discipline was to educate consumers in all manner of daily life, thus ensuring that consumer health and safety were not sacrificed for producer wealth. These scientists-cum-consumer advocates analyzed foods, drinks, and drug product composition. Laboratory tests often revealed the presence of wholesale impurities: chicory in coffee, dyes in brown sugar, sawdust in flour. Without such tests, consumers could not check the veracity of manufacturer claims and might inadvertently squander family resources and contribute to the family's ill health. Home economists pursued the campaign for "pure food" because it meshed with their new field of endeavor in incorporating science in the home, and because it reinforced the ideology of woman to protect her family.[23] Mobilizing via academic constellations, social organizations and moral concerns, millions of ordinary women motivated by the science of home economics or their sense of womanly duty worked to ensure consideration, if not passage, of a pure food and drugs bill.

Other women joined the fight for pure food and drugs. As Karen Blair has demonstrated, many women's organizations in the nineteenth century shifted from individual self-improvement and cultural uplift to communal concerns about social conditions.[24] The women who belonged to many of these groups, upper-class and white, would most likely not have worn (visible) cosmetics at the beginning of the century. After all, these were respectable women. When Congress first began to consider regulating foodstuffs and drugs in the late 1880s, cosmetics were among those manufactured items whose days of unchecked freedom seemed numbered. Cosmetics fell within the rubric of "drug" in an 1897 version of a food and drugs bill, but that section of legislation was dropped in 1900 in exchange for the support of a grocers' association and never appeared again.[25] Three women's organizations, whose members may have worn powder or used creams, that were involved in the long battle for pure food legislation were the Women's Christian Temperance Union (WCTU), the General Federation of Women's Clubs (GFWC), and the National Consumers League (NCL). The actions of each group reflected the founding principles of that particular organization.

The WCTU began near Cleveland, Ohio, in 1874. Combining evangelical religious fervor with recurring ideas about alcohol, women picketed, occupied, and (temporarily) shut down saloons one at a time, city by city. The WCTU opposed alcohol, citing religious and family claims, and judiciously played on woman's role as the moral guardian of her family. As the WCTU expanded, departments within the organization developed to better direct the flow of information. Of particular importance in the fight for pure foods and drugs were the Departments of Social Purity, Hygiene (later Health), Heredity, Scientific Instruction, Legislation, Medical Temperance, and Narcotics.[26] The WCTU's campaign for scientific instruction in physiology and hygiene in the public schools taught members to lobby effectively for changes in the education curriculum.[27] In accordance with its mission for temperance (and later abstinence), the WCTU embraced removing alcohol and narcotics from all proprietary drugs. By 1905, however, membership in the WCTU was declining, and the WCTU ceded leadership in the pure food and drugs campaign to the GFWC and NCL.[28]

The WCTU was, at the turn of the century, the largest women's organization in the United States. There was also significant crossover of members between the WCTU and the GFWC, a common situation for women committed to and involved in social change. More than the WCTU, the GFWC helped unite women for a common cause.[29] The GFWC, founded in 1890, united several extant regional women's groups, notably Sorosis (a New York group founded in 1868), the New England Women's Club (in Boston, also founded in 1868), and the Chicago Women's Club (founded 1876), and shifted the emphasis to community service.[30] The national organization loosely unified local chapters into a national entity while emphasizing local autonomy. The national board might suggest campaigns or issues for a given year, but each local chapter decided which topics suited their particular situation. The GFWC, unlike the WCTU, did not have semi-autonomous departments, although committees for legislation and other areas existed. In response to increasing concern by its members on the food and drug issue, the GFWC established a Pure Food League, headed by Alice Lakey.[31] A member of both the GFWC chapter and a consumer protection league in Cranford, New Jersey, Lakey embraced the cause after Harvey Wiley gave a speech on the need for food and drug regulation. In her role as head of the GFWC's Pure Food League, she coordinated action with other women's organizations. Anna Kelton, another GFWC member, was similarly inspired. Following her marriage to Harvey Wiley, Anna Kelton Wiley's continued presence and commitment to food and drug legislation demonstrated her loyalty to consumers' rights for protection even as she started a family. In contrast to the WCTU, which received little public attention, for reasons that shall become clear later, the GFWC was visible.

The third important women's organization in this fight was the NCL. Similar to the GFWC, in 1899 the NCL consolidated local consumer leagues in New York (founded 1890), Brooklyn and Philadelphia (founded 1896), and Boston (founded 1897).[32] The NCL, open to men and women, was a consumer organization that acted on behalf of its members, some of whom had a personal interest, as members of other women's or temperance groups, or a professional interest, as public health officials, journalists, or physicians.[33] The NCL existed to benefit and improve life and production for both the worker and the consumer. Members of the NCL protested—often by economic boycott—workers' unsatisfactory wages, long hours, and unsanitary working conditions. League concerns expanded to include conditions for employees at public utilities, in clothing and food production, sweatshops and homework, and child labor.[34] Local leagues devised a "white list" of stores where sales help had optimal working conditions to encourage patronage of those establishments. A label was also created for food and clothing that "wedded the social and political potential of middle-class women's organizations with an emblem devised by the union movement."[35] Although its primary concern was labor and labor conditions, the NCL endorsed pure food legislation, because they believed in consumers getting their money's worth.

The heavy emphasis on social welfare by women's organizations unconsciously applied middle- and upper-class morals and solutions to the food and drug problem. These women had resources to purchase sensible foods and might summon a doctor rather than buy and rely upon proprietary medicines; these women had the time and education to investigate the problem at hand. The NCL, which ostensibly benefited consumers by assuring them sanitary products, sought to improve working conditions for employees without fully considering the economic ramifications of fewer hours of work at the same pay, or a minimum wage that became, de facto, the maximum wage. As the history of food and drug laws demonstrates, however, this cause is one in which all consumers were directly involved and everyone had a vested interest; eating is, after all, a universal activity.

• • •

Simultaneous with this activism by women's and consumer groups, some federal officials concluded that adulteration was a serious threat to business success. When European markets threatened to boycott

American meat because of unsanitary meat and manufacturing conditions, Congress passed the 1890 Meat Export Act, which combined
inspection of packing plants with the threat of vigorous tariff retaliation,
should European countries prohibit American meats.[36] The "embalmed
beef" scandal of the Spanish-American War and the attendant newspaper coverage of soldiers sickened by meat, during the heyday of
yellow journalism, gave credence to the popular belief that meat
packers had made enormous profits selling the U.S. government an
inferior product.[37]

Unregulated and untested drugs provoked a crisis as well, albeit
one with a quick resolution. In 1901, thirteen children in St. Louis died
after being inoculated with diphtheria antitoxin containing tetanus
bacillus; a similar episode in Camden, New Jersey, killed nine children.[38]
The 1902 Biologics Control Act regulated antitoxins at the federal level,
thus establishing a national standard.[39]

The federal agency most affected by and concerned about food and
drug adulteration was the Bureau of Chemistry. In his annual reports,
bureau chief Harvey Wiley asked Congress for extended powers and
warned Congress of the dangers of various adulterants. This came on
top of the almost yearly bills being submitted in Congress. Wiley
believed that Congress gave more attention and priority to industry
than to the average citizen; the Meat Export Act did nothing to dissuade
him of that belief, as it protected foreign consumers but ignored those
stateside. Despite the sweeping power of the Biologics Control Act, the
bureau had insufficient monies and staff for adequate enforcement. In
1902, Congress allocated an additional $5,000 to the bureau to test adul-
terated foods and drinks. Wiley assembled a group of a dozen men,
known jocularly as the "Poison Squad," who ate courtesy of the bureau
in exchange for frequent medical examinations, laboratory tests, and
collection of urine and fecal samples. The experiment to assay the
effects, benign or otherwise, of some ubiquitous food preservatives
began in December 1902 and continued for five years. In the first round
of sampling, food was adulterated with borax, a common food preserv-
ative, to assess its effects. Wiley concluded that borax, unpleasant in
large doses, was far gentler than other common preservatives, including
salicylic acid and salicylate, sulfurous acids and sulfites, benzoic acid
and benzoates, and formaldehyde.[40] The publicity and details of the
results of the Poison Squad's diet swayed many people to be wary of
preservatives and other hidden dangers in unregulated food.[41]

The Bureau of Chemistry (and Wiley) became one of the best-known
government agencies at a time when most people were distanced from

the workings of government.[42] The conclusions about food additives, preservatives, and (common) adulterants—that they were not beneficial at best and harmful at worst—enraged some consumers. Not only were these products present in food, they were completely legal and consumers had no way of knowing which products contained which adulterants.

Even though there was crossover of membership among women's organizations, Wiley fostered a coalition of these groups at the turn of the century. By 1902, the GFWC's Pure Food League was the most active among the women's organizations working for legislation, but the legislative experience and repeated success of the WCTU hinted at the need for a broad (and cohesive) alliance of like-minded groups. The myriad women's organizations, with their hundreds of thousands of members, organized letter-writing campaigns and tried to exert the same moral suasion on legislators that had worked so successfully on the local level. In addition, these various groups remained active and well informed about causes important to their membership; for example, the WCTU sent a delegation to the 1898 National Pure Food Congress.[43] Wiley failed to realize, however, that others had their own agendas as well. The usefulness of recruiting so many women's organizations may have backfired: Wiley wanted the law passed, but he also wanted full credit for its passage.

Physicians were another concerned cohort, particularly about drugs in the marketplace. The allopathic medical community was still working to demonstrate its superiority over other medical systems at the turn of the century and also to target specious remedies.[44] In 1900, the American Medical Association (AMA) began a campaign against the "nostrum menace." In a series of eight articles in the *Journal of the American Medical Association (JAMA)*, the editor explained the insidious and deceitful nature of these potions, from forestalling (competent) medical help to aggravating the condition to bankrupting the patient. Even as the AMA was encouraging the medical community to be aware of the "nostrum menace," it was reluctant to commit in the ongoing congressional tussle for food and drug legislation. In 1904, Charles Reed, head of the AMA's Committee on National Legislation, threw his full support behind pure food and drugs bills. Reed, claiming to speak for over 2,000 medical societies and 135,000 physicians, urged AMA members to write to their congressmen expressing support for the proposed bill.[45] Reed also asked Senator Heyburn, one of the bill's sponsors, to make members of the House aware of the many petitions he had received from individual physicians and medical societies.[46] Dissension among *JAMA* editors and the AMA officers about a drug provision in the bill, however, threw AMA support in doubt, and the association stayed on the sidelines in the spring of 1906, just when their help was most needed. Uninformed about decisions and strategies of legislators, the AMA seemed ready to quit.[47] However, during the AMA's House of Delegates meeting in June, the association assented to rejoin the fight for pure food and drugs.[48] Discussing the 1906 Pure Food and Drugs Act in subsequent years, selective collective memory prevailed, and the AMA recast itself as a significant, constant, and ardent supporter in the fight for pure food laws.[49]

Perhaps the most critical element in the fight for pure food and drugs was the media, particularly print journalism. Magazines and newspapers exposed readers to the world beyond their neighborhoods, and the competition for readers was fierce. High literacy rates, cheaper production costs and advertising symbiotically sustained a wide variety of publications, providing a mass-market exchange of information.[50] As Jennifer Scanlon demonstrates in her study of *Ladies' Home Journal*, editors shaped what their readers saw, thought, and knew; in the case of *Ladies' Home Journal*, "proper womanhood" met the limits and vision of journalism.[51] Editor Edward Bok's determination to investigate the thriving empire that was Lydia Pinkham's Vegetable Compound was a calculated risk as he depended heavily on advertising revenues for profitability. The article unmasked a carefully concealed truth: Pinkham, who personally answered letters from those seeking advice and aid, was merely an advertising phenomenon; letters were answered by a large (female) staff as the good lady herself was long dead. The accompanying photograph of her tombstone was presented as incontrovertible evidence.[52] In concert with the WCTU, the journal also revealed the alcohol content of various remedies, such as Mrs. Winslow's Soothing Cough Syrup with 18 percent alcohol.[53]

At the same time that some magazines were willing to print these sorts of stories, a cadre of journalists emerged who were interested in researching and writing them. Muckrakers—journalists who exposed corruption, particularly in big business and government—took advantage of the myriad publishing options and had a significant impact on public opinion and knowledge.[54] The exposés of muckrakers served to reinforce the importance (and need) for Progressive reform of government, political systems, labor systems, and other pertinent social issues. In a recent introduction to Upton Sinclair's *The Jungle*, a muckraking classic, Ronald Gottesman notes that "Americans have always responded to writing that calls attention to discrepancies between the ideal and the actual, but with the growth of literacy and the spread of mass-circulation magazines and newspapers at the turn of the century, shocking news about corporate and political wrongdoings—usually interrelated—became big business."[55] One investigation into publishing and advertising practices explained why WCTU activities received little press. Journalist Mark Sullivan discovered that advertisers inserted a "red" clause in contracts with magazines and newspapers that stated, "It is mutually agreed that this Contract is void if any law is enacted by your State restricting or prohibiting the manufacture or sale of proprietary medicine."[56] This provision encouraged publishers to give little (or minimal) coverage to organizations trying to do just that, and it encouraged publishers to lobby against such bills. This clause only gradually lost force; William Allen White's *Emporia Gazette* alerted its readers to the hazards of patent medicines but was among the few to do so.[57]

No subject was safe from the inquisitive and curious, from corrupt municipal government in the "wholesome" Midwest to oil trusts, from lynching to everyday items.[58] In 1901, muckrakers cast their curious and incisive gaze on the highly profitable and entirely unregulated food and drug industries. After a six-month promotion, *Collier's Magazine* ran a series on drugs by Samuel Hopkins Adams from October 1905 through February 1906. Adams investigated patent medicines, scrutinized claims that liquids were antiseptic, analyzed ingredients of patent medicines, and determined the actual effects of these "medicines."[59] Adams's series stirred and outraged the public, who spent more than $90,000,000 each year on nostrums.[60] Few readers were pleased to learn that their trusted medicines contained mostly water, sugar, and food coloring. For those already enmeshed in these issues, the series offered additional justifications for drug regulation: users might unknowingly become addicted to patent medicines containing narcotics, alcohol, or both; people wasted money on non-efficacious remedies; mildly unwell people who self-dosed often delayed seeing a physician.

The day after Adams's series finished, Upton Sinclair's *The Jungle* was published. A Socialist critique of the lives of immigrant workers in Packingtown (Chicago), the research had been underwritten by *Appeal to Reason,* where it had initially appeared in serial form. Revisions and changes (including the ending) did nothing to "sell" the book to publishers, who shied away from the book's controversial agenda and graphic depiction of the slaughterhouses. The possibility of a costly libel suit was a detraction; Edward Bok of the *Ladies' Home Journal* had already lost a lawsuit because an article had relied upon old and inaccurate information.[61] To deflect the possibility of a lawsuit—and because

Doubleday expected to profit handsomely from publishing the shocking exposé in novel form—the press agreed to publish the book only after private investigators confirmed that the workers' lot was every bit as dirty, grim, and bleak as Sinclair's portrayal.[62] Reviews of the book were not, on the whole, favorable, but *The Jungle* quickly became a best-seller. Although the doomed romance between Jurgis and Ona ostensibly serves as the central plot device, the most captivating (and revolting) section was the twenty-page description of the meat-packing process, which turned many a stomach and heightened the call for regulations. As Sinclair himself wryly noted, "I aimed at the public's heart and by accident I hit its stomach."

Two passages in particular struck a nerve (or stomach). In the first, Sinclair described slaughterhouse practices—floors slippery with blood, men swiftly scooping out entrails—and injuries the men incurred— swollen knuckles, lost fingernails or fingers. In the second, he described how bad meat was disguised and foisted upon a hapless and hungry public. In addition to disguised but legitimate meat, there was another concern: what was actually in meat products? Men who fell into the vats disappeared from the work floor and often "went out into the world as Durham's Pure Leaf Lard." Readers began to question the quality of meat they bought.

● ● ●

The book upset digestion nationwide and shocked President Theodore Roosevelt, who had received an advance copy. Roosevelt and members of Congress received numerous copies, frequently accompanied by letters from outraged and concerned citizens. To determine the veracity of Sinclair's charges, Roosevelt privately sent Charles Neill, a labor commissioner, and James Bronson Reynolds, a New York social worker, to Chicago to investigate the working and living conditions in the stockyards. Much as Doubleday's investigations had, Neill and Reynolds confirmed Sinclair's charges. Roosevelt responded to public and political pressure: the current food and drugs bill finally appeared to have a chance, if it could survive passage in both houses of Congress and a compromise measure.

But the debate over meat packing was only half the story. While the Meat Inspection Act and the Pure Food and Drugs Act have become inextricably intertwined in our memory, they had different legislative paths. A pure food and drugs bill was introduced by Senator Weldon B. Heyburn in December 1905.[63] In his December State of the Union address, President Roosevelt also expressed his support for the bill. "I recommend that a law be enacted to regulate interstate commerce in misbranded and advertised food, drink, and drugs. Such a law would protect legitimate manufacturers and commerce, and would tend to secure the health and welfare of the consuming public. Traffic in food-stuffs which have been debased or adulterated so as to injure health or to deceive purchasers should be forbidden."[64] The usual machinations of stalling, blocking, and refusing to allow a discussion had occurred over and over again. In February 1906, after floor debate on a variety of pro-posed food and drugs bills, letters from both the AMA and GFWC arrived just as the Senate was about to vote on a pure food and drugs bill.[65] The Senate passed Senator Heyburn's version on February 21 by a 63 to 4 vote, with twenty-two members abstaining.[66] The House Com-mittee on Interstate and Foreign Commerce reported out a bill on March 7 similar to the Senate version. And then, silence.

After years of effort, and more success in one congressional session than any since 1879, members of many women's organizations were surprised that pure food and drug legislation, seemingly so close to vic-tory, was suddenly relegated to a legislative back burner. The uproar over the just-released novel *The Jungle*, however, aroused public senti-ment far more than women's groups had been able to do.[67] After pri-vately reading the Neill-Reynolds report, Roosevelt requested an amendment in the Department of Agriculture's appropriations bill to cover the cost of meat and factory inspections. The amendment pro-vided that meat packers, rather than the Agriculture Department, bear the costs of inspection. When changes made to this proposed amend-ment essentially gutted it, Roosevelt did what he had both threatened and feared to do: he released the Neill-Reynolds report, which damned the meat trust.[68] The report did not identify specific slaughterhouses. Those responsible parties inadvertently revealed themselves, and their shoddy practices, however, when they wrote and signed a letter to Con-gress protesting the Neill-Reynolds findings.[69]

In late May, just as members of Congress began responding to public and presidential pleas urging passage of a bill ensuring some modicum of consumer protection, the GFWC held its biannual meeting. The chair of the legislative committee explained the latest discussions in Wash-ington and urged each chapter delegation to write in support of the leg-islation to their representatives, the sponsors of the bill, and the Speaker of the House.[70] On June 21, the House began three days of debate over the extent and definition of food adulteration.[71] The bill passed the House on June 24, on a 241 to 17 vote, with 112 members abstaining on grounds of states' rights, and then went to conference to reach a compromise between the two versions.[72] The House and Senate approved the compromise version of the Pure Food and Drugs Act and the Meat Inspection Act on June 29. Roosevelt signed both acts into law on June 30, 1906.[73]

● ● ●

What had been achieved with this law? The Meat Inspection Act regulated slaughterhouse practices and subjected factories to inspection. The Pure Food and Drugs Act, though, had a different legislative intent. The former was designed and implemented to protect consumers. The Meat Inspection Act ensured that meat products purchased domestically were disease-free, slaughtered, and packed in a (relatively) sanitary environment. The latter act, however, gave consumers information so they could make smarter and more informed purchasing decisions about increasingly mass-produced items. Robert Allen, food and drug chief for Kentucky, a Pure Food League member, and an ardent Wiley supporter, stated, "When purchasers know *where* a product was made, *when* it was made, and *who* made it, and are informed of the *true nature* and *substance* of the article offered for consumption, it is almost impossible to impose upon the most ignorant and careless consumer."[74] Congress protected consumers and enabled them to better protect themselves by requiring specific information on the label. Armed with this information, consumers could accept more of the responsibility for safe food and drug choices; if they felt they were being inadequately protected, the government offered a layer of protection and aid. What this law did not do, though, was cover non-food or drug products, a fact about which the public remained woefully ignorant for many years.

The 1906 law defined food, drug, adulteration, and misbranding. "Drugs" had to meet standards proscribed in the *United States Pharmacopoeia*.[75] "Adulteration" was a deviation from standards, while "misbranding" meant deceptive labeling. In addition, food and drug products needed to state the presence (and proportion) of alcohol, morphine, opium, cocaine, heroin, alpha or beta eucaine, chloroform, cannabis indica, chloral hydrate, acetanilide, or any derivative of any of these substances. Although Bureau of Chemistry Chief Harvey Wiley had lobbied for a bill for two decades, he was far from satisfied with the final version of the law. On the positive side, that regulation and enforcement of the law was possible was clearly delineated.

If the Bureau of Chemistry could prove that a company violated the law, that company could be charged with prosecution or seizure. To prove that a product was misbranded, for example, federal prosecutors had to prove intent—that manufacturers knowingly engaged in deceitful labeling, deliberately intending to trick or harm the public. And only those drugs enumerated in the *Pharmacopoeia* were under jurisdiction. Despite the wording of the 1902 Biologics Control Act and the emphasis on "pure" drugs, there were no provisions for testing new products for efficacy or safety. Any drug or combination of drugs could be sold, passing directly from laboratory bench to home medicine cabinet. Another limitation—necessary given the limits of congressional powers—was that the law applied only to interstate commerce. Companies so charged were guilty only of a misdemeanor. A first conviction carried a maximum fine of $200 or possible imprisonment; subsequent violations carried maximum penalties of a $300 fine or a year's imprisonment. Adulterated or misbranded products could be removed from the market altogether if there was sufficient proof that said products were in violation of the law. The bureau had little money and inadequate manpower to enforce the laws. To maximize its effectiveness, bureau inspectors scrutinized one product or industry at a time. The low rates of conviction for violating either law seem to suggest that most manufacturers toed the line, or made sure their products fell within acceptable parameters.

The act was amended five times between 1906 and 1938.[76] These amendments, and others that did not survive the legislative process, hinted at the problems in the rapidly expanding food and drug market. Some flaws in the 1906 law such as the definition of "mislabeling" were immediately apparent but common wisdom held that some consumer protection was preferable to none at all.[77]

The zeal and determination of women's organizations, including the nascent Home Economics Association, to ensure better food and drug standards did not abate with the passage of the 1906 act. If the justification for involvement had been extending the role of mother under the guise of domestic feminism, the continued activism of women belied this: they wanted and intended to continue to use the political system. In the years after passage of the act, local chapters of the WCTU, GFWC, and other organizations diligently pursued enforcement of the law in their areas, and often ensured that local and state food and drug officials were in compliance.[78] In several states women's organizations asked for the appointment of lady inspectors, arguing that not only were women uniquely qualified to undertake the task of inspection, given women's multiple daily interactions with food, they were extremely knowledgeable about the wording and intent of the law.[79] The dedication and attention to the enforcement particulars of this hard-fought battle spoke of a commitment to the political process, and the desire to enact change. Their effort had not gone unnoticed.[80] Women had proven to themselves, time and again, that they could effect social and political change. But that was only the first step.

In the year between passage and implementation of the law, Harvey Wiley conceived of and instituted a system to investigate adulteration, helped devise standard methods of analysis, continued to test the effects of chemical preservatives, and assisted in organizing a pure food congress.[81] He created a system of enforcement for the 1906 law and its subsequent amendments that in its basic components remains unchanged. The Bureau of Chemistry divided the country geographically into three divisions—Eastern, Central, and Western—each with a district chief. These districts were further subdivided into branch or field offices, located in cities with sizable populations, near manufacturing and shipping routes.[82] Each branch office reported to the appropriate district chief. Staff in each branch office included chemists to conduct analysis and investigators to inspect factories and collect samples, and typically delved into goods of local interest. The New Orleans office, for example, analyzed coffee for the presence of chicory in so-called (or so-labeled) "pure coffee."

In March of 1912, after six years of implementing and enforcing the 1906 law he had long sought, and faced with increasing resistance from Secretary of Agriculture James Wilson, Wiley tendered his resignation as chief of the bureau. At the time of his retirement from government service, Wiley was sixty-seven years old and had recently married and become a father.[83] After several months' vacancy, Carl Alsberg, a chemist in the Bureau of Drugs and Plants, replaced Wiley as chief.[84] No longer responsible for protecting the country's health, Wiley did not simply abandon his quest for food and drug products free from adulteration. Named chief chemist of *Good Housekeeping*'s test laboratories, he continued his self-imposed mission. As advertising became more important as a selling tool for consumers and the amount of advertising in all magazines increased, Wiley's task in assessing whether products lived up to their billing became more important.[85] *Good Housekeeping* only accepted advertising from companies with honestly advertised products, tested in the *Good Housekeeping* laboratories, which substantiated the claims made. The *Good Housekeeping* Seal of Approval, coming out of Wiley's laboratory analysis, became a marketable and relied-upon commodity for the magazine.

The active enforcement of (and education about) the 1906 act reflects on Theodore Roosevelt's commitment to this and other Progressive legislation. Roosevelt's enthusiasm, coupled with Progressive ideals and a healthy respect for business, allowed for many measures to pass into law protecting both the nation's and the public's health. The wide-ranging legislation passed during his terms of office did much to improve the lives of and government for Americans while simultaneously giving business a great deal of (self-regulatory) power.[86] Although Roosevelt might not have defined himself as a trust-buster, nor a Progressive (until it was politically expedient to do so in 1912), his legislative legacy argues otherwise. In the case of food and drug legislation, Roosevelt threw his weight behind Wiley's cause with direct pleas to Congress in his 1905 State of the Union address and his threat to release the Neill-Reynolds report. Subsequent reorganization within the Board of Chemistry, however, made Roosevelt's dislike of Wiley abundantly clear; the cause, however, was distinct from the people involved.[87]

Roosevelt accorded himself well as regards other Progressive concerns.[88] Aided by Gifford Pinchot's vision of scientific and agricultural forestry, Roosevelt helped enhance the national park system with large tracts of land, purchased by public and private organizations, set aside for future generations. In 1903, Roosevelt also suggested a Bureau of Corporations to gather information on certain areas of industry, particularly large corporations and trade associations. The bureau, located within the Department of Commerce, was "to regulate all state corporations involved in commerce and report directly to the president."[89] On some level, the bureau recognized the inevitability of a concentration of business. Unlike the 1890 Sherman Antitrust Act, which theoretically repressed industrial interaction "in combination or in restraint of free trade," the bureau sought to understand and regulate these concentrations of industrial power. The bureau's three largest investigations examined the petroleum industry (Standard Oil), the tobacco industry (American Tobacco), and International Harvester.[90]

Much like the Bureau of Chemistry, interpretation of the laws central to its mission determined the Bureau of Corporation's course of action. For the latter, the question was how to interpret the restraint of free trade, as per congressional intent of the Sherman Antitrust Act. Some people believed that certain business combinations were acceptable if they promoted efficiency within a field, and were unacceptable only if the sole aim was the elimination of competition.[91] In succeeding congressional sessions, Senator Francis Newlands introduced bills to elevate the bureau to a commission that would do more than merely investigate "antitrust" allegations.[92] In his 1914 State of the Union address to Congress, President Woodrow Wilson melded Democratic and Progressive platforms and implored Congress to take action on antitrust laws.[93] In response, bills were drafted in both the House and Senate within the week.

Ultimately, Congress passed not one but two bills establishing a commission charged with regulating interstate commerce. The Federal Trade Commission (FTC), created on September 26, 1914, enforced a law declaring that "unfair methods of competition in commerce are hereby declared unlawful."[94] The Clayton Act, passed October 14, 1914, prohibited certain trade practices and authorized the FTC to discourage them.[95] Enforcement procedures for the FTC and the Bureau of Chemistry were similar. When a complaint was lodged, the agency conducted a preliminary investigation or "conference ruling" to determine whether the complaint was legitimate. If affirmative, the complaint was docketed as an "application for issuance of a complaint" and assigned a team of investigators, comprised of one or more lawyers, plus economists and accountants. After a formal investigation, cases were either dismissed—two-thirds of FTC cases were disposed of in this manner— or a formal complaint was issued against the company. For the first two years of FTC enforcement, there were no formal hearings because the charged parties agreed to "cease and desist" the practice in question. In 1917, the FTC began to investigate foodstuffs in cooperation with the Agriculture Department.

The 1906 Food and Drugs Act and the 1914 formation of the FTC were two significant pieces of consumer legislation. These laws demonstrated presidential concern for consumers, respect (if not support) for Progressive causes, and political acuity. Progressive ideas and issues, including reform and social justice, particularly for the disenfranchised or unenfranchised, and for more responsible (and responsive) government were nurtured at the local level.

The passage of the 1906 Pure Food and Drugs Act had the paradoxical effect of being the first significant piece of consumer legislation and almost ending all concerns about food and drugs. The medical community turned its attention to internal organizational matters. The Bureau of Chemistry, led by Harvey Wiley and Carl Alsberg, enforced the law but was often restrained by both language and fiscal and personnel constraints. Wiley's resignation from the bureau did not end enforcement, nor the desire of many at the organization to strengthen the law and close more loopholes. Although some women's organizations did continue to pressure state and local agencies to enforce the national law, many other organizations soon lost interest or found other causes. Women were more active, more visible, than ever before. And in their new visibility, women were making their faces more distinct and visible as well.

chapter two

"The arts and crafts of the modern flapper"

IGNORING COSMETICS in the 1906 Pure Food and Drugs Act was as much a political decision as an economic one. Grocers' support had been gained by deleting the cosmetic provision. Sales of cosmetics were so slight that this omission did not appear to have an impact, or negative health repercussions, the way food and drugs so obviously had. Cosmetics—products rubbed, patted, powdered, or by any alternative method applied to the skin to alter, enhance, or otherwise beautify its wearer—were small, mostly inexpensive items purchased and consumed by only half the population. In other words, they were extremely easy to overlook. Within two decades, or one generation, however, manufacture and sales of cosmetics soared beyond anyone's wildest dreams, fostering a new industry and creating new employment opportunities for women.[1]

Because "only" women used beauty aids, cosmetics and their impact on the economy have been almost wholly ignored in historical analyses about consumption.[2] Not everyone, however, was oblivious to the volume of cosmetics sales: advertisers promoted items manufactured by others; beauty editors and advertisements in women's magazines touted various aids to beauty; pharmacies and department stores sold cosmetics. The impact of these seemingly insignificant items was, in fact, quite significant for a store's fiscal health. A druggists' trade journal noted in 1918 that "ten years ago it would not have been such a hard task to select a line of toilet articles to stock, but today, the great number of manufacturers of this class of merchandise through their extensive advertising have made it necessary that you stock a rather comprehensive line of various toilet articles."[3] The effects of cosmetics also inspired fear. A proposed 1915 law in Kansas would have forbidden women less than forty-five years of age from wearing cosmetics "for the purpose of creating a false impression."[4] The law failed to pass, and these products remained free of government scrutiny.

Who, then, ensured the safety, or healthfulness, of cosmetics? The chief target of early Bureau of Chemistry enforcement of the 1906 act was foodstuffs rather than proprietary medicines.[5] The Federal Trade Commission (FTC) and the U.S. Postal Service (USPS), charged with enforcing trade practices, rather than specific industries, did prosecute cosmetic companies, among others. FTC and USPS enforcement was proportional to the size of the industry: the larger the industry and the more companies involved, the greater the likelihood that (at least) one company would violate the law. There had long been prescribed beauty tips, from pinching or slapping one's cheeks for color to altering one's physique with corsets and bustles. As more and more women discovered in the early 1900s, the trick to wearing cosmetics lay in the duality of appearing natural while using (nearly invisible but critical) artificial aids. At the heart of the cosmetics industry was the changing perception of women who wore makeup, or more accurately, who *visibly* wore it.[6] Cosmetics as commodities in the marketplace grew in economic importance from the late nineteenth century onward. The changes that accompanied mass production in the 1910s reflected the shifting ideas about cosmetics use by American women.

In the latter half of the nineteenth and the early part of the twentieth centuries, "beauty" meant clear, fair skin free of blemishes, pocks, or acne scars. This aesthetic had profound and unintentional implications in a country peopled by women from southern and eastern Europe, Asia, and Africa, as the standard of beauty inherently assumed a northern European face.[7] This reflected the country's growing obsession with cleanliness. White represented purity and healthfulness, freedom from the dangers of dirt.[8] The relationship between science and health could easily be discerned by "reading" a woman's face, ideally smooth and free of beauty aids. Fair or unspeckled skin also bespoke a life of leisure. Women who worked outside, even if protected by a hat, often colored at best, freckled at worst. If fair skin was the ideal, however, few women actually possessed it. Many quietly, and secretly, resorted to face powder that they made, typically from orris root or crushed rice, to provide the pallor nature had neglected. The trick was subtlety—to use powder without looking as if one did. Complicating the economic and class assumptions inherent in the beauty standard, women who visibly wore cosmetics in the last third of the nineteenth century were morally suspect and liable to criticism.[9] Blatant cosmetic use had been associated with prostitutes and actresses, neither secure or reputable professions, and cosmetic use in the early twentieth century was still tainted by this association.

This lack of visible cosmetic use, and the negative opinion of women who wore it, is not to suggest, though, that women did not employ artificial means to enhance their appearances. Powders, creams, and lotions had long been, and continued to remain, staples of many a woman's vanity. If artfully applied, cosmetics were unobtrusive and went unremarked upon by others. The beauty standard changed at the end of the nineteenth century; unlike future standards, this one did not require use of cosmetics, although they could be helpful. Lois Banner distinguishes three visually distinctive modes of beauty between 1865 and 1921, in which the tall, athletic Gibson girl of the 1890s supplanted the voluptuous woman, "buxom, hearty and [a] heavy model of beauty" of the 1870s, and in the 1910s in turn gave way to the small boyish model of beauty.[10] The newly fashionable "look" reflected changing expectations about a woman's demeanor and acceptable range of activities. With the rise in popularity of outdoor sport and athleticism in the 1890s, such as playing lawn tennis or bicycling, the desired look evolved from one of languor to vigorous activity; the pale face gave way to ruddy cheeks and sparkling eyes.[11] Accustomed or unwilling to discard their powders for artificial pallor, women relied upon rouge to bring back—or add—the tamped down glow of health to their faces.

The Harriet Hubbard Ayer Company was one of many companies to manufacture and sell cosmetics. Soap manufacturers expanded their business by slightly altering the formulation to transform a solid (soap) into a liquid (lotion) or semisolid (cream) emulsion. Other companies were created with the express purpose of making and purveying cosmetics. At least five enduring companies got their American start in the first fifteen years of the twentieth century. Each company took advantage of women's (and society's) changing perceptions and conceptions about beauty. These companies effectively parlayed a standardized, homogenized perception of beauty into a multimillion dollar business. Helena Rubinstein, Elizabeth Arden, and Max Factor, and their eponymous companies, each illustrate the power of the media and the aura of class in selling beauty. The illusion of exclusivity conjured by these names, from salons catering to a select few to an artist creating Hollywood beauties, successfully translated to mass-market sales, without tarnishing or losing the exclusive image. Two other companies—California Perfume Company (later renamed Avon) and Madam C. J. Walker—sold products door-to-door. Their success rested firmly upon the personal integrity and dedication of local agents coupled with a national reputation for trustworthy products and good value. The differing strategies for prestige among the first three companies and local credibility for the latter two were successful. And these were but five of many companies whose items were sold in beauty salons, pharmacies, department stores, and door-to-door.

Helena Rubinstein created a beauty empire based on a sense of elitism, privilege, and wealth, all the more interesting given her unassuming background. In 1898, Rubinstein fled or was sent from a broken romance in Cracow to live with relatives near Coleraine, Australia.[12] Unhappy with the situation in Coleraine, either because of an uncle's unwelcome advances or because of the isolation, she relocated to Melbourne, determined to earn a living. Rubinstein's smooth, pale skin impressed the Australian women with their wind-roughened, sun-chapped skin. Rubinstein claimed that the secret to her smooth visage was a cream used by women in her family; as luck would have it, she possessed twelve jars. After a chemist analyzed the constituents of the cold cream, she manufactured and sold the familial beauty secret, named Creme Valaze. Showing true signs of entrepreneurship, she sold not only the cream but also a day of beauty instruction in which she taught Australian women how to care for their skin. Rubinstein hired female attendants to service customers in her salons, thus also fostering a new occupation for women—beautician. By 1912, Rubinstein had salons, or Houses of Beauty, in Melbourne, Paris, and London, and an impressive clientele. In 1915, she moved to New York City, which served not only as her North American base but the hub of all operations. The expense and time required to go to Rubinstein's salons, and her own flawlessly smooth skin, bolstered the cache of her name and her products.

In creating salons that catered to the wealthy, Rubinstein was not alone. Her longtime competitor Elizabeth Arden, née Florence Nightingale Graham, had similarly humble beginnings.[13] Born to a poor lumberjack and his wife in a small town outside Toronto, Graham worked and contributed to the family's meager income early on. She too was blessed with fair skin, and intrigued by chemistry and skin care. In Toronto and New York City, Graham worked in beauty salons where she learned how to give facials and other beauty treatments. Eventually, she pooled her resources and talent with another woman to open up a salon. When her entrepreneurial ambitions outpaced the flexibility, limits, and financial means of the partnership in 1909, she bought out her partner and became sole proprietor. She changed her name and that of the salon to one more upscale; she chose Arden because she enjoyed the novel *Enoch Arden,* and Elizabeth because it had been the name of

her former partner and did sound elegant. Next, Arden created and promoted her own products, packaging them as part of a day of pampering
and leisurely beauty at her finely appointed New York City salon, the
"Red Door." As the years progressed, Arden added hairdressing,
millinery, clothing, and a full makeup line to her salons.[14] Two upscale
salons, Rubinstein's and Arden's, catering to the same group of women,
were bound to cause tension and competition. It did.

Because he was not in New York City, did not cater to the same
strata of society, was male, or a combination of these factors, Max Factor
was not (initially) a threat to Helena Rubinstein and Elizabeth Arden.
Ironically, he should have been taken more seriously by these two cosmetic doyennes. In addition to fabulous (and frequent) publicity in
movie credits and Hollywood magazines as *the* makeup artist to the
stars, and an Oscar in 1929 for his makeup work, his product lines were,
by the mid-1930s, available in drugstores and thus more accessible to
the consuming public than those items found only in salons and select
stores. Exclusivity was one thing, but sales quite another; the former
should never overshadow (or inhibit) the latter.[15] An accomplished wig-
maker and cosmetic artist, Factor fled Russia for St. Louis, where he displayed his wares at the 1904 World's Fair. Intrigued by the new film
industry, Max Factor hooked his star to Hollywood and moved west. He
had done makeup and wigs for the Russian Imperial Grand Opera, so
he transferred that skill to both stage and film. In 1909 he founded Max
Factor and Company, devoting his talents and creativity to theatrical
makeup. His particular genius lay in his ability to develop or alter "old"
makeup in response to new technology. As lighting techniques and the
film itself physically changed, he adapted his stage makeup to new conditions. For example, he changed conventional greasepaint for the
stage—heavy and almost mask-like when dry—to a slick form that was
lighter and did not crack as it dried, thus allowing film comedians a
broader range of facial expression, a necessity during the silent film era.
His inventiveness was not limited to cosmetics: he designed the first
powder puff (as opposed to a brush) for the application of loose powder,
false eyelashes, kits for theatrical makeup, and a kissing machine (to test
lipstick).[16] Perhaps his signal contribution, however, was changing the
popular name of beauty aids. As Fred Basten, Robert Salvatore, and
Paul Kaufman note, "In 1920 Max Factor began referring to his beauty
products as *makeup,* rather than *cosmetics.* The term eventually caught
on to such an extent that his competitors were forced to use it as well."[17]

Not all cosmetic companies relied upon prestige and celebrity. Personal, door-to-door sales also generated sales for cosmetics and other

consumer items.[18] One of the older cosmetic companies in the United States, founded in 1892, relied upon this sales technique. David McConnell sold books, silverware, and perfume as an agent for a publishing house. When he bought the company, he continued to employ its traveling sales force.[19] As a bonus gift to boost sales, he developed a set of three perfumes and an atomizer, but soon realized people were more interested in the gift than the sales item. A friend suggested calling the business the California Perfume Company "because of the great profusion of flowers in California," and the California Perfume Company (CPC) was born.[20] Buoyed by the success of the perfume, McConnell increased the variety of perfumes (different odors) and the product line as a whole.[21] Gradually the CPC dropped most of its other lines until the main categories sold were perfumes, cosmetics, cleaning agents, and flavored extracts (vanilla, almond, etc).

An early key to success was hiring an outstanding (and tireless) "general agent" or leader of the sales force.[22] Perseus Foster Eames Albee, the first "Avon lady," sold products door-to-door, and subsequently recruited, trained, and supervised other members of the sales force. The sales force was unique in that its agents were independent contractors rather than company employees, as was typical in other, similar operations; also, most agents were female.[23] Each woman had an assigned territory.[24] The longer an agent serviced the same territory, the more her customers began to rely upon and trust her beauty advice. The orders, submitted once a month, were shipped to the agents who then delivered them and (hopefully) got paid. Contact with a local (and known) person, the company's guarantee policy, and the *Good Housekeeping* Seal of Approval helped increase sales. By 1903, only eleven years after its founding, the company employed forty-eight general agents (district supervisors) and over ten thousand depot managers (sales representatives).[25]

A second element, a sound business decision, contributed to CPC's success. McConnell decided in 1895 to build his own manufacturing plant to control quality and costs, rather than rely on an outside jobber for products. In 1897, the plant and a research laboratory opened in Suffern, New York. In addition, the company opened regional offices and warehouses in Luzerne, Pennsylvania; San Francisco; and Kansas City to expedite delivery.[26] The Kansas City office soon served as headquarters for midwestern and western agents, issuing directives, filling orders, and sending out daily encouragement to its traveling sales force.[27] In 1915, the company entered the perfumes, toilet articles, and extracts division of the Panama-Pacific International Exposition and won a gold medal. For years, pride in this achievement "for excellence in quality of goods, display, and artistic design" was visible on letterhead, catalogues, and order forms. Continual tinkering with the sales force calendar and new products kept Avon in many homes as the preferred beauty product. Also, for women in remote areas, the convenience of sampling in and delivery to one's home was immense.

A second cosmetic company also relied on door-to-door sales. When Sarah Breedlove, a black laundress, turned twenty years old, she began to lose her hair. Recently widowed, she also needed to support herself and her young daughter. Dissatisfied with the available hair remedies, she experimented in her kitchen, testing various recipes' ability to restore and straighten her hair.[28] With patience, she finally discovered the right combination of lotion and application with a hot steel comb. In 1905, she began to peddle her method from house to house in St. Louis. She continued to sell her product and method when she moved to Denver a year later. There, she married Charles J. Walker, a newspaperman who is credited with much of her advertising strategy. Like women in the beauty business had done before her, Walker gave the product her name, perhaps using the titular "Madam" to deflect common nicknames given to black women at the time, perhaps for the same aura of authority that Helena Rubenstein had. In 1910, Walker moved to Indianapolis, where she set up a laboratory, factory, and beauty school. Walker stipulated that women who sold her method needed to be properly trained, which meant taking courses at Lelia College. Soon, Madam C. J. Walker beauty schools were established in other cities with growing or sizeable black communities, including Chicago, Kansas City, and Philadelphia.

The image and professionalism of its saleswomen helped to sell Walker's products. Walker agents demonstrated how to use the hair care products, and taught prospective customers how to achieve maximum benefits. Pride in one's appearance was critical both to Walker personally, and to her company; only women who prided themselves on their appearance would avail themselves of her products. From the date of incorporation in 1911 until Walker's death in 1919, the company grossed over $100,000 per year and employed thousands of agents. Walker agents had a sense of community: they had attended beauty school classes together. To further this cohesion and instill a sense of pride, Walker created a series of local "unions" for the agents, which resembled social and philanthropic clubs more than labor unions. These associations, part of the Madam C. J. Walker Union of America, provided a pool for beneficiary payments in case of death of an agent.

These local associations were also encouraged (and expected) to engage in civic and philanthropic endeavors, extending the motto "to be a credit to their race" from Walker agents to Walker customers. Much as domestic feminism transcended the confines of the home, Walker's belief and pride in personal appearance transcended the need to transform the individual woman's appearance, thus transforming a community.

There were similarities and differences between the two door-to-door companies. The Walker Company stressed local involvement, while CPC did not. On the other hand, CPC embraced national campaigns, such as its offer of a commemorative booklet on President William McKinley shortly after his assassination.[29] Another difference between the two companies was the gendered power structure. David McConnell founded CPC, succeeded by his son and then another man; only recently has a woman headed the company. Although the majority of the sales force and their direct supervisors were women, men oversaw the agents and supervisors from regional offices and held the important offices at company headquarters. At the Avon's Suffern manufacturing plants, men's and women's jobs were distinct and on different pay scales. Although the products were targeted for women consumers, or women purchasing for their family, the management structure of Avon was indistinguishable from that of any other manufacturing firm, irrespective of item of manufacture. By contrast, the structure at Madam C. J. Walker was decidedly female. Walker hired a male lawyer, but decreed that women head the company after her death. The beauty colleges, named for her daughter A'Lelia, and the accompanying salons were run and managed by women. Who did what in each company depended more on who founded it than on what it manufactured.[30]

• • •

In the first few decades of the twentieth century, the ability to purchase cosmetics in stores, salons, or from a visiting sales agent instead of using homemade products facilitated cosmetics use. Two cultural phenomena influenced this discretionary purchase. First, the film industry with its emphasis on appearance gave rise to instant celebrity, both to actresses and their makeup artists. Second, the emphasis placed on youth, particularly after the First World War, accorded the younger generation more influence in setting fashion, and in challenging their

mothers' conventions of beauty and cosmetic use.[31] Movies and magazines provided many models of beauty for young women, who were
ready, as the younger generation is always wont to do, to rebel against
their elders. Surveys of purchasing habits indicated that younger
women were less hesitant to purchase cosmetics openly, in a department or drugstore, than were their mothers.[32] As noted by Cornelia
Comer in *Atlantic Monthly* before the war, "Modern girls are louder-
voiced and more bouncing than their predecessors, and their boy-
associates are somewhat rougher and more familiar toward them than
used to be thought well-bred."[33]

Young men and women in urban settings who provoked this worry
worked hard and wanted to enjoy their leisure time to the fullest. Those
women not compelled to seek paid employment often found their time
consumed by voluntary activities that reduced their leisure time.[34] With
paychecks in their pocketbooks, time at a premium, and mass-produced
commodities getting more inexpensive many young women chose to
buy rather than make their own clothing, and likewise began to purchase rather than make their own cosmetics. Young women, particularly
those who moved to larger cities, were free of community and familial
scrutiny of behavior and criticism of purchases. More women with
income to spend as they saw fit, plus mass production of cosmetics and
increasing media presence, coalesced in a growing consumer impulse to
buy.

The visibility of the postwar younger generation—in advertising, in
the popular press, in fiction—and their portrayed sensibility firmly
established an image that had only limited basis in reality. Parents in the
1920s worried about this very different young generation, and emphatically declared that they had not been so rebellious at a similar age, nor
had the world offered so many temptations.[35] In the popular imagination, flappers and sheiks (their male counterparts) did things "good
girls and boys" did not.[36] As with most social trends, young people were
more comfortable and willing to experiment than were their seniors.
Prohibition created new sanctions and meanings for alcohol even as traditional support for temperance was quickly disappearing; cigarettes
became newly fashionable for men and women; jazz began to attract a
white audience in the 1920s, and radio brought new audiences into the
fold. With an absence of all things female—breasts, hips, waist—
women's clothing hinted at androgyny; paradoxically, their visibly
made-up faces and bobbed hair reflected a new and very feminized
beauty aesthetic. The flapper's costume was taken by many to be her
true self, rather than an acceptable persona donned for public viewing.

"The flappers," historian Frederick Allen recounted, "wore thin dresses, short-sleeved and occasionally (in the evening) sleeveless, some of the wilder young things rolled their stocking below their knees, revealing to the shocked eyes of virtue a fleeting glance of shin-bones and knee cap."[37] The ensemble alone did not define the flapper, however. "The intoxication of rouge," explained Dorothy Spear in *Dancers in the Dark*, "is an insidious vintage known to more girls than mere men can ever believe."[38]

Not everyone was as intoxicated with cosmetics as Spear's statement might suggest. The religious periodical *America* inveighed against the flapper who "depended daily on a row of pots of paints and pomades, whose lips imitated a gash hastily inflicted by an unskilled surgeon, who sat in bondage to a parcel of barbers who put mud on her face and pull at her eyebrows." An editor at the *Presbyterian Banner* thought that it was "pitiful to see the face painted and overlaid with all manner of these artificial enhancements that are not even skin deep and will wash off like whitewash, while the deeper face of the soul is unadorned and marred with an unhappy disposition and evil spirit."[39] Mainstream women's periodicals, independent of an overtly religious agenda, depended heavily on advertising dollars generated by these very items. *Ladies' Home Journal,* for one, described cosmetics as "the arts and crafts of the modern flapper."[40]

Although cosmetic use among younger women was practically de rigueur for this highly stylized look, "older" women who visibly wore cosmetics were regarded with some suspicion. In 1912, when cosmetic use was not yet widespread, one article concluded that a positive attitude, coupled with a sunny smile, gave one sufficient beauty.[41] Three years later, the attitude and smile were no longer sufficient, and sales were clearly not limited to the younger set: $50 million worth of cosmetics sold in 1915.[42] "The intelligent selection and proper use of the . . . face or talcum powders, cold creams . . . and toilet waters are necessary in preserving health and affording much *legitimate* daily comfort," an article on chemical analysis of cosmetics in *McClure's* concluded.[43]

The appeal of legitimate and daily comfort, coupled with 1920s sensibilities about leisure, beauty, and vanity, coalesced to make toilet goods one of the largest industries in the United States, behind food, clothing, and automobiles.[44] Some speculated cosmetic sales were propelled by "sheer, unadulterated woman's vanity running riot in times of prosperity," but writer Frances Kaye believed otherwise. Woman's new role in the political, social, and economic world outside the confines of her home heightened her awareness about aesthetics and beauty in general, and her own face in particular. "Intelligent care," Kaye wrote, "is making and keeping beauty."[45] For the new generation of business women, their faces (not their brains) might very well be their fortunes, education and new political powers to the contrary. "The woman who fails to avail herself of these [beauty aids]," Mary Winslow believed, "never looks so well-groomed as the woman who applies them wisely."[46] According to job manuals and etiquette guides for women (not to mention the numerous beauty columns and beauty books), good grooming became inextricably linked with business success.

Good grooming also became linked with the country's economic success. The value of cosmetics in the larger U.S. economy became glaringly apparent when the government relied upon sales of this "insignificant" item to raise money. Congress passed a war revenue tax requiring "stamps" on proprietary medicines, cosmetics, perfumes, and other items with an anticipated yield of $7 million.[47] The Revenue Bill, passed on October 22, 1914, became effective December 1. The idea and the language of the bill were not unique. As *Weekly Drug Markets* noted, it "is identical with the Spanish-American War Tax" of 1898.[48] In September 1915, the U.S. Treasury announced that cosmetic manufacturers had paid $34,000.[49] In 1921, rather than rescind this tax, however, Congress proposed a 4 percent "luxury tax" on all toilet goods to continue generating money from the sale of beauty products. Soap manufacturers argued that this was essentially taxing cleanliness and would have an adverse effect on the public's health. "Adjuncts of cleanliness and decency, absolute necessities in the humblest home, the greater portion of toilet goods now on the market can no more be classed as luxuries than ordinary soap."[50] Congress passed the luxury tax but excluded soaps, thus establishing a legislative pattern of omission that would continue vis-à-vis cosmetics and soaps.

● ● ●

In addition to changing how a woman looked, cosmetics also changed what women did or could do in terms of possible employment. The new beauty standard and the changing hair fashions presaged the beginning of a job niche for women. Each of these early companies contributed to this growth—Rubinstein and Arden with their salon attendants, Factor with his wig makers and makeup artists, CPC and Walker Company with their traveling sales force. Not all beauty salons bore women's names, but an essential element of the salon experience was being pampered and indulged, often by other women. Other employment emerged as the beauty industry evolved, including demonstrators in department stores and clerks in drugstores.[51]

The pursuit of beauty, then, provided countless new job opportunities for women.[52] Beauticians were not insignificant in the economy: over two hundred thousand women were employed in such positions in 1937.[53] Popular and professional trade literature suggests that cosmetology was a serious, profitable, and respectable profession for women. In numerous "career guides for girls" of the 1910s and 1920s, beauty work was among those listed. Reasons for becoming a beautician included status, cleanliness of the work environment, money, and stability. The beauty industry provided some women with jobs and others with a personal service. Both upscale salons and their lower-class beauty shops fed on and catered to women willing to pay a fee for beauty.

Helena Rubinstein, for example, did not want "just anyone" to become a beautician. Rather, she regarded the profession as one combining scientific rigor, educational training, and an artist's eye for style and color. As such, she envisioned the beauty industry as a lifelong job for women, not a temporary bridge between girlhood and marriage; the skills that made for success in the industry were either always or never present. In a 1920 career manual offering "a general view of the kinds of positions women are filling" she described employment in beauty culture.[54] "The career of beauty culturist," Rubinstein wrote, "has increased in scope within recent years and has attained the dignity of a major profession for women."[55] Just as nursing, a traditional woman's role, had struggled to attain professional status, Rubinstein hoped to do the same for beauty culture.[56] Rubinstein's characterization of the knowledge necessary for the job elevated the beautician to the pinnacle of professionalism. Her description of salon work detailed the enthusiasm, business sense, interpersonal skills, determination, and knowledge of chemistry, dermatology, physiology, anatomy, and hygiene necessary. "This work, therefore, offers more opportunities for women than perhaps any other field of endeavor," she concluded. "Furthermore, women are becoming increasingly aware of the importance of good grooming, and the demand for beauty culturists is becoming correspondingly larger."[57]

As Rubinstein so accurately prophesied, the ranks of beauty culturists swelled in the post–World War I period to meet the demand. As women became increasingly visible in economic and social roles outside the home, appearance and good grooming became more important as well. Like other vocations in the first three decades of the twentieth century, cosmetology became increasingly professionalized, with educational requirements, licensure laws, national professional associations, and trade journals.[58] The National Hairdressers and Cosmetologists Association (NHCA), founded in 1919, united cosmetologists and manufacturers of appliances and products used in beauty shops. In a critical move, the NHCA had an official, nationally circulated publication from its inception. Charles Kozlay, publisher and editor of *American Hairdresser,* and co-founder of the NHCA, allowed his journal to become the official organ of the NHCA. Immediately, then, the NHCA had a means of communication with its members, a platform from which to inform members of potential legislation, call for lobbying on state and national levels, present news within the industry, and relay the latest hair fashions. The NHCA's mission, recapitulated twelve years after its founding, was to "bind together the various independent associations of hairdressers, cosmetologists, and allied activities into one comprehensive organization, in order to procure uniformity of standards and harmony of results."[59]

The national organization aided in the increase of professionalization of this service and maintaining standards. Beauticians in each state spearheaded drives for licensing boards and laws to clearly distinguish between those with, and those without, the proper training. This mirrored changes in other professions as well, with the shift from haphazard apprenticeships to one more systematic. Although the specific requirements for obtaining a license varied from state to state, the general elements—hours of supervised practical training, formalized education from accredited schools—did not vary. The NHCA suggested key components of a "model bill" and published various state laws as examples. A license in cosmetology, almost nationwide by the late 1920s, signaled that the holder had attended an accredited beauty school; had learned about circulation of the blood, general anatomy, and skin care; had hands-on training; and had passed a state-sponsored test consisting of written and practical sections.[60] Endorsed and fully supported by the NHCA on both the national and local levels, the license-granting boards in each state usually sought stricter and tougher policies than the state legislature was willing to pass.

Legislation was always an important and pressing issue for local and national chapters to follow. In 1931, a tax bill before the Illinois Senate effectively proposed to tax beauty shops twice (for providing a personal service and for using "luxury items," already carrying a 20 percent surtax). Not only did Ann Steele, president of the Illinois State

Society, testify before the state senate, but every member of the Illinois Senate received telegrams from local chapters opposing the legislation.[61] As frequently published charts and the "Beauty School" column in *American Hairdresser* made clear, virtually every state had laws regarding beauty practices in place. During the early years of the New Deal, *American Hairdresser* assiduously reported on legislation, out of both self-protection and self-interest. The NHCA hopped on the (short-lived) National Recovery Act train, set standards for its workers, and proudly displayed the blue eagle at salons nationwide, proclaiming "We do our part."

The downside to this professionalism and attempt at universal licensure was that these efforts were little-known outside the beauty industry. In *The Truth about Cosmetics*, the author challenged the conventional wisdom about the lack of sophistication and education of beauticians. "In spite of the scoffing once heard directed at the intelligence of this group, a close study of their training would lead one to greater appreciation," physician Everett McDonough wrote. "Most operators take a very intensive training course; this does not take in the entire field of dermatology, but it makes her limitations clear and teaches her logically the proper things to do for skin conditions she is permitted to treat and why they should be done. Most states have laws requiring every operator to show her knowledge by passing a state exam before she can practice."[62]

A critical component of the licensure process was learning about and respecting the parameters of one's expertise. Although licensure laws defined what one could and could not do, they seldom explicitly prohibited activities. This omission in the law created tension and competition between the old guard already cutting hair—barbers—and the new group also cutting hair—beauticians. Barbers, an older, established, and esteemed profession, disagreed with cosmeticians about which profession could perform which personal care routines, and about the gender of the patron. Most state laws for the licensure of barbers did not specify the sex of the patron, but had been written at a time when only men would patronize public haircutting establishments. In the 1920s, as women began to get their hair cut, however, barbers' associations tried to ensure that licensing laws limited beauticians' clientele to women only. A 1931 article in *American Hairdresser*'s legislation column noted that the NHCA helped defeat 150 barbers' bills at the state level, most of which attempted to extend the province of barbers to encompass women's hair and makeup.[63] It was not so much that the barbers actually wanted (or knew how) to cut women's hair and apply their makeup so much as barbers did not want to lose more ground to beauticians who were cutting women's hair, and occasionally, men's hair. A report on the monthly meeting of the Chicago and Illinois Hairdressers' Association noted that readers' belief that "the Supreme Court ruling allowing beauty culturists to cut hair without a barber's license has settled the controversy for all times" was erroneous; the 1931 victory was temporary.[64] No sooner were beauty culturists in Illinois allowed to cut women's hair than a new pending Senate bill, S.197, threatened to make it illegal for beauty schools to do facial work, a service that accounted for a significant portion of beauty shop income.[65]

The conflict or overlap between cosmetologists and barbers was clearly defined, and both tried to alter licensure laws to protect their patron base. An unanticipated third party in this world was the physician. Regardless of state or local licensing law, beauticians carefully observed their professional boundaries. Part of the conflict with the medical community was economic: physicians feared they were losing (or never getting) patients who discussed their facial flaws with beauticians; a larger part of the problem was medical care: most physicians viewed the beauticians as ill-trained to treat skin problems. Rather than advance the potentially sticky monetary issue, physicians focused their attack on the skill, or lack thereof, of beauticians. Some dermatologists encouraged their medical colleagues to establish cordial working relationships with beauticians in their community, on the grounds that such connections could be mutually beneficial. After exhausting all possible treatments to eradicate or minimize a beauty flaw or skin problem, a beautician allied with a physician often encouraged her patron to visit the medical professional.[66] Conversely, dermatologists occasionally referred patients to beauty shops for facials and skin treatments.[67] One dermatologist, G. Alexander Ward, noted that 90 percent of beauty shop customers were under thirty-five years of age, and therefore particularly prone to acne. In the beauty trade literature, he encouraged beauticians to treat acne and other simple skin conditions. Cleanliness was of primary importance, Ward believed; he also endorsed beauticians executing X rays and chemical peels.[68]

Skin peeling, a process in which caustic acids were applied to the face and the burned layers of skin subsequently removed, reached its zenith the early 1920s. At one time recommended as a correction for oily, shiny, or dirty-looking skin, as well as large pores and freckles, peeling was not a procedure to be undertaken casually.

Skin peeling is the removal of the horny outside layer of skin by means

> of masks or chemicals, which makes the average girl think she is getting
> a new skin. There is nothing miraculous in this; the outside layer is
> always being shed. The skin underneath is new and may look softer
> and smooth for a very short time, then it resumes its usual appearance.
> Skin peeling sometimes results in improved looks in acne, for the time
> being at least. This practice means a few days in seclusion. It may be
> dangerous. If the treatment is allowed to act too long, the real skin
> beneath may be injured and scars result

warned a dermatologist in the late 1930s, long after the practice had
shifted from salon to surgical suite.[69] First practiced by cosmetologists,
many physicians appropriated this treatment and suggested that only
qualified medical personnel perform this lengthy (and possibly dangerous) process. In the 1920s, the process was administered over a
course of weeks and the typical patron remained shrouded and swathed
in bandages for six to eight weeks following the application of the chemicals. "For those who doubt the seriousness of proceeding with these
applications as cautiously as advised, it should be mentioned that if the
peeling is done too deeply, by the solution being too concentrated or left
on too long, there is danger of scarring," a physician warned in 1932.[70]

State and local boards of public health did their best to keep dangerous cosmetics out of the hands and off the faces of consumers. They
were not alone, however, in their efforts. The NHCA had long recognized the risks women undertook when submitting themselves to the
ministrations of a cosmetic. If anything, beauticians had a professional
and personal interest in safe beauty aids. In the event of a disaster, the
beautician had liability. The combination of increasingly dangerous
chemicals in beauty products and electrical-based appliances raised the
possibility of a lawsuit filed against individual operators or appliance
manufacturers.[71] Even seemingly innocuous processes were fraught
with potential risk. "In many of these operations [permanent waves,
curling, crimping, and straightening] there is the danger of burning the
scalp and thus causing the permanent loss of hair," a dermatologist
noted, "and in recent years there have been many damage suits against
hairdressers by women whose hair and general health were ruined by
such operations as the 'permanent' wave."[72] Articles in *American Hairdresser* urged readers to employ safe beauty practices and obtain insurance to protect customers and themselves from any possible injury.[73]

In an attempt to make education and other key concerns more interesting, *American Hairdresser* took an innovative approach. "Peggy in
Uniform," a serial novella, appeared in *American Hairdresser* from July

1933 through July 1934, and encapsulated many of the trials and tribu-
lations encountered by modern beauticians. "Here," the teaser read,
"begins the challenging and up-to-the-minute novel by Merlet and
Deane, in which Peggy Black, fresh from beauty school, encounters
many difficulties in love and business with which beauticians are often
faced."[74] As the reader followed the raven-haired heroine through her
shaky and uncertain professional beginnings at a variety of highly
unsatisfactory beauty parlors, certain ethical and behavioral codes of
the profession were subtly reinforced, from scientific and hygienic standards taught in beauty schools (but often not implemented in shops) to
patch-testing clients to determine sensitivity to dyes, from the proper
demeanor of a beautician towards a patron to working with jobbers to
promote certain product lines.

In the early episodes, Peggy frequently sought guidance from Mrs.
Hewlett, her mentor at Hampton Beauty Academy, where she had been
a star pupil. Each discussion bolstered the lessons of the beauty school.
Many of Peggy's early problems, and source of unhappiness, were
because of her inability to negotiate between the high standards she had
learned at Hampton and the patrons she encountered once employed.
In her first position, in an old-fashioned beauty shop, she was repri-
manded for applying her newly acquired ideas of cleanliness—ideas
that ran counter to established shop policy. Similarly, Peggy's reluctance
to apply and push inappropriately bright blush, lipstick, and eyeshadow colors at another salon was because of her training about use,
type, and appropriate shade of color.[75] Peggy, transformed into Madame
Margot Noir by the end of the saga, ultimately held fast to her teaching,
her professional image, and her high standards, all of which also happened to be endorsed by the NHCA. Equipped with a beauty school
education, certified and licensed under state law, a member of her local
NHCA chapter, Peggy ran her salon with scrupulous hygiene and
enhanced her inherent professionalism with an air of elegance and chic,
thus providing the perfect role model for both her (fictional) clientele
and the readers.

● ● ●

Pressure to be well groomed has always stimulated cosmetic sales, especially facial creams, lipstick, and hair dyes. In the 1920s and 1930s, older
women purchased cosmetics to look young(er), and for added job security; younger women purchased cosmetics for a psychological rather

than an economic boost. Cosmetics were so embedded on women's vanities by the end of the 1920s that the Great Depression failed to alter established patterns of consumption and application. If anything, more rather than fewer women wore makeup during the Depression than had previously. For some women past the bloom of youth, economic necessity—the need to look younger to get and keep a job—won over vanity and ideas about who did and did not wear cosmetics. The effort to look one's best did not abate during dire economic straits; although women were conscious of money spent on these "luxury items," many were loath to change to cheaper brands or give up cosmetics.[76] "I think that when we . . . have found that combination of cosmetics that we think ideal for us, we do not care to experiment unless we are reasonably certain that we are going to improve our appearance, for what woman does not want to look her best?"[77] Despite the pervasive use of cosmetics, men preferred veiled knowledge or ignorance about cosmetic use, even though the "look" to which they responded was possible only through judicious use of makeup. A survey of male undergraduates revealed that they did not approve of evident makeup. "Practically 100 percent no. How they hate it! They want to be fooled by artificial aids to beauty—never to be made aware of them."[78] Nor did young men want to see their female companions "apply their complexions in public."[79]

The beauty industry stood to profit twice from the resurgence in the necessity of cosmetics. First, sales increased. Second, business at beauty salons increased also, thus keeping cosmetologists employed and increasing sales of beauty products at salons. Once women were in the salons, hairdressers were encouraged to capitalize on their presence and sell them more items by emphasizing pride in one's appearance. "Even in these days of pinch-penny economy," G. W. Vanden speculated in 1932, "women are not running around with wan cheeks and shiny noses. WOMEN ARE NOT GOING WITHOUT COSMETICS, even if it takes the last spare change from their pocketbooks to buy."[80] Advertisements in women's magazines also began to tout the importance of regular salon visits, and the wonders they could do for women. Many of these advertisements were sponsored by, or in conjunction with, the NHCA, which had a vested interest in keeping beauty shops open, and beauticians working. The rationale behind this campaign was explained to NHCA members in *American Hairdresser,* the official trade organ. According to editor Hazel Kozlay in 1932, many women had not yet been sold the doctrine of beauty cultivation by experts and therefore did not yet have the beauty habit. However, with the right persuasion, she believed these women could learn the correct beauty habits and contribute to what was sure to be guaranteed growth of the beauty industry. "The beauty industry is weathering the economic crisis in a manner which is the envy of other trades and professions," she wrote. American women "may get along with a little less service in their beauty shops, they may seek more for their dollar, but give it up they will not. It is as necessary to them as the clothes they wear and the food they eat."[81]

Men may have chosen to remain blissfully ignorant, but retailers did their best to ensure visibility of their products. In a 1925 article on strategies on sales of toiletry items in beauty salons, Anne Kellogg suggested that the beauty ideal would be sufficient: if the idea of glamour and beauty appealed to the customer (as it must have to women patronizing beauty salons), the beauty aids would sell themselves. "Beauty is something to preserve, or it will take unto its wings. And the woman who is not attractive can easily make herself so, by cultivating her best points and strenuously improving her bad ones."[82] Cosmetologists and cosmetic manufacturers were not alone in promoting this image, although they did so in their quest for sales of beauty products. In 1932, the president of the Chicago Medical Association spoke at a meeting of the Chicago and Illinois Hairdressers' Association and emphasized the importance of beauty via cosmetics. "In its psychological aspects," Dr. John Hager told his audience, "the work of the beauty profession is very closely related to that of the medical profession: to make your customers *feel* they are looking their best is equally as important as actually to make them look the best that is within your power."[83]

The continuing and escalating growth of cosmetics during the Depression can partly be attributed to the same psychology that propelled sales in the 1920s. A 1932 appraisal of the cosmetics industry by the Chemical Division of the Department of Commerce found increased production in 1931 compared to that between 1920 and 1929; further, the 17 percent decline in cosmetics sales from its 1929 sales peak was small given the 41 percent decline experienced by most other industries. Manufacturers quietly expressed surprise that in a year of economic depression cosmetics were purchased in greater rather than lesser quantities. Cosmetics, industry observers decided, were regarded by consumers as essential for civil life and good grooming. C. C. Concannon, chief of the Commerce Department's Chemistry Division, postulated that continued high sales were due to "a psychological factor—the conviction that the race is to those who feel fit, and a large part of feeling fit is looking fit. So far as cosmetics act as an aid to that end of really making people feel fitter, they have ceased to be a 'non-essential' and have become a necessity."[84] And feel better women clearly did, if market share is any indication.

Certain products from specific companies dominated women's vanities. A 1935 comparison of cold, cleansing, and vanishing creams revealed that Pond's dominated all three markets, accounting for 27.4%, 21.4%, and 19.6% respectively, of all sales; Lady Esther's sales figures were close behind, with 22.2%, 12.8%, and 5.5% of all sales. These two companies accounted for 25% to 50% of all retail sales in cream. In facial powders, Lady Esther, Coty, and Woodbury claimed over 30% market share, with 20.6%, 7.6%, and 5.9% of all powders purchased. Similar figures emerged for other cosmetics: Princess Pat dominated dry rouge sales with 10.2%; Angelus accounted for 7.8% of the paste rouge purchased; and Tangee sold 10.5% of all lipsticks. In the hand lotion market, three companies—Campana, Jergen, and Hind's—captured over one-half of all sales.[85] Variety and product options, it seems, opened the cosmetics market to new possibilities for customers and manufacturers.

How cosmetics successfully increased market share is a testament to good advertising agencies and clever campaigns. The strategy employed and the success of Pond's Cold Cream in the 1920s serves as an excellent example of a company trying to gain market share in a category of product—cold cream—that previously lacked identity.[86] In 1886, the advertising firm J. Walter Thompson Company won the Pond's account to promote Pond's Extract. For fifteen years, the extract was the primary focus, and the sole product advertised. When the company introduced a vanishing cream in 1907, it quickly became the segment leader and dominated vanishing cream sales. According to an internal Pond's product history, "In 1916, sales figures showed that the Vanishing Cream was well entrenched, and it was considered time to begin developing the *Cold Cream.*"[87] Before launching the advertising campaign for cold cream, however, the agency conducted a survey which revealed confusion about the distinctions between cold and vanishing creams.[88] This confusion posed a potentially serious problem: because Pond's sold both creams, the agency feared that the merits and benefits of one cream might cannibalize the other cream's sales. The success of the cold cream might well come at the expense of the vanishing cream. "The campaign of these two Pond's products is designed to have a real news appeal to women," J. Walter Thompson internal memoranda revealed. "It has been found upon investigation that the skin needs 2 creams. . . . The reason for this, and the ways whereby Pond's products satisfy these needs, are featured in every piece of copy. This is again a case of *selling an idea rather than a product* [emphasis in original]."[89] J. Walter Thompson's advertising campaign explaining the need for both creams boosted sales from $307,000 in 1916 to $1.6 million in 1923.[90]

Pond's cold and vanishing creams became the victim of their own advertising success, however, as the idea of two creams became more important than the particular brand. The public embraced the message—the necessity for two creams—but did not apply it to Pond's creams in particular. As public confidence in all cosmetics and creams rose, Pond's profits fell. Upscale cosmetic companies began to offer "treatment lines," in which individual items complemented each other much the same way Pond's vanishing and cold creams did. To pull Pond's out of its profit slough, and to increase advertising dollar outlay, the advertising firm created a new series of advertisements harkening back to those of Harriet Hubbard Ayer, in which leading American society women and European royalty endorsed Pond's creams. "If," account executives speculated, "endorsements could be secure [sic] from *women of social prominence as well as beauty*, then, indeed, Pond's would be lifted out of the class of its active competitors."[91]

The wrinkle in this strategy was how to secure these endorsements. The women who ultimately endorsed Pond's were approached through intermediaries—women who were part of society and also knew about the proposed advertising campaign. The "personal contacts," as the go-betweens were called, earned $1,000 for each endorsement they helped to obtain. The women who endorsed Pond's were rewarded for their efforts as well, although many donated their stipend to charity. American endorsers included Mrs. William Borah, wife of the Idaho senator; Mrs. Condé Nast, renowned hostess and the wife of the magazine publisher; Mrs. Nicholas Longworth, née Alice Roosevelt, Teddy's redoubtable daughter and Washington hostess; Mrs. Marshall Field, wife of a Chicago shopping emporium magnate; and Mrs. Alva Belmont, socialite turned suffragist and president (and chief financial support) of the National Woman's Party.[92] The advertising campaign was waged in middle-class periodicals: *Ladies' Home Journal, Woman's Home Companion, McCall's, Delineator,* and *Good Housekeeping*.[93] Once again, the strategy to increase sales of Pond's vanishing and cold cream succeeded: revenues surged from $1,600,000 in 1923 to $3,508,000 in 1932, the duration of the campaign.[94] This campaign vividly illustrates how commercial appeal was created: sales tactics, diverse advertising, and repetition of the key message. Each advertisement featured a different woman with different text, endorsing Pond's creams. The success of Pond's creams, as evidenced by market dominance, was linked to

advertising dollars. The advertising was carefully conceived and exe-
cuted, placed in magazines that reached the target audience. And
Pond's was only one of many products on the market.[95]

The increased sales of Pond's and other cosmetics strongly suggest
that women did a considerable amount of reading (and shopping) in the
1920s and 1930s. Advertisements, which soon accounted for 65 percent
of magazine revenues, targeted women, the primary purchasers in the
household.[96] Advertising firms charged with promoting and enhancing
sales used space in magazines, along roadsides, and on radio to incul-
cate consumer demand.[97] In 1900, women made 80 percent of all purchasing decisions. In 1920, when one-fourth of all women worked outside the home, women's purchasing power was even greater.[98]
Advertising, particularly in magazines, encouraged a cultural homogeneity of trends, fashion, and politics.[99]

Mass media was a critical component of increasing homogeneity
and uniformity in American culture. American aspirations of a better (or
different) life were fostered equally by the articles and advertisements in
magazines and newspapers. Newspapers increasingly relied on syndicated features such as gossip columns and newswire services for everything from sports scores to national news. And the public voraciously
consumed all types of magazines, from the sex and confession genre to
literary and news magazines. Bernarr MacFadden's *True Story,* launched
in 1919, had an initial circulation of 300,000 and increased threefold in
seven years, to almost two million readers in 1926.[100] To stay competitive,
many women's magazines originally established as fashion and pattern
books, such as *Woman's Home Companion* and *Delineator,* recast themselves as worldlier and less domestic, with editorials, news, and literature.[101] The number of magazines and magazine circulations escalated
rapidly.[102] According to a 1923 survey of 9,200 homes in Muncie, Indiana,
one in five families subscribed to *American Magazine* or *The Saturday
Evening Post;* one in six homes subscribed to *Delineator, Ladies' Home
Journal,* or *Woman's Home Companion;* 200 to 500 families subscribed to
Good Housekeeping or *Cosmopolitan;* thirty-five received *Atlantic Monthly,*
fifteen received *The New Republic,* and four received *Survey.*[103]

One trend in women's magazines was a regular commentary
devoted solely to enhancing (or creating) beauty—the beauty column.
This feature became a staple in many magazines, from regional publications such as the West Coast periodical *Sunset,* to those with national
distribution such as *Harper's Bazaar Monthly, Good Housekeeping,
Woman's Home Companion, Delineator,* and *Ladies' Home Journal.*[104] Mary
Foster Snider's column, one of the first of this genre, appeared in

Woman's Home Companion in 1905; the trend continued with twists or accommodations, as with Jean Eaton's mother-daughter good grooming column in *Parents' Magazine*.[105] Antoinette Van Hoesen's beauty column in *Harpers' Bazaar* began in 1907 and was taken over by Marie Montagne in 1912; *Good Housekeeping*'s two editors—Nora Mullane and Ruth Murrin—dictated beauty fashion for a long time: Mullane edited the column from 1915 until 1927, when she was replaced by Murrin. *Ladies' Home Journal* essentially had an editor a year between 1922 and 1927, when Ethel Lloyd Patterson, Mary Brush Williams, and G. M. Georges held the position. The *Delineator* retained Celia Caroline Cole's services in 1923; after Jean Felts took over the column in 1930, Cole continued to write columns on gracious living for the magazine. *Sunset* hired Marise de Fleur and Jean Ashcroft in 1926 and 1929 respectively for its column.

Each beauty editor offered advice and information on proper skin care, evaluated new products on the market, and suggested seasonal skin-care regimens (extra moisturizer in December, suntan creams and freckle removers in July). Beauty advice was recycled within a magazine from year to year, as well as from magazine to magazine. Despite "new" and "improved" products, the basic tenets of skin care did not change. The very availability and multiplicity of merchandise that sustained these authors simultaneously provided fodder for new columns and generated advertising revenue for the periodicals.[106]

Beauty columns should be read with a jaundiced eye, however. As the beauty and film industries grew in the 1920s, and the power of celebrity became a marketable commodity, the names of various starlets began to adorn both columns and cosmetics.[107] Readers could not assume that the column had actually been written by the person credited in the byline. Fame did not translate into automatic beauty knowledge, particularly in the film industry, with its invisible phalanx of makeup artists. Responsible and hard-working beauty editors worried that the powers of invention outweighed the powers of reason and research. The popularity—and possibly unsound advice—of these features also raised some eyebrows in the medical community as early as 1910. "In nine cases out of ten, the information they [columns] give is harmless, for, in order to be safe, they confine themselves to obvious suggestions, often bordering on nonsense," dermatologist William Woodbury wrote, "but in the tenth case they may give absolutely injurious advice."[108]

● ● ●

A confluence of events—changing ideas about femininity, the rise of the New Woman, the growth of advertising and mass media—worked in conjunction to foster the cosmetics industry. In visible and invisible ways, makeup provided goods- and services-related jobs. Cosmetics were often made, and assembled, by women. Makeup purchases helped women define who they were—a generation distinct from their mothers'. But cosmetics also provided employment for beauticians, saleswomen, copywriters, and beauty editors. None of these jobs was possible without the other. Women bought items, and beauticians employed them, to create a "look," based on advertising, articles in women's magazines, and beauty editors' columns. Only the barest hint of tension between doctors and cosmetologists was palpable, and only then if one was looking for it.

chapter three

"Marring the fair face of nature"

AS THE COSMETICS industry continued to grow through the 1920s, the move to protect consumers from cosmetics grew incrementally. The involvement of government agencies—the Food and Drug Administration (FDA), the Federal Trade Commission, and the U.S. Postal Service—in protecting the public's physical and economic health really only began toward the end of the 1920s as consumption increased. The near invisibility of consumer activism among women's organizations, and their lack of concern about cosmetics, was understandable: cosmetics were widely regarded as safe—a perception shattered in the early 1930s. The movement by the medical community to protect women from unsafe cosmetics occurred on an individual rather than an institutional basis: individual physicians encouraged legislation and regulation of cosmetics and cosmetologists. Even the increasingly visible (but small) consumer movement, embodied by Consumers' Research, paid little attention to cosmetics.

The response to the letter little Hazel Fay Musser wrote to President Franklin Roosevelt pulled these disparate groups together, forcing government response to a medical injury that was receiving national attention. What happened to the letter was a little out of the ordinary. As per procedure in dealing with the tremendous volume of White House mail, the letter was sent to the appropriate authority, in this instance, the FDA. Ruth deForest Lamb, an FDA information officer, was so taken with the letter and its heartfelt plea that she rerouted it back to the White House and encouraged a personal response from the president. "The human interest of the whole thing," she wrote to Stephen Early, on White House staff, "would have a far reaching effect. It has us tied up in knots."[1] The timing of the letter, and a presidential response, were such that it could have influenced negotiations over a revised food and drugs bill. Senator Copeland's bill had just, on January 4, been submitted, copied, and circulated with a date set for hearings before the Senate Commerce Committee when this letter arrived back at the White House.[2] Had the president responded to Miss Musser, or made the letter public, it might have affected more than just a few government personnel and physicians.

• • •

As cosmetic sales increased in the 1910s and 1920s, social and political activism, so vital just ten years earlier, decreased. Progressive reform is generally regarded as ending by 1920.[3] Activism continued, but the focus shifted to the local level and local causes, rather than a national agenda. The efforts of some women's organizations had been rewarded with the passage of the Eighteenth and Nineteenth Amendments—Prohibition and woman suffrage. In the absence of a visible national agenda in the 1920s, until recently many historians assumed that women's activism disappeared altogether.[4] The days of grassroots campaigning that had been successful (if not pivotal) in the fight for the 1906 Pure Food and Drugs Act seemed long gone. This position fails to take into account the exception to this lull in activism: the consumer movement. In the midst of sustained prosperity and economic growth beginning in 1922, some consumers began to question the value and comparative worth of products on the market. The same market forces that fostered increased sales of radios and rouge sparked a movement for activism and protection on behalf of and to benefit unwary consumers.

One of the most profound political changes of the 1920s was the new power given to women. Women had long been politically active on social issues ranging from abolition to temperance to protecting child labor, but, prior to suffrage, had had little more than moral suasion on their side.[5] With the passage of the Nineteenth Amendment, the National American Woman Suffrage Association, an organization dedicated solely to suffrage, transformed itself into the League of Women Voters (LWV). The LWV's mandate was to educate and encourage the newly enfranchised women voters. Maud Park, LWV president, formed the Women's Joint Congressional Committee (WJCC) to capitalize and harness the nascent political power of women voters. The WJCC, representing a broad coalition of women's organizations, who in turn represented a large number of new voters, had greater political clout when speaking and petitioning members of Congress than would a woman appearing as a representative of only one association or organization.[6]

In a demonstration of the power (or fear of power) of the perceived women's bloc vote, Congress passed the Sheppard-Towner Act in 1921. The act, which provided maternal and infant care at federally funded clinics, passed by significant margins in both the House and the Senate, with funding for five years.[7] Some women (and the WJCC) regarded its passage as a testament to their lobbying strength and to women's issues being accorded respect and consideration in Congress.[8] For most physicians, however, the Sheppard-Towner Act represented a dangerous step in giving the federal government increased power and control over state public health issues.[9] The rights of the state versus federal government to provide health care were an ongoing battle. The American Medical Association (AMA) had two other complaints. First, they objected to the administrative agency, arguing that Public Health Services, rather than the Labor Department (in which the Children's Bureau belonged), should be directing the program.[10] Second, in a period of changing medical practice and an increase in specialization, physicians argued that they were being economically displaced by "free" care provided at the clinics. Some physicians also questioned the level and competence of care at the clinics, which were staffed largely by nurses and women physicians.

The Sheppard-Towner Act had a five-year life of funding. When the possibility of extending the funding came up for debate in Congress, the AMA urged its membership of more than 83,000 to write the president, senators, and representatives urging no further funding.[11] In *JAMA*, William Woodward, of the AMA Bureau of Legal Medicine, formally explained the AMA's opposition, arguing in part that maternal and infant health had declined, and mortality increased, between 1921 and 1926. Despite AMA opposition, the Sheppard-Towner Act was funded for an additional three years, contingent on funding ending at that point. The WJCC remained concerned, but its attention diminished and its campaign for continued funding was less vigorous than it had been earlier. Also, the much vaunted "woman vote" had not materialized and was insufficient to hold representatives or senators hostage. When the act again came up for extension in 1929, the AMA prevailed.

The AMA was not alone in monitoring and policing health policy. In a new step for women's activism, various groups formed to tackle specific problems, armed with the real threat of voting someone out of office. In 1931, the New York Protective Committee of Women established a committee to investigate conditions in beauty shops and hairdressing parlors. In their activism and goal, they echoed National Consumers' League investigations of the garment and candy industries twenty years previously.[12] The committee found much in the beauty industry in disarray: deplorable sanitary conditions; widespread exploitation of beauticians; little regulation of beauty schools, with some providing little training despite tuition fees; and too few insurance policies. The final, and perhaps most serious, area of negligence was the disastrous results wrought by inadequately trained operators. "Severely burned scalps often result from inexpert permanent waving, and infected fingers often cause danger of blood poisoning or cancer," the investigative committee's indictment read.[13] In enumerating these glaring deficiencies, the Protective Committee hoped the National Hairdressers and Cosmetologists Association (NHCA) would clean up its own shop rather than force state intervention.

Not everyone was preoccupied with beauty and health, however. The concern of a newly emerging consumer movement in the mid-1920s centered on the health of one's wallet. A loosely constructed consumer movement had been vibrant and active up to and following passage of the 1906 Pure Food and Drugs Act. Like many other reform movements, the wave of activism subsided with the onset of the First World War, when "concerns for war supplanted those of consumption."[14] One critical problem facing the consumer movement—an ongoing problem for the movement, it turned out—was the inherent difficulty in organizing consumers. Unlike other activist causes with clear agendas and easy (or obvious) solutions such as had existed for child labor, there was seldom legislation on specific issues around which consumer activists could rally. Also, many citizens viewed Congress as disposed to treat business hospitably, often at the expense of the consumer. Instead of fighting for (or against) legislation, most consumer activists were concerned with broad, less concrete issues such as getting value for a dollar. Although getting one's money's worth ought to have been a pressing and daily concern, the American public seemed resigned to the market economy, willing to accept false advertising and shoddy merchandise. The abstract nature of "consumer consciousness" helps explain one of the paradoxes of the consumer movement: most of its supporters were educated middle- and upper-income families. Those who presumably needed to get the most for their money appear to have had the least amount of interest, time, or education.[15]

One organization, the American Home Economics Association (AHEA), taught students (mostly women) how to be better, smarter consumers. Despite the AHEA's concern for healthy and wholesome foods, however, they did not engage in product testing; luckily, other groups did. During World War I, Herbert Hoover, an engineer-turned-director of the Food Administration, realized that the government suffered large financial losses due to faulty or defective products. When he became head of the Federation of the American Engineers Society, Hoover suggested developing product standards to ensure more uniform and consistent products. The American Engineer Standards Committee, renamed the American Standards Committee in 1928, moved to address this problem. Realizing the potential cost savings, most companies either created in-house laboratories to test their own products, or hired outside firms, including the American Engineer Standards Committee. Hoover's appointment as secretary of commerce under Presidents Warren Harding and Calvin Coolidge helped strengthen his argument for standards and aided in promulgating industrial product testing.[16]

As conceived by Hoover and implemented by private companies, product testing benefited corporations more than it did consumers. In *The Education of the Consumer,* author Henry Harap urged consumers to learn more about the products they purchased to enable them to make sound, educated, and economical buying decisions. Harap stopped short, however, of comparative education and product testing.[17] Stuart Chase, an engineer with the American Standards Association (ASA), began to consider the larger implications of Harap's message: science could benefit the consumer. Using his work at the ASA as a starting point, the year following Harap's publication Chase wrote *The Tragedy of Waste* in which he searched for more economical solutions to wasted materials and dollars.[18] Encouraged by the reception of that book, Chase and another staff member, Frederick Schlink, wrote *Your Money's Worth* in 1927. Unlike his first book which he had done entirely on his own, Chase provided background information and test results, and Schlink wrote most of the text. *Your Money's Worth* called for "an extension of the principle of buying goods according to impartial scientific test, rather than according to the fanfare and trumpets of the higher salesmanship."[19] Chase and Schlink's book struck a surprisingly responsive chord in the prosperous late 1920s: it became a Book-of-the-Month Club bestseller, and many readers wrote Chase and Schlink complaining about or enumerating defects in specific products.

In response to the book's reception and the subsequent flood of mail requesting more information about various products, Chase and Schlink transformed a small existing consumer group into Consumers' Research (CR) and incorporated it as a nonprofit consumer testing organization in 1929. For annual dues of $2, members received a Confidential Bulletin containing information gathered as the organization "investigate[d], test[ed] and report[ed] reliably concerning hundreds of common items purchased." Membership grew rapidly, from 565 in 1927 to 42,000 in 1931.[20] The spike in membership may have been a reaction to the Depression and a renewed awareness of the need to spend wisely. A sticky problem for CR regarded a central aspect of its existence: product testing. A limited budget and lack of adequate testing facilities greatly constrained what (and how) CR examined various items. Many products tested were small and inexpensive, such as razors or silk stockings, which could, if necessary, be tested by staffers in their homes. Larger items were tested in commercial or academic laboratories, often those of CR supporters, typically at no or minimal cost. The bulletins for members were always marked "Confidential" or "Members Only" for fear of libel suits from companies who might argue that their manufactured goods were being unfairly maligned.[21]

Not all of the product information in CR bulletins was original to the organization. An April 1931 article, "Hair Removal Presents New Hazard," derived the bulk of its information from, and properly attributed, the AMA. The final sentence, a scathing criticism of Koremlu (a depilatory), largely on public health grounds, was a direct quotation from a *JAMA* column.[22] Consumers' Research found itself changing its stance on some issues. "Although Consumers' Research realizes that cosmetics are luxury goods, and has in the past declined to spend money for tests in this field," CR members read in October 1932, "we have become increasingly aware of the fact that it is a subject of great interest to many consumers, and a field in which a large amount of money is spent annually. In view of this fact, we are planning to make analyses, from time to time, of outstanding products on the market."[23] After this initial foray into astringents, none of which were recommended, CR analyzed cream rouges, hand creams, shampoos, and toilet soaps.[24] Consumers' Research first brought attention to the deficiencies in the 1906 act in 1930.[25]

As the consumer movement grew, it was too small, too elite, and too localized to force wholesale changes in business practice. Some manufacturers themselves wanted formal, externally imposed legislation creating uniform standards within the industry. Recognized and sanctioned standards would make it easier for companies to compete for wholesale buyers who were too far away to personally examine the merchandise, particularly if there were federally established "grades" or levels of quality.[26] These standards also would reassure the public, who could expect a certain level of consistency and quality from items, such as canned tomatoes; government regulations, if enforced, carried more weight and a better guarantee than informal and internally controlled association "standards." For example, before the passage of the 1930 McNary-Mapes Act, or "Canners Bill," an amendment to the 1906 Food and Drugs Act, several trade associations established standards by which all members abided.[27] The Association of New York State Canners created guidelines for fruits and vegetables in 1924; the Canners League of California, the California Olive Association, and the Northwest Canners Association followed suit in 1925 and 1926 respectively.[28] Butter manufacturers received federal permission in 1924 to place grades on their retail packaging.[29]

• • •

Physicians saw the aftereffects of poorly produced food, dangerous drugs, and unregulated cosmetics in their offices. The use of soaps or other beauty aids only became an issue of import when a patient appeared because of a rash, discomfort, or other ailment caused by these products. The manner in which these cases were relayed in the medical literature often betrayed an attitude of impatience and a distinct lack of sympathy. Some case reports criticized women for applying products of uncertain provenance to their faces. In a 1924 keynote address, a doctor labeled as "foolish the women who use paint and powder and remain ignorant of their dangers."[30] Three years later, doctors were no more sympathetic. "From the use of cosmetics the writer has not seen any good at all. They are to be condemned from every point of view."[31] Most physicians were at a loss to understand why women wanted to apply these unknown, untested, and possibly dangerous products to their faces, and why women were so foolish or ignorant to rely on these beauty aids when a natural look was "better."[32] One doctor, though, finally figured it out: "The medical profession . . . has maintained an attitude of indifference or aloofness from the question of hair dyeing, probably [because] practically all of the available preparations are either unsuitable or dangerous." And then he treated an older woman who had had a reaction to a hair dye. "Any hesitation I might have felt . . . was immediately dispelled by the sincerity and poignancy of that simple statement: 'It is almost impossible for a woman with gray hair to get a job!'"[33] Only gradually did this point of view take hold.[34]

The typical article in the medical literature followed one or more of several patterns: an historical overview of cosmetics; a chronicle of ingredients, dangerous or otherwise; a reference to previous literature; a simple case report; or a call for regulation or legislation of, variously, cosmetics, cosmetologists, or other doctors. Whatever the reason, or whatever the format, articles in medical journals clearly had a service component. One doctor noted that he had difficulty identifying the causative agent in his patient's rash until he read the weekly issue of *JAMA*.[35] Another noted that a patient came to his office, diagnosis in hand, because she had read an article in a woman's magazine and had already determined what caused her rash.[36]

Early articles on cosmetics were primarily of the first two genres. Most articles in the medical literature through the mid-1920s were entirely or largely historical in nature. Authors went to great lengths to present a history of cosmetics, seemingly proving that these were not, alas, so new. Almost every author noted that Galen, the celebrated and revered ancient physician, invented cold cream, although he may have been considering its properties to sooth burns rather than remove makeup; Cleopatra also merited mention. Given the frequency with which history was offered, the use of medical history did not end with the rise of "scientific medicine" in the late nineteenth century as some have argued, but persisted in helping frame professional arguments in early-twentieth-century medicine. After a flurry of articles simply detailing this history, this genre almost wholly disappeared.

The issue of ingredients in cosmetics was critical, particularly for those trying to establish the field of dermatology. The ingredients in manufactured cosmetics could be innocuous or lethal, depending on the combination and amount used. An article on ingredients might list harmful ones and detail the products in which they could be found; or, alternatively, it might list products and the possible hazards they might pose based upon possible ingredients. A comprehensive listing in the former style, given as part of a presentation on dangers in cosmetics at a meeting of the Section of Dermatology and Syphilology in 1925, ran as follows: face powder—barium sulphate, anilin dyes, perfumes; rouge—zinc oxide, anilin dyes; lipstick or liquid lip rouge—anilin dyes; wrinkle removers—phenol.[37]

Because hair products (shampoos, dyes, tints, and, after 1939, cold permanent waves) contained more "bad" products than any other cosmetic, some articles detailing ingredients focused solely on this category of beauty aid. In this instance, dyes were ranked from most to least innocuous. The latter were also the least permanent; the stronger and more colorfast dyes were more toxic. Hair dyes derived from organic vegetables (henna, indigo, wood extracts, herbs including pyrogallol);

metallics (lead, arsenic, copper, cobalt, tin, bismuth, cadmium, nickel, mercury, and iron); metallic compounds; and anilines (most notoriously, paraphenylenediamine).[38] Once the basic list was established, subsequent case reports assumed readers knew the level of hazard the dye presented.

The third classification of articles, case reports, came about because women were appearing in doctors' offices. Most of the time women suffered allergic reactions to one or more of the ingredients in their toilette. The typical reaction was dermatitis, a red and itchy swelling of the skin, often (but not always) in the area in which the product was applied. The reaction was often induced: initial contact with the allergen served to sensitize, the second exposure heightened sensitivity, and the third exposure elicited a reaction. This happened frequently with perfumes.[39] Given the abundance of cosmetics available, with more and more appearing on the market in the 1920s than ever before, women appeared in doctors' offices with nails peeling or separating from the nail bed, itchy scalp, swollen-shut eyes, odd rashes, pus-filled sores, dry and cracking lips . . . the exact opposite of beauty and glamor.[40]

In some case reports, doctors admitted that it was difficult to determine what had caused the dermatitis. The attitude of physicians could also be a deterrent of patient honesty. One patient mounted a "subconscious defense" against her makeup causing any problems, leading her physician to note that "denial" by patients often was a hindrance in determining the cause of the rash.[41] Women would often forget that they were wearing cosmetics—a true sign of the success of beauty products!—or discount these items as causative agents. One woman, who had been hospitalized because of paralysis and nausea, seemed to be on the rebound, until she suffered a mysterious relapse. Her friends, her doctor later discovered, had brought her some items from home, the indispensable items from her vanity including the face cream responsible.[42] Another doctor only realized what was causing the problems for his patient when he read a case report uncannily similar to what he was seeing in his office. Problem solved, he importuned others to pay attention to what women were wearing, and to ask specific questions about their cosmetic products. "A warning should be broadcast in regard to the dangers of depilatories containing thallium."[43]

Either because formulations often changed, or because one case report caused a cascade of others related to the first, specific products appear in the pages of medical journals over and over again. Papers presented at meetings and subsequently reprinted in medical journals often also included subsequent discussion; not atypical is the comment in which physicians from the floor professed encountering similar cases in their practices, which had gone unreported (until now).[44] After another presentation, audience comments ranged from the AMA's responsibility to keep the public informed about poisonous cosmetics to the FDA's exemption on this front to not blaming women for wearing these products.[45]

Despite this, some physicians wrote skin care guides that appeared alongside those written by beauty editors and beauticians. According to physician William Pusey, his volumes on skin care offered "what everyone of intelligence should know of these subjects, both because of their practical personal importance and as a part of one's general knowledge."[46] Almost all of the beauty guides proffered the same advice—wash the face, frequently, with hot soapy water.[47] Some physicians wrote informal (and popular) beauty guides.[48] Dr. Lulu Hunt Peters, for example, trained as a pathologist before turning to dietetics, practicing first in Los Angeles and later in New York City. In 1923 she contracted with a news service to write a syndicated column on diet and health.[49] In addition, she wrote two popular books on diet, health, and general well-being.[50] Her columns frequently cited physical fitness and overall good health as the way to achieve real beauty. Although many of her columns were indistinguishable from those of beauty editors, she frequently suggested that readers consult their doctor for problems of a more physical nature. Health was not the only reason to pay attention to one's complexion, however. "A woman who neglects her appearance is like an heiress who spurns her inheritance. . . . It is invaluable in pursuing the path to a goal, be it matrimony or a career," Dr. Mary Mac-Fadyen wrote in *Beauty Plus*, a 1938 book-length treatment on skin care. "Doors will open to a handsome girl that are shut to her more careless and less attractive sisters. The girl whose appearance is unprepossessing has an extra hurdle to get over and so is handicapped before she starts."[51]

The authority of physicians and the wisdom of beauty editors paled in comparison with years of experience, however. Helena Rubinstein claimed, in the introduction to *The Art of Feminine Beauty*, that patrons had repeatedly asked her to write about beauty. "These women feel that my experience, stretching as it does over a period of thirty years, must have given me a knowledge on the subject which should be invaluable to them," she wrote, "especially since the period of my professional life happens to have been the most significant thirty years in the development of beauty culture." Rubinstein's book contained basic and essential rules of health and hygiene, almost identical to those in books written by doctors, which she believed would be as true in fifty years as when she wrote them.[52]

For physicians, the health of the patient was of paramount importance. At the conclusion of the chairman's address to the AMA Section of Dermatology and Syphilology in 1924, Herman Cole concentrated on protecting the female consumer. "We should do everything in our power to call to the attention of the public the damage resulting from [cosmetic] use."[53] Cole hoped that women, informed about the ingredients in cosmetics and the limitations of cosmetologists, would use cosmetics, beauticians, and physicians accordingly. Ten years later, John Godwin Downing, assistant professor of dermatology at Boston City Hospital, suggested that a little knowledge about what women actually put on their faces might go a long way towards making women want to clean up their cosmetics, if not their faces. "American women are rapidly ceasing to look like barbarians and agree that the best face is the natural face."[54] Downing, like other physicians, thought the best solution to dangerous ingredients and endangering public welfare would be to convince women to discontinue cosmetic use.

The continued medical reports suggest otherwise. Some women suffered allergic reactions, or other mysterious health problems that coincided with the application of a new hair dye or cosmetic cream and sought medical relief. As most physicians perceived the situation, there were two problems with the beauty industry. The first problem was the lack of regulation of cosmetic products; unlike food and drug products, cosmetics could contain anything and everything. Limiting what could and could not go into cosmetics was seen as a necessary part of consumer protection, but not one that the AMA as a whole was willing to embrace. In the 1920s, the AMA had other, more pressing issues on its public health agenda than what amounted to a minuscule problem affecting a marginal number of patients each year.[55] Alert doctors warned patients about certain products and determined the cause of reactions sooner, based on a close reading of the professional literature. The daunting task of education—of patients and other physicians—only increased as more beauty products flooded the market. Physicians gradually realized that government regulation of cosmetics offered a better solution than education and offered patients the personal margin of safety they deserved.

All of the accidents that arose from cosmetics use were discussed not only in the medical literature but also in the professional beauty literature. Although the former would have been surprised to learn this, the concerns of both groups were remarkably similar: neither wanted women harmed in the pursuit of beauty. Physicians may have disdained women who wore cosmetics; the more realistic among them suggested regulating cosmetics or (depending on the injury) cosmetologists. Cosmetologists, for their part, had far more to lose than physicians if the application of some product caused a rash or untoward reaction to a steady and faithful customer. Neither side fully understood the nature of what the other side had to offer, but physicians more so than cosmetologists were reluctant to cede any power in the realm of skin and facial care. In essence, a turf war broke out over who had the right to tend a woman's face and offer the proper care (whatever that might mean).

But physicians viewed some of the beauty injuries as inflicted by beauticians. The critical issue was who was allowed to do what, as woman patients would appear with a problem from some minor procedure that the physician viewed as a medical, not beauty, procedure. Most physicians, unaware of the licensing procedures for beauty shop operators, believed that unqualified and ignorant women were performing procedures for which they were ill-equipped, and caused more harm than good. Given the difficulties dermatologists had in establishing themselves as specialists, and the disputes between dermatologists, allergists, and general practitioners for patients and treatments, competition with another group proved an added and altogether unnecessary complication.[56] By delineating what cosmetologists should and should not consider acceptable beauty treatments, physicians hoped to move mole removal, acne treatment, and other aesthetic procedures out of the beauty salon and into the doctor's office.[57] Much as barbers had, physicians thought that an effective way to establish acceptable boundaries was through licensure. The difference from barbers, however, is that most physicians did not know that licensing laws were already in place for beauticians. In relying on state licensing laws, physicians replicated earlier an AMA strategy to control or eliminate certain kinds of practice.[58]

In trying to limit (and establish) the boundaries of medical practice, physicians argued among themselves what the boundaries should be. In a talk, dermatologists Lawrence Taussig and Hiram Miller opposed regulating cosmetic ingredients on a national level, and instead urged physicians to engage in direct, local public education of their patients and each other. They indirectly argued for the professionalization of cosmetology; their condemnation of "unlicensed" individuals suggested that a trained group performing these tasks would be much easier to educate and guide to (or away from) certain practices. "It would be unwise for the medical profession to combat charlatans and 'beauty specialists,' who are responsible for most of the ill effects from wrinkle removers," they argued. "More can be accomplished by educating the public or by enacting proper legislation against the injection of paraffin and the application of 'phenol packs,' by these unlicensed individuals."[59] The problem, they believed, was not the beauty specialists themselves so much as it was the wrinkle removers they employed.

Although Miller and Taussig's talk needs to be given serious consideration (as much for what they did not say as for what they did say), it is clear that they used their platform to advance their personal agenda. They wanted cosmetic products regulated and cosmetologists permitted to perform a limited (and clearly defined) number of skin care treatments. Miller and Taussig were concerned about the safety, health, and well-being of beauty patrons and did not want patrons to become patients. In their presentation, Miller and Taussig were fairly well informed about licensure law and could distinguish between product-induced and person-caused accidents. Unfortunately, however, their knowledge did not extend to the AMA's Bureau of Medical Legislation. William Woodward, head of the bureau, commented from the floor on beauticians and the problems they caused; his accusations against them were glaringly inaccurate. First, he believed that beauticians were regulated and cosmetology licensure laws were passed only when outside forces pressured state legislatures to act accordingly. Second, he claimed that only "one or two states have already enacted such legislation" for the licensure of cosmetologists.[60] According to *The New Medical Follies*, written by Morris Fishbein, *JAMA* editor, nine states had licensure laws in 1925, all at the insistence of state NHCA chapters.[61] Woodward also stressed that licensure alone was no guarantee of public safety, although the laxity of licensing boards seemed to apply only to cosmetologists, as opposed to physicians. "Do not presume that because the licensing is to be under your state board of health there will be no danger to the public or to the status of the dermatologist," he admonished the audience.[62] If laws regulating cosmetologists went unenforced, Woodward predicted, these women might evolve into "quasi-dermatologists" to satisfy their patrons and in these new roles unintentionally injure them.[63] In their call for increased control and adherence to licensing, physicians inadvertently strengthened the position and authority of cosmetologists.

Licensing laws for cosmetologists did not satisfy all concerned parties. Those physicians who knew about the licensure process thought it both too lenient and too broad, as it allowed treatments too similar to medical practice, granting beauty operators the authority to remove warts and moles "indiscriminately" and to perform electrolysis.[64] In a pair of case reports, dermatologists Lawrence McCafferty and Serafino Genovese recounted incidents which lent credence to physicians' fears. They worried that patients with skin afflictions would mention it to a cosmetologist and have it "treated," rather than consult a physician. For minor rashes this practice had no foreseeable detrimental consequences, but for more serious problems, such as pigmented moles or manifestations of secondary syphilis, this course of inaction might prove fatal. In their first case, a woman with pigmented moles went to a well-known beauty shop in New York City and purchased a mole removal cream. She sought medical attention only when her skin reacted to this cream; the cream, a mercurial compound, might have stimulated the moles to malignancy had she continued to use it. In the second case, a woman told by her physician to obtain radium as treatment for pigmented moles visited a beauty parlor to buy the radium. In the course of the sale she mentioned that she was buying it on her doctor's recommendation. "The attendant, who was dressed as a nurse, replied that radium was not the thing to use, and if it were, they would advise her as they always had a physician in attendance. She was given some cream and told to apply this to the lesion and it would disappear."[65] Despite the attendant's advice and good will, the problem was not resolved and the woman returned to her doctor for additional medical aid.

Physicians' impressions to the contrary, however, beauticians' education did not end once a woman had obtained her license as a beauty operator. Just as other professionals had requirements for continuing education after licensure, so did cosmetology. Many cosmetologists belonged to the NHCA and read professional periodicals to keep abreast of new products, innovations, practices, and news. As cosmetics became more chemically complex, it became increasingly important to know the ingredients of products used regularly in the salons. Good business practice and legal consequences dictated that salons operate as accident-free as possible: return customers were the lifeblood of salons, and a lawsuit could easily destroy the business. To avoid catastrophe, articles and their educational training exhorted beauticians to perform patch tests prior to applying hair dyes and tints. This simple test could prevent larger problems that might arise if a patron were allergic to a dye applied to her scalp.

● ● ●

Cosmetics were big business. Prior to the 1930s, the Department of Commerce did not distinguish between cosmetics and other toiletries (including perfume, dentifrices, and soap). Figures submitted by various companies on their profits diverged wildly. J. Walter Thompson Company, responsible for promoting Elizabeth Arden, Cheseborough-Ponds, Andrew Jergen Company, Northam Warren, and Coty products, estimated retail cosmetics sales of $18,000,000 in 1909, $90,756,063 in 1921, and $117,175,741 in 1923.[66] It is highly probable that the Thompson figures reflect soap sales also, as the Jergen advertising campaign initially boosted soap sales before progressing to creams and lotions. Using U.S. Census data, a dermatologist claimed that in 1909, 429 firms manufactured cosmetics worth $14,211,969; by 1931, he asserted, the number of firms had increased to 657, and the value of cosmetic output to $156,375,744, with wholesale figures in excess of $250,000,000.[67]

Some cosmetic firms reported profits in trade magazines, albeit sporadically. Procter & Gamble, primarily a soap concern, announced sales of $105,655,386 for the fiscal year July 1, 1921 through June 30, 1922. The sales were disappointing compared with those of the previous year—$120,019,327—but not surprising given the depression of 1921–22.[68] Eleven years later, in 1933, Procter & Gamble's net profit was $3,738,572.[69] In 1932, Noxema announced a 1931 profit of $172,871.33, and a 1932 net operating profit of $229,716.59.[70] Similarly, after depreciation, federal taxes, miscellaneous items, assets of $1,348,810, and liabilities of $184,043, Helena Rubinstein (the company) had a 1931 net income of $120,904.[71] Coty, a purveyor of face powders, claimed $415,662 income in 1934.[72]

An unanticipated side effect of the boom in cosmetics sales (and use) was the cosmetic-induced "accident." Many authors duly noted that most cosmetics were safe for most people; an idiosyncratic, or allergic, reaction to a particular ingredient—often the cause of the reaction—was the exception rather than the rule. Known allergens, materials that sensitized the skin so that subsequent exposure provoked irritation, were frequently the problem.[73] More than one doctor emphasized the extremely small percentage of women affected by makeup. In 1925, Howard Fox, a New York dermatologist, thought it was advantageous and "interesting to quote the *Druggists' Journal*, which says that at present the public uses nearly eighteen million packages of rouge, generally harmless, I think; 240 million packages of face powder, which in the main is also harmless, and many million jars of cream and other cosmetics."[74] Fox attempted to introduce common sense into a discussion that typically focused on the injured individuals at hand and ignored the larger (and for the most part harmless) picture.

The AMA in its own way added to the discussion. The organization had long been concerned with quackery and health fraud. In 1906, Arthur Cramp was hired to write a regular column in *JAMA* on health fraud. In 1913, he became head of the newly organized Propaganda Department, renamed the Bureau of Investigation in 1925.[75] In addition to Cramp's work and regular columns, the AMA also published three volumes on *Nostrums and Health Quackery,* in 1906, 1912, and 1936.[76] Essentially a compilation of articles from *JAMA* and additional information from the Bureau of Investigation, these volumes reached a wide public audience. The AMA used the information from these (and other) departments to educate both physicians and the larger American public. The AMA's concerns about quackery were not unfounded: people spent vast sums each year on ineffective or detrimental cures. Physicians read about quackery and products to avoid in the Bureau of Investigation's *JAMA* column and in *AMA Bulletin.* The public read *Hygeia,* an AMA-sponsored public health magazine geared toward a lay audience; listened to AMA-sponsored radio broadcasts; and perused AMA booklets and pamphlets.

The Bureau of Investigation became a clearinghouse of sorts. Physicians wrote to the bureau for help, or for more information. Dr. Kathryn Whitten, preparing to give a talk before local cosmeticians, asked for "leaflets, booklets or any literature giving analyses or exposures of harmful or useless cosmetics." In a handwritten postscript, she added, "I do not keep the Journal after reading them so I cannot look these matters up."[77] Manufacturers large and small also wrote, both for help and to help. Miss Isobel Dupray requested an analysis of Desert Bloom Pack, a beauty clay. In reply, Cramp noted that, "We cannot undertake to make an analysis of your product, as we have never had any inquiries about it and there is no reason why we should spend the time and money on determining, by analytical methods for your information, what you already know—or should know."[78] On the other hand, a chemist at Elizabeth Arden supplied Cramp with information regarding a henna product to enable Cramp to respond to a query from a woman in Iowa.[79]

The call within the medical literature, both case reports and the bureau's own column, for regulating ingredients in cosmetics viewed legislative oversight as a necessary public health action to protect the populace from unscrupulous manufacturers and powerful advertising.

Assessing the growth of cosmetic dermatology, which was directly proportional to the growth of cosmetics, Herman Goodman in 1933
observed that "the industry . . . has reached its healthy, nay legendary
growth under the untutored supervision of industrial barons, midwife
advertisers, and sundry soothsayers, to win the support of millions of
women."[80]

• • •

On the federal level, consumers were offered some level of protection by
three different federal agencies. The FDA enforced the 1906 Food and
Drugs Act with a combination of enforcement activity and public education.[81] Toward that end, the FDA's Office of Information took advantage of all media, including radio, magazines, and films, to educate,
inform, and stir the public to action.[82] At the conclusion of an FDA-
sponsored radio broadcast in 1930, for example, listeners were told how
they could participate in the legislative process, make the law more
effective, and aid themselves. "[Listen] to our radio talks, read our
newspaper articles and write for our free booklets," the public was
urged.[83] In early 1930, William Wharton, the FDA Eastern District chief,
and Wendall W. Vincent, the FDA Western District chief, launched a
series of radio broadcasts. On "Safeguard Your Food and Drugs" and
"Uncle Sam at Your Service," the Eastern and Western District shows
respectively, Wharton and Vincent elucidated the FDA's regulatory
powers (and limitations) under the 1906 act, reported seizures of fraudulent products, explained laboratory analyses, and urged consumers to
shop carefully. As the broadcasts repeatedly emphasized, "the *most
important* activity of the Administration—the one *always* given first
attention—*is the suppression of practices that are a menace to public health.*"[84]
     But the FDA could not be everywhere, nor could it do everything.
Two series of accidents caused by cosmetics—not regulated by the
FDA—highlighted both the agency's power and its lack thereof.
Koremlu, a depilatory, relied upon thallium acetate, an ingredient com-
monly found in rat poison, to destroy and remove hair. The company,
founded by Kora M. Lublin in April 1930, did not come to the attention
of the medical community, or the FDA, until later that year. In
November, the AMA Bureau of Investigation received a query from a
large department store, followed by physician requests, and soon began
an investigation. Laboratory tests revealed a product in excess of 7%
thallium, far higher than the 0.5% level recommended by Raymond

Sabouraud, the French dermatologist who first discovered its hair-removal properties.[85]

A 1927 experiment on two young girls had conclusively demonstrated that thallium acetate poisoned the nervous system.[86] As the number of case reports in the medical literature grew, it was clear that Koremlu was problematic. Symptoms of thallium acetate poisoning included progressive discomfort, epigastric pain, cramps, nausea and vomiting, foot pain, numbness spreading in the lower extremities, and dizzy spells.[87] Even though Koremlu was applied mostly to women's upper lips, the problems manifested themselves elsewhere: loss of axial or pubic hair; baldness; temporary or long-term paralysis; and optic nerve damage. Despite the Bureau of Investigation column, and some press about Koremlu, not everyone immediately knew what was happening. One physician noted that "a warning should be broadcast" about Koremlu because he "didn't realize the cause [of dermatitis] until [he] read the *JAMA* article."[88]

Fortunately, women consumers and public health officials paid attention to rumor, innuendo, and newspaper stories about this new and wildly popular depilatory. In early 1931, the FDA received letters requesting information about Koremlu; in both cases, the writers were referred to *JAMA*.[89] Many people, unaware that the FDA could not regulate cosmetics, wrote for information, from housewives to city public health officials to congressional representatives on behalf of their constituents. Again, the standard reply noted that Koremlu did not fall within the definition of "drug," and as such the FDA could do nothing.[90] Complaints and questions continued to be directed to the FDA throughout 1932, when the company declared bankruptcy. Women who had been injured sued the company and were awarded damages in excess of $2.5 million. Not only did they not receive money after Koremlu failed, some physicians blamed the women themselves for the injuries. "Anyone who buys products of unknown composition for application either to the surface or to the interior of the human body in the treatment of human disease is trifling with health and with life. Moreover, he [sic] cannot, in the vast majority of cases, hope to recover anything in the way of monetary compensation for damages should. harm result."[91]

And then, a little over a year later, history seemed to repeat itself, this time with an eyelash and eyebrow dye. Lash Lure, concocted by Isaac Dellar, contained paraphenylenediamine (PPD), an aniline dye that repeatedly achieved the rating of "most dangerous" in the list of hair dyes. "The dangerous possibilities of certain types of dyes has [sic]

. . . been known . . . for many years. Extending their use to the eyelash field is new and a reaction as severe as that which occurred in this patient deserves more than the passing comment ordinarily given by dermatologists," wrote one physician. His patient was lucky: she only experienced mild discomfort.[92] In benign cases, women suffered temporary nausea, discomfort, or vision problems; in more severe cases, women were blinded or died. One woman, who died, had had her eyebrows plucked by her beautician (and her daughter) preparatory to the application of Lash Lure. Quickly, swelling developed, followed by pain; before a complete battery of tests could be completed, she was dead of a staphylococcus infection.[93]

Dramatic as this death was, a woman blinded by Lash Lure ultimately proved far more effective as a living warning to the dangers of makeup. Mrs. Musser was blinded by Lash Lure, applied at the beauty shop in preparation for an award she was to receive acknowledging her efforts on behalf of the Parent-Teacher Association. Her daughter, ten-year-old Hazel Fay, wrote to President Roosevelt, "because I don't want anything to happen to other ladies like it has happened to my mother. My mother suffered a great deal by the cause of some poison which was put in the dye and those applied to lashes."[94] Ruth Lamb, the FDA information officer who read the forwarded letter, was "tied up in knots" and began correspondence with Hazel Fay's mother. Over time, a friendship of sorts developed between the FDA information officer and the blinded mother of Hazel Fay in Dayton. Lamb commiserated when multiple operations failed to restore Musser's sight. Musser supported Lamb's work at the agency to rally public support and further the cause of food and drug reform. On some level, Lamb saw her penpal friendship as part of her job, because the letters remain in FDA correspondence files, which suggests that Lamb might have been cultivating Musser as evidence to counter claims that present laws were more than adequate. In a January 1936 missive, Lamb offered hope that the operation was a success, noted that no more hearings would occur in the present congressional session (which ran 1934–36), and added a final comment indicating that the battle was far from over. "It was not Judge Goodwin [chair of the Federal Trade Commission] . . . who said he believed that every woman injured by cosmetics was fully compensated, but Dr. Ralph Evans, the manufacturer of 'Inecto.' . . . Of course he knows better."[95]

Some letters between Musser and Lamb contained updates on the progress of the legislation, while others were just friendly chitchat.[96] A visit Musser made to Washington "deeply affected and captivated both

Senators Donahey and Copeland," Lamb reported.[97] The relationship
was reciprocal: Musser was used as a particularly egregious example of
the flaws in the law for Lamb, and Lamb engineered a visit with the
First Lady when the latter was in the Dayton area. After the nearly forty-
minute visit, Musser was, if anything, more discouraged about the fate
of legislation. "Please advise me the status of the Congressional Bill,"
she wrote Lamb. "Mrs. Roosevelt seemed just a little bit doubtful about
it—the lobby being so immense."[98]

A flurry of Lash Lure cases appeared in the medical literature, with
four separate and successive reports in *JAMA* in November 1933.[99] But
more queries were directed to the FDA than reports appeared in the
medical literature. Once again, the FDA could sympathize but do
nothing. "I share your opinion that this product should not be permitted, or at least should be very definitely controlled," a clerk replied
to the Georgia state chemist, "as will be the case if the proposed Federal
food and drug act becomes a law."[100] Time and again, as it had so often
in the past, the official FDA response to anxious queries was to urge
writers to consult *JAMA,* contact the AMA, or recall that the FDA did
not have power over cosmetics.

What the FDA could, and did, do was remind the public of its limitations. A 1932 press release noted that "so long as cosmetics are labeled
solely as cleansing agents, beauty enhancers, etc., they will not become
subject to action under the Federal food and drug act."[101] Radio broadcasts, including "Uncle Sam at Your Service" and local shows, reinforced this message. The narrator of "Uncle Sam," who considered "cosmetics have been a boon to womankind," was tempered by the more
sober talk given by Wendell Vincent, in which he pointedly discussed
Koremlu and other depilatories.[102] And when Lash Lure was a national
story, FDA Chief Walter Campbell issued a press release, noting that "at
present, the Administration has no legal power to take such action. . . .
In spite of our inability to direct regulatory action against Lash-Lure,
Koremlu, and numerous other dangerous cosmetics, we firmly believe
that we would be seriously remiss if we did not inform the public by
every means in our power of the danger involved in using such poisonous 'beautifiers.'"[103] Happily, the FDA's message got out, as radio correspondent Elsa Todd attested. After she heard a 1933 broadcast on cosmetics, she inventoried her medicine chest.[104] "I'm mighty glad I heard
the statement [on the dangers of Koremlu]. . . . Thanks to you I shall no
longer use [Koremlu] and be safe from its poisons and expenses."[105]

The FDA's mandate to protect the public did not include cosmetics, so
the agency could do nothing to stop the traffic of harmful or deleterious

makeup items. Two government agencies charged with consumer protection—the Federal Trade Commission (FTC) and the U.S. Postal Service (USPS)—could and did charge cosmetic companies with fraudulent
practices when such practices violated interstate trade or postal codes.[106]

According to its 1914 congressional mandate, the FTC was charged
with maintaining fair trade practices in interstate commerce.[107] It
charged more than one hundred cosmetic, toiletry, and beauty firms
with violating this standard between 1914 and 1938. Each company
charged with breaking the law underwent an investigation and hearing
process; however, a company could continue to sell the item(s) in question while under investigation. In 1928, for example, the Marsay School
of Beauty Culture in Chicago was charged with employing business
practices that might harm competitors. The FTC believed the school
made false and misleading advertising claims that bordered on deceptive and unfair practice. In scrutinizing the advertised claims about the
success of Marsay graduates, the FTC challenged the very premise of its
educational program. The advertisements implied that students who
took the school's correspondence beauty course would be able to "earn
a big salary," upwards of $5,000 to $25,000 a year, as beauty culturists.
The materials failed to state that board certification in each state
required an apprenticeship period of not less than 625 hours, under the
tutelage of an experienced (and registered) beauty culturist, something
not possible through a mail-order beauty school. Also, few cosmetologists earned $5,000 a year. In 1928, the FTC determined that the com-
pany fell woefully short of its claims and ordered the Marsay School to
cease and desist its business practices.[108] Another case involved Pond's
Extract Company and its endorsement campaign. In 1932, the FTC
decreed that the company's advertising campaign might confuse the
public, who understandably might assume that the paid testimonials
were unsolicited, given freely and spontaneously. Because other companies employed similar advertising strategy, the proceedings were suspended, and the charges against Pond's were ultimately dismissed.[109]

The USPS, like the FTC, concerned itself with advertising, ensuring
that mail was not used for false and fraudulent purposes. A promise to
mail a cream, which guaranteed to melt fat in exchange for a sum of
money when such a feat was scientifically impossible, and the cream
contained only glycerin and rose water, constituted mail fraud. Consumer complaints to the USPS were taken seriously. Like the FTC, companies accused of misusing the postal system were subject to a lengthy
hearing process; often they were ordered to cease and desist their current practice. The USPS had fewer cases than the FTC related to cos-

metics, because most business was transacted in person or through advertising, not sent in the mail. Madam C. J. Walker's company was charged in 1919 with using the mail system fraudulently. Coupons assured potential saleswomen that, for twenty-five dollars, they would receive a $12.50 "outfit," a steel comb, and a diploma from the Leila College. Nowhere did the advertising indicate that this was all the training the sales force was to receive, nor did it hint that the "outfit" only cost ten dollars, the replacement cost. After a USPS ruling, the wording of the advertisement changed accordingly.[110]

• • •

Consumer groups and manufacturers were not alone in this movement for uniformity and consensus for protection. Physicians also had concerns about the quality of food products on the market, as they often treated illness resulting from adulterated or poorly processed food. They also were concerned with related items, including drugs and cosmetics. In 1924, one of the first calls for safeguarding cosmetics appeared in the medical literature, when one physician suggested "protecting the public through proper legislation. This should include laws to enforce placing of the names of poisonous ingredients on the label. Moreover, laws prohibiting the use of the most harmful types of ingredients in cosmetics would be of great value; and to these there should be added a criminal liability to enforce recognition."[111]

Pieces of the puzzle were starting to fall into place. A consumer's movement gathered the momentum lost by the women's groups for protection of health and pocketbook. Physicians were increasingly concerned with cosmetics, or, more precisely, the injuries they caused. Although doctors and the AMA, particularly general practitioners, dermatologists, and allergists, bemoaned a lack of regulation of beauty aids, they in turn became a resource for the FDA, which by law could not regulate or ensure the safety of these same products. Would the quest for beauty ever be a safe one?

chapter four

"Some protection to our health, our looks and our pocketbooks"

THE YEAR 1933 was an important one for the American people, especially for those concerned with consumer safety. Franklin Delano Roosevelt used the interregnum between the November 1932 election and the March 1933 inauguration to formulate policies to help solve, or resolve, the ongoing economic depression. The first hundred days of his administration saw an unprecedented number of laws passed by Congress. Almost as an afterthought, revision of the 1906 Pure Food and Drugs Act was submitted, on one of the final days of the special legislative session. Introduced into Congress in the flurry of New Deal legislation, the revised food and drug act became, after five long years, one of the final of the Second New Deal.

The first ripple, or hint, of change occurred with the publication of *100,000,000 Guinea Pigs*, by Consumers' Research (CR) founders Arthur Kallet and Frederick J. Schlink. If the subtitle "Dangers in Everyday Foods, Drugs, and Cosmetics" was not enough of a hint about the contents within, the blurb below the authors' name on the jacket would have been a clue: "'Pure Food' laws do not protect you. This book names and describes scores of 'standard' products that are either dangerous or worse than useless for the purposes advertised."[1] Much of the book illustrated the many shortcomings of the 1906 Pure Food and Drugs Act, using the best (and most damning) examples, from Koremlu to ginger jake, from "acceptable" levels of arsenic to antiseptics. The law was weak from the start: "We have already noted that the very first months of enforcement were marked by appeals to officials, including President Roosevelt himself, by manufacturers seeking relief from the operation of the law."[2] Immediately preceding the chapter "To make the best of a bad law," the authors apologized to the reader: "We regret the space it has been necessary to devote to the dubious practices of this Federal Department; but without the specific evidence that we have presented concerning the misrepresentation, evasion, and misconception of the legal function of officials charged with a high responsibility, it would be difficult to understand how the wholesale poisoning of the public can go on practically without restraint, and why a complete new deal is emphatically called for."[3] The final chapters exhorted consumers to action, encouraging them to "bother your congressmen and senators and state legislators . . . write to your newspapers and magazines."[4]

Bother their congressmen readers did. Almost as soon as the book appeared in bookstores, concerned readers took pen in hand and wrote letters: the first printing was January 12, 1933, and the first letter to a Food and Drug Administration (FDA) official arrived on January 16, 1933.[5] The FDA received so many letters that it created a category within its filing system solely for correspondence generated by this book. The reactions ranged from outraged to pleas for help. "Even in these times," wrote Earnest Lux to President Roosevelt, "I don't think I have ever read a more brutal indictment of a government regulatory body than is contained in these pages, fortified and supported with a maze of figures and statistics."[6] The first lady also received letters, because, as Mrs. E. H. Winters explained, "Knowing of your interest and your husbands' interest, in the welfare of mankind, I feel that you would want to read the book entitled '100,000,000 Guinea Pigs.'"[7]

As was FDA policy, each letter writer received a reply. In response to an attorney who "subscribe[s] most heartily to the opinions and conclusions set forth in . . . 100,000,000 Guinea Pigs," assistant FDA chief Paul Dunbar did note that "our report in 1931 called for specific attention to the crying need for strengthening amendments designed to give more adequate protection to consumers," as they had done in preceding congressional sessions as well.[8] What is not obvious from the letters—and these continued to arrive for the next three years—is that many postcards also arrived. It appears either that early editions of the book contained a postcard to be filled out and mailed, or that some organization (CR itself?) instigated a postcard campaign. Approximately 2,500 postcards were received, 2,000 from consumers and 500 from "professionals."[9]

Only one chapter of 100,000,000 Guinea Pigs was specifically about "dangers in cosmetics." That gap in coverage was rectified with the publication of Skin Deep: The Truth about Beauty Aids—Safe and Harmful a year later. Its cover, much like its predecessor, promised to "'name names.' It tells you the facts, hitherto reported only in trade circles or among scientists, about face powders, rouges, talcum powders, soaps, cold creams, lipsticks, nail preparations, hand lotions, hair 'restorers,' depilatories, eyelash dyes, astringents, sunburn preventives, etc., etc."[10] Dedicated to "all who suffered grave injuries from *Koremlu, Lash-Lure, Dinitrophenol,* and other dangerous cosmetics," the book sought to fill the vacuum of consumer knowledge, and answer all the queries CR had received from "numerous women readers" following the publication of *100,000,000 Guinea Pigs.*[11] The author, Mary Catherine Phillips, was a CR member and wife of Frederick Schlink. *Skin Deep* was arranged by topic or product, and also concluded with a chapter outlining "what consumers can do." These books, and others like them, a new generation of muckraking books, became known as "guinea pig books." And one of the most potent would be written by an FDA insider, which will be discussed later.

What the popularity and response to these books concealed, however, was turmoil within CR. *100,000,000 Guinea Pigs* ran through at least nineteen printings, and *Skin Deep* at least eleven. *Publishers' Weekly* speculated that the former "will continue its best-selling career until the evils exposed in this exploited book are stopped."[12] Without consulting the board, Schlink and Kallet decided to move CR headquarters from New York to New Jersey. The move, for financial reasons (cheaper rent), caused financial hardship among staffers and some hard feelings for those who were terminated by the move or would be if they did not also move across the Hudson. This rift was exacerbated in 1935 when the printers went on strike in a bid to unionize. Accusations of Communism within the union and a lack of willingness to negotiate even through intermediaries led to a split within CR. The strikers formed a new organization, Consumers Union. This internal division within one of the most visible organizations dedicated solely to consumer issues, coupled with the sometimes abrasive manner of Kallet and Schlink, might help explain why members of Congress so readily dismissed CR representatives at the hearings.

● ● ●

In the frenetic emergency congressional session called by the president in the spring of 1933, smaller pieces of legislation are easily overlooked or forgotten. Proposed programs and laws offering immediate agricultural and industrial relief took center stage, dominating legislators' attention, time, and discussion.[13] Helping farmers by championing their

FIGURE 2. Rexford Tugwell, Assistant Secretary of Agriculture, 1933–36. (Courtesy of FDA History Office)

cause and implementing the Agricultural Adjustment Act (AAA) occupied Henry Wallace, secretary of agriculture.[14] The intense (and deserved) focus on agricultural recovery meant that other issues within the purview of the Agriculture Department (USDA) were relegated to other officials within the department. Revision of the 1906 law, long favored by the FDA, was given some measure of prominence in that it was on the New Deal agenda at all. FDA officials dexterously used to their advantage a new administration to try to further their goal. Oddly enough, given the upheaval and chaos of those first hundred days, Rexford Tugwell, assistant secretary of agriculture, formerly an economics professor at Columbia, began examining the problem almost immediately.[15] Conceived as a way to close the loopholes in the 1906 act, strengthen the law, and increase consumer protection, Tugwell—and the FDA—sought to include cosmetics and therapeutic devices, grant the FDA control over advertising, and increase penalties and fines for companies violating the law.

As he contemplated the 1906 law, Tugwell sought presidential approval for this project. With Roosevelt's assent, Tugwell created a commission to investigate and propose possible amendments. The committee, composed of FDA officials, USDA solicitors, and legal experts outside government, quickly concluded that only complete revision, rather than overhaul, in the form of additional amendments would do.[16] Two early decisions by the commission profoundly impacted the bill's reception. First, the committee desperately wanted the bill to be submitted for consideration in the emergency session, suspecting it might fare better in the special rather than regular session of Congress. Given this necessary but self-imposed time constraint, the committee decided to draft a bill with only limited input from affected industries. Typically, drafts of a bill were shown to trade groups, which allowed the associations time to respond with suggestions or draft their own version of the legislation. Instead, the committee merely solicited input.[17] The repercussions of this decision were profoundly clear at the subsequent public hearings: industries balked and protested in congressional hearings at language they regarded as unfair, overly harsh, or too constraining. In the final analysis, many of the changes proposed by industry became part of the law; industry would have objected regardless, and some FDA officials wondered whether the legislation might have proceeded faster had the "normal" process not been circumvented. A second, far less important, consequence was that the bill in its 1933 incarnation was referred to as the Tugwell bill, even though Tugwell was almost wholly removed from the revision and drafting process, acting in a cursory supervisory capacity.[18]

In the final week of the hundred days, the committee completed revision of the 1906 Pure Food and Drugs Act and Senator Royal S. Copeland of New York submitted it. Copeland was in many respects the ideal person to sponsor and champion this bill. A homeopathic physician, he formerly had directed the Food and Drugs Division of the New York City Public Health Department. In addition, he had previously submitted bills to strengthen food and drugs laws.[19] The committees on agriculture in both the House and Senate refused to accept the bill. Copeland then redirected it to the Senate Committee on Commerce, on June 12, 1933; Representative William Sirovich did likewise, introducing the same bill to the House Committee on Interstate and Foreign Commerce.

The public introduction of this bill—even though it was "referred" until the regular session commenced—produced diametrically opposing results. On the one hand, affected industries, including publishing concerns, advertising firms, and food, drug, and cosmetic man-ufacturers, claimed that this was their first introduction to or knowledge of this bill. This, however, is simply untrue. Industry representatives had been apprised of developments throughout the spring. Reports, speculation, and criticism of the revisions appeared in drug and cos-metic journals in late March 1933, almost as soon as the committee began working on their appointed task and well before the law's "offi-cial" public debut in mid-June 1933. In April, less than three weeks into the new administration, *Drug and Cosmetic Industry* noted in an editorial that, "The 'New Deal' appears to have gotten around to this industry with the proposal that a new Federal Food and Drugs Act throwing much more stringent restrictions around the industry be enacted."[20] At the annual Drug Chemical and Allied Trades meeting, the executive board discussed the proposed food and drugs bill.[21]

The Tugwell committee's decision to maintain contact only with industry meant that this proposed legislation was almost wholly unknown by most consumer groups. "The new bill is already drafted, and long before consumers and the few local consumer organizations could be heard from, or their views considered and collated, has been submitted to Congress (June 1)," an article in *Consumers' Research Bul-letin (General)* pointedly noted in July.[22] In the midst of a newspaper strike in the spring of 1933, this kind of news—decidedly not a radical New Deal program—did not generate much excitement. This was, then, a piece of consumer legislation of which most consumers were igno-rant.[23] Some women's organizations, particularly those based in Wash-ington or which were part of the Women's Joint Congressional Com-mittee, and a few consumer groups knew of these developments, but they were the exception rather than the rule. And, as the FDA was pointedly demonstrating in Chicago at the World's Fair, most people did not know how little protection the FDA offered.[24]

The World's Fair in many ways proved the salvation of this bill, pre-venting it from disappearing entirely. The Tugwell bill barely had time to be acknowledged in the waning days of the emergency session of Congress; like other legislation, it was shelved until the regular session. In a brilliant stroke of luck, however, the FDA was receiving national attention on the deficiencies of the 1906 law, which served as the cor-nerstone of arguments for revision.[25] In the summer of 1933, Chicago hosted the World's Fair; the theme, a tribute to the host city, was "A Cen-tury of Progress."[26] Planning for the event had begun several years ear-lier, with commitments from sponsors, vendors, agencies, and organi-zations, and companies willing to build and be a presence at the fair.

Local backers hoped that this large construction project and potential vacation destination would aid a depression-stressed economy.

The FDA, like other government agencies, had been invited to participate in the United States Government Building at the Chicago World's Fair. Under normal circumstances this would have been an easy decision: the FDA had long maintained an active and visible presence at state and county fairs.[27] Times were not normal, though: the "standard" FDA fair exhibits had gotten rather shabby and worn; rather than incur the expense of replacement, the FDA curtailed this educational service. Once before since the onset of the Depression, the agency declined an opportunity for public display: the 200th anniversary of George Washington's birth, which was held in the nation's capitol in 1932. On that occasion, the FDA pleaded poverty. "While I believe in normal times such an exhibit would be thoroughly worth while and the expenditure justified," wrote the FDA director of extension work, "under our present circumstances trying to make every dollar work overtime in actual enforcement of the law, I do not believe that we should undertake the time or expense which such a visit would entail."[28] Faced with a similar request for the World's Fair, the FDA acquiesced. This decision, for all the advance planning required by the Chicago organizing committee, was fairly last minute. A commitment for the government building was secured in 1931, but the list of federal agencies, departments, and bureaus participating was only made public in early 1933.[29]

Once the FDA accepted the offer, the agency quickly needed to determine what exactly to *do* in its limited space. The government building was divided by departments, each of which was further subdivided amongst its constituent agencies. The floor space allocated to the FDA was fairly limited. In trying to determine how best to utilize its space, the agency had several factors to consider: What was the focus of the exhibit? Should an "old" exhibit be reused, or an entirely new one created? What were other, related government agencies such as Public Health Service planning? Early discussion focused on practical public relations issues. "Since this Exposition will be visited largely by the general public," the head of FDA information services wrote, "I think we should make our display as popular in its nature as possible."[30] The FDA returned to a familiar theme: deficiencies of the 1906 act, including some of the very issues under discussion in Washington such as lack of coverage for cosmetics and therapeutic devices, lack of control over advertising, and deceptive packaging practices.[31]

All told, an estimated thirty-nine million people visited the World's Fair, June through November of 1933, making it the first commercially

FIGURE 3. 1933 Chicago World's Fair exhibit. (Special Collections, Vassar College Libraries)

successful World's Fair.[32] The fair was promoted as a tourist destination, an educational experience, and an opportunity to explore the world beyond this country's borders. Some innovations, such as the first fair-based radio station, and some entertainment, such as the midway attractions, received much press. Some exhibits received press attention as well. Few government exhibits received the attention and scrutiny that the FDA exhibit did. In seventeen short panels, the FDA mercilessly attacked those products that committed particularly egregious breaches of ethics in marketing or that narrowly skirted the law. The panels and examples ran the gamut, from "safe" cosmetics containing lead, mercury, and arsenic to X rays of children with prizes lodged in their gullets.[33] And industries complained. Many items displayed were no longer on the market; the exhibit was overly sensational; the exhibit highlighted a minor number of "dangerous" products versus the many safe products on the market.[34] The antagonism of the drug and cosmetic industry mirrored what was—or was not—happening with the postponed revision of the 1906 act. Although virtually everyone used these products daily, there was no organized reaction in support of this exhibit; nor would there be a consumer presence to match that of industry at subsequent congressional hearings on the proposed bill.

In spite, or because, of industry complaints about the FDA exhibit, many of the eight million visitors to the United States Government Building at the fair went up to the second floor to see the exhibit.[35] During the FDA broadcast of "Uncle Sam at Your Service," which aired at the beginning of the fair's run, the narrator described the exhibit and encouraged listeners to see it should they attend the Century of Progress World's Fair.[36] In several letters of reply, the FDA encouraged people to see the exhibit as well. Dr. Harry Krasnow inquired about food and drug legislation. "We have at our Chicago Station, and also at the Century of Progress Exposition, some exhibits in which I think you will be interested. They show the weaknesses of the present food and drug law."[37]

An unintended consequence of the exhibit was its long "legs." Along with other participants, the FDA declined to remain at the fair for a run the following summer. Miniature (photographic) copies of the "Chamber of Horrors" exhibit were sent to FDA branch offices. Stories in local newspapers, repeated mention on FDA broadcasts, and suggestions in FDA correspondence heightened public awareness of the exhibit on view at local FDA branch offices. The high-profile (and greatly courted) visit by Eleanor Roosevelt to FDA headquarters specifically to look at the exhibit also increased demand.[38] Walter Campbell's decision to bring "Chamber" panels with him when he testified before Congress about a revised bill kept the exhibit in the spotlight. Even if Campbell merely wanted good visuals to illustrate why revision was important and necessary, opposing interests always noted the "Chamber's" resurrection, even when the general press and public did not.[39]

• • •

When Congress reconvened in the fall of 1933 for its regular session, Senator Copeland duly resubmitted Senate Bill 1944 (S 1944), which he had introduced in the final days of the spring's emergency session. Hearings on Copeland's measure were held in early December before a subcommittee of the Senate Committee on Commerce, whose members included Senators Copeland, chair; Hattie Caraway of Arkansas; and Charles McNary of Oregon.[40] Copeland and others vastly misjudged public interest in the proceedings. "We have a crowded room. I am sorry we do not have enough chairs for everybody," he apologized on the first day. "Perhaps we can secure enough after a while to fill the room. We had to go from a room which we had arranged into this larger one, and even this seems to be crowded."[41] Eighty-four people testified or submitted briefs at the hearing on S 1944. Only seventeen people or institutions explicitly supported the bill. Those supporting the measure were in one of three categories: government, women's and consumer groups, or public health personnel. The remaining sixty-seven people, including representatives from food, drug, and cosmetic manufacturers and advertisers, began their testimony in much the same way: agreeing in principle with S 1944, to protect consumer health, BUT. . . .

The strongest advocates for improved standards and increased safety were USDA Secretary Henry Wallace and FDA Chief Walter Campbell. Wallace was the first person to testify. He acknowledged that "my time has been taken up . . . exclusively with emergency matters in the field of agricultural and national recovery," and suggested that Campbell could speak to the finer points of the bill.[42] He then discussed the innovations and added protection S 1944 offered. "There is greatly increased traffic in food and drugs today as compared to 1906. The cosmetic industry has become of first importance, whereas when the present law was written the cosmetic industry was in its infancy."[43] The Agriculture Department, Wallace made clear, fully supported the bill. His time-constrained testimony got to the heart of the matter, by delineating—in plain, non-legal jargon—the new or improved features: the updated Food and Drugs Act extended protection to include cosmetics and mechanical or therapeutic devices, prohibited false advertising, redefined "adulterated" drugs, required specific information on labels, established tolerance levels for insecticides, and increased penalties for repeat offenders. "I doubt that anyone will wish to appear before this committee in defense of the many abuses which cannot be remedied under existing legislation; there is too much grim evidence of the tragic effects that almost daily result from the Government's inability to prevent the shipment and sale of dangerous and worthless products."[44] The improved bill, Wallace concluded, "was intended primarily to protect consumers. At the same time, it should operate in the interest of all honest manufacturers."[45]

Campbell followed Wallace. He testified far longer than anyone else, speaking for almost the entire first day of the two days of hearings. His testimony was deliberate: he cited specific examples of products that violated or eased their way around the law. The very first item Campbell showed to the subcommittee was "'Bred Spred,' which has the appearance of a preserve." The product contained less than half the amount of fruit required to be labeled a preserve or jam, but the general public would likely purchase it assuming it was a jam; as the absence of fruit made it cheaper to produce, the company was perpetuating economic fraud on unwary consumers.[46] Campbell also explained the rationale for the "new additions" to the bill. "It may be of interest, however, to the committee to know that in the first drafts that were prepared of the existing Act the term 'cosmetics' was included. In the bill submitted originally by Dr. Wiley, the definition of drugs included cosmetics. That was eliminated in the progress of the measure in Congress."[47] The power of his presentation cannot be underestimated; rather than discuss theoretical implications of the proposed law, he offered tangible proof how the law was (or was not) currently working to protect consumers and how the proposed bill would solve these problems. To further emphasize his points, Campbell used several panels and samples from the "Chamber of Horrors" exhibit.[48]

After many depositions and much testimony from representatives of pharmaceutical firms, women began to testify. As Mrs. William Sporburg noted, she was the first woman to testify, and claimed to do so on behalf of consumers.[49] She reiterated the need for a stronger bill to help consumers and the need for cosmetics to be covered by federal fiat. "I want a law with teeth in it—but with *real teeth* gripping hard and relentlessly into vulnerable spots threatening public safety and public health—not one with false teeth that may slip into unintended corners and nibble into honest healthy spots with results that might finally defeat some of its own purposes and obstruct the ultimate desired protection of the consumer by its possible abuses rather than its uses."[50] Although she was a member of several women's organizations, most notably the General Federation of Women's Clubs (GFWC), she portrayed herself as merely an interested consumer. "May I say in passing," she concluded, "that I am glad to see a woman on this Senatorial Committee, whose decisions and recommendations will affect so many women who are users of drugs, cosmetics and foods."[51]

Women's organizations, including members of the Women's Joint Congressional Committee (WJCC), came in force to the hearings. Those who testified included Mrs. Gladys Irene Hendrickson, District of Columbia Home Economics Association; Mrs. Sarah Vance Dugan, director of the State Bureau of Food and Drugs, Kentucky; Mrs. Franklin W. Fritchey, Maryland Home Makers' Association; Mrs. Malcolm McCoy, New York City Federation of Women's Clubs and a letter submitted on behalf of Home Makers Forum; Mrs. William Bannerman, National Congress of Parents and Teachers. Mrs. Hendrickson, the first to speak, noted that "The District of Columbia Home Economics Association wishes, therefore, to go on record as endorsing all the provisions of S. Bill 1944 as protective of the best interests of its members and needful to the well-being of all consumers."[52] While not especially emphasizing cosmetics, these women were acutely aware of their role as purchasing agent within the family.

Arthur Kallet and Frederick Schlink, authors of *100,000,000 Guinea Pigs*, spoke on behalf of the 50,000 members of their organization, Consumers' Research. Both men criticized the bill for not extending enough protection to consumers, an argument forcefully made in their book.[53] "With respect to the bill," Kallet said, "I wish merely to say that while we believe the bill far too weak to give consumers the adequate protection to which he has every right, it is nevertheless infinitely superior to the present act, and if a stronger act cannot be obtained, this at least should be passed."[54] This was the calmest, and most conciliatory, representatives from Consumers' Research would be over the course of the four sets of hearings.

Public health personnel supported both "the purpose and scope of this revision of the pure food bill," Allen Freeman, professor of public health at Johns Hopkins, succinctly stated. On all levels, the current law was inadequate. "So far as cosmetics are concerned, I think that every one who has seen the results of some of the cosmetics now on the market will agree that some form of regulation is necessary; and, while we do not want to interfere with anybody paying $3 for a small amount of perfumed lard if they wish to, we do not want them to be sold anything that is going to take the hair off their head or ruin their vision or produce horrible scars."[55] Dr. Haven Emerson, representing the American Public Health Association, concurred: "I believe that there is practically unanimous opinion among physicians . . . that we are unable at the present time to protect our patients and our families against the hazard of poisoning and the damage to health by cosmetics and drugs . . . without the provisions that are made in this proposed law."[56]

In spite of these women's and consumer groups claiming to speak on behalf of the consumer, most consumers remained wholly oblivious to this possible legislation. Given the far-reaching effects it could have on daily life, this might strike some as more than a little surprising. However, consumers are not, as a rule, organized around the mere fact of consumption, nor do most people watch legislation the same way trade organizations do. The press, in their capacity as disseminators of information, played a role as well. Many publishers feared a drop in advertising revenue if the bill passed, and a drop in revenue if they endorsed the bill while it was still under discussion. In some respects, this echoed the "red clauses" thirty years earlier, which served to muzzle periodicals from engaging in discussion about possible food and drug legislation.[57] A study of the Tugwell bill, undertaken by the National Publishers' Association (NPA), found similar anxieties, if not legal language in advertising contracts. C. C. Parlin, the association's representative, stated that, "[l]eading magazines actively worked for the Food and Drugs Act of 1906. They would today, I believe, be actively working for this bill if it had been confined to phrases needful to protect health and to stop false advertising."[58] Under "Provisions are vague and sweeping," the first section of the NPA critique published in *Toilet Requisites*, the association concluded that "the only safe course of information for a director of a food, drug, or cosmetic corporation, if he wishes to keep out of jail, is to vote against all proposals that his company advertise."[59] The penultimate section, "Publishers are not exempt from prosecution," noted that "[i]t may be the intent of the Bill to exempt publishers . . . from prosecution, but the wording of the Act does not do so."[60] With this attitude, and the possibility of loss of advertising dollars, what magazine editor would choose to support this legislation? At the same time, a news strike helped keep this and other not-so-pressing news from the papers, let alone the front page.[61]

The testimony of Ray Schlotterer, speaking on behalf of business organizations, reinforced this lack of consumer knowledge. Testifying for the New York Board of Trade, "the second oldest civic organization in the country," he argued that S 1944 was anti-NRA and therefore bad for business.[62] To bolster his argument, he submitted responses from local chambers of commerce in response to a query about the reception or perception of S 1944 in their areas. To a city, the reply was uniform: the local chambers could detect no interest or knowledge on the public's part about improved consumer protection under consideration.[63] Typical was the note from Winfield Clearwater, manager of the Allentown, Pennsylvania, Chamber of Commerce: "Frankly, I know of no demand on the part of the public for a change from the present Pure Food and Drugs Act. I believe firmly, however, that the general public is solidly behind the Federal Government in the administration of the act now in force which seems to give ample protection. Any lessening of this protection would be a serious mistake. On the other hand, as I said, I know of no demand in this territory for any change in the present law."[64]

Those who produced and used cosmetics had an abiding interest in this attempt by the federal government at regulation. Northam Warren, head of Northam Warren Corporation (manufacturer of Coty), spoke on behalf of the Associated Manufacturers of Toilet Articles. In recent years, Warren explained, "our activities have been largely those of policing the toilet goods industry and attempting to drive the crooks, the scoundrels, the adventurers, and keep them out." In other words, self-regulation was already in place, and a few rotten apples were spoiling a barrel of profits. "I want to make it perfectly plain," he added, "that the two instances of injurious products that [Dr. Campbell] brought up [Koremlu and Lash Lure] do not represent any large part of the cosmetics of this country."[65]

After two long and physically packed days of hearings, the subcommittee sent the bill to the Senate Committee on Commerce. S 1944, the subject of the December hearings, had itself been a modification of S 5, the bill Copeland had submitted half a year earlier. Over the winter recess, Copeland and Ole Salthe, his legislative assistant, again modified S 1944 in response to suggestions and criticisms raised at the hearings.[66] Bowing to industry complaints, Copeland decreased the power of the secretary of agriculture by establishing two committees—Public Health and Food Standards—to establish regulations. Many consumer groups, including Consumers' Research, believed that this provision emasculated the bill and increased the sway of industry groups by asking them to set their own standards, and decreased the power of consumers to get assurances of protection.[67] No sooner had Campbell submitted S 2000, his modification of S 1944, in January 1934, than Representative Loring Black of New York and Senator Hubert Stephens of Mississippi submitted HR 6376 and S 2355 respectively, nearly identical bills written by James Beal, counsel for the National Drug Trade Conference. Both men had a vested interest in Beal's version. The Toilet Goods Association and many other manufacturing and trade organizations had headquarters in New York City; Vicks Pharmaceuticals was based in Mississippi. Responding to this challenge, Salthe and Copeland revised again, producing S 2800 on February 14, 1934. Representative Virginia Jenckes of Indiana and Senator Pat McCarran of Nevada submitted HR 7694 and S 2858, written by Charles Dunn, counsel for the Associated Grocery Manufacturers of America. And thus another round of hearings began.

One consequence of the continual revision and shuffling of bills immediately prior to the hearings was that prepared statements from organizations and industries were often based on the "older version" rather than the one under consideration. Copeland's primary concern was to maintain enough support that people did not shift their allegiance to a bill written by industry counsel, such as the McCarran-Jenckes bill. (The McCarran-Jenckes bill would benefit industry at the

Bill Number	Submitted by	Date	Written by
S 1944	Royal Copeland (NY)	June 1933	USDA: Tugwell and Handler; Cavers
S 2000	Copeland	January 1934	Salthe S1944 with December revisions
HR 6376	Loring Black (NY)	January 1934	National Drug Trade Conference: Jame s Beal
S 2325	H. D. Stephens (MS)	January 1934	National Drug Trade Conference: James Beal
S 2800	Copeland	14 February 1934	Salthe revisions as response to above
HR 7694	Virginia Jenckes (IN)	February 1934	Assoc. Grocery Manu. of Am: Charles Dunn
S 2858	McCarran (NV)	February 1934	Assoc. Grocery Manu. of Am: Charles Dunn
HR 8316	Patrick Boland (PA)	February 1934	Consumers' Research
S 5	Copeland	Early 1935	
S 580	McCarran	January 1935	Dunn (food and drug concerns)
H 3972	James Mead (NY)	January 1935	Proprietary Association
H 6906	Mead	Spring 1935	Proprietary Association
HR 8805	William Sirovich (NY)	Spring 1935	
H 8941	Jenckes	Spring 1935	
S 5	Copeland	1937	
HR 300	Virgil Chapman	1937	
HR 5414	Frank Towney (NY)	1937	Medical Society of New Jerse y
HR 5854	Lea (CA)	1937	(To become Wheeler -Lea Bill)
HR 5286	John Coffee (WA)	1937	

FIGURE 4. Origins and path of legislation resulting in 1938 Food, Drug, and Cosmetic Act

expense of consumers, from decreased enforcement powers of the FDA to fewer restrictions on industry.) David Cavers, who had helped draft the "original" bill in the spring of 1933, believed that so many changes were introduced into the whole revised bill that serious concessions were made, sacrificing consumer benefits for a decrease in industry opposition.[68]

Even though the newest version of legislation under consideration at the hearings, S 2800, was friendlier to and privileged the food and drug industries at the expense of consumers, the hearings suggested precisely the opposite. This second round of hearings spanned five days instead of two; twenty-five more people submitted briefs or testified than had done so at the subcommittee hearings the previous December. FDA Chief Campbell's testimony was significantly shorter than it had been several months earlier, and Agriculture Secretary Wallace did not testify at all. The number of women's organizations testifying on behalf of all consumers was almost half of what it had been two months earlier. Most testimony was from industry lobbyists who supported bills other than the one technically under consideration.

If the first person to testify sets the tone for the hearings, as Wallace and Campbell had done in December, then the Senate Commerce Committee hearings on S 2800 were not destined to support consumer measures. Representative Arthur Lemneck of Columbus, Ohio, opposed passage of the bill. "[I]n my district I have large wholesale houses. I have many manufacturers engaged in the manufacture of drugs, foods, and cosmetics, and if I reflect their sentiments, I believe I am safe in saying that there is no public demand for this bill."[69] Of concern to Lemneck were the forty-six cities and states whose laws were based on the 1906 Pure Food and Drugs Act: to change the federal act would, he feared, invalidate those laws. In his closing statement, he captured the pervasive sentiment about whose interests were worth protecting (and why). "I represent the manufacturers of food, drugs and cosmetics and the only expressions that I have had favoring this bill come from the university professors at Ohio State University, and some of the students that they have asked to write letters supporting the original bill."[70] Testifying shortly thereafter was Charles Dunn, counsel for the Associated Grocery Manufacturers of America, the National Drug Trade Conference, the American Pharmaceutical Manufacturer Association, the National Association of Manufacturers of Dog Food, and others. Much of Dunn's testimony extolled the superiority of other bills, including the McCarran-Jenckes bill (that he had written), over S 2800, the (technical) subject under discussion.

Consumer concerns were given voice by two disparate groups, and, as usually happens, the smaller but shriller voices overrode the larger consensus-building attempts. Mrs. Harris Baldwin, chair of the National League of Women Voters' Living Cost Department, pointed out to the senators that "I failed throughout the testimony today to hear any real recognition of the stake of the consumer."[71] She reminded them who did most of the shopping and got to the heart of the matter: consumer protection:

> It is said that between 85 percent and 90 percent of all retail purchases in this country are made by women, which makes the woman consumer a very great factor in the industries which are represented in this bill, yet the woman consumer is part of a very large unorganized group. She is not organized. She is not vocal. She has no money for organizing. She has no research bureau. She has no means of setting up specifications by which she may buy those things which she needs. She must depend on protection of some kind, of guarantees of some kind. . . . They are asking for protection for the things which they buy.[72]

In the first round of hearings, representatives from many different women's organizations had testified. This time Baldwin entered into the record a letter from the League supporting S 2800, including some suggested revisions. In addition, she submitted letters with similar sentiment from the American Association of University Women (AAUW), the American Dietetic Association, the American Home Economics Association (AHEA), the Medical Women's National Association, the National Congress of Parents and Teachers, the National Service Stars Legion, and the National Workers Trade Union League (NWTUL).[73]

Each woman who spoke suggested that she did so on behalf of the consumer. Mrs. Harvey Wiley noted that "[y]ou have had now 9 hours of hearings, of which 25 minutes have been for the consumer. We have heard mostly from the drug industry and advertisers."[74] Consumers' Research representatives, however, adopted quite a different strategy. Before the hearings had begun, they developed a defeatist attitude toward the bill; such support that they might have rendered in preventing the far more damaging changes that were still to come was largely withheld.[75] The women's organization representatives had a realistic understanding of the possibility for passage of this legislation, and, while disappointed with several changes, they increased rather than diminished their efforts to secure the best possible bill.[76] Arthur Kallet, the Consumers' Research representative, began aggressively and grew increasingly hostile. He first read aloud and placed in the record a telegram he had sent to President Roosevelt protesting the lack of equal time for all sides at the hearings.[77] Kallet next personally attacked Senator Copeland for touting Fleischmann's Yeast on radio. Kallet's opening salvos effectively torpedoed anything else Consumers' Research might have said. His vitriolic attack weakened whatever support and sympathy consumers might have gained through the diligent efforts of the women's organization representatives and other consumer advocates.[78]

In addition to diminishing support on behalf of, or by, consumers, other hints of opposition began to appear. On the third day of the hearings, the Honorable Ewin Davis, head of the Federal Trade Commission (FTC), testified about the potential problem or redundancy inherent in allowing the FDA to oversee advertising of food, drug, and cosmetics products, as advertising already was the province of the FTC (and, to some extent, the U.S. Postal Service).[79] Ewin submitted amendments to S 2800 "that require false advertising cases brought before the FTC rather than the courts."[80] In his second appearance before the Commerce Committee, on the final day of the hearings, Walter Campbell was "reluctant to commit further" to S 2800, for fear that additional testimony might raise more opposition following his use of "Chamber of Horrors" panels two days previously.[81] Nonetheless, a bit of his testimony centered on the before-and-after pictures of Mrs. Musser previously exhibited at the Century of Progress Exposition in Chicago.

> Mr. CAMPBELL: . . . I confess I know little or nothing about cosmetics. They are not included in the terms of the present law. We haven't had to deal with them in such circumstances, but facts of a disconcerting sort have come to our attention from time to time about the necessity for the protection of the public from certain types of cosmetics.
>
> [. . .]
>
> Senator HEBERT: What did it [Lash Lure] do—destroy eyesight?
>
> Mr. CAMPBELL: Oh yes, yes; just corroded the eye. This product is on the market now. At the time of the preliminary hearing I made known to you that there was a store on Fourteenth Street—with a window display of that very product.
>
> [. . .]
>
> The CHAIRMAN (Hubert Stephens): It appears that the eye of the lady was badly affected. Did she recover the full use of her eye?
>
> Mr. CAMPBELL: Absolutely blind, Senator.

The CHAIRMAN: Permanent injury?

Mr. CAMPBELL: Yes; just a complete corrosion, the eyesight entirely destroyed.[82]

The Chamber of Commerce, whose members' letter excerpts had been entered into the record in December, now officially opposed S 2800. Echoing Representative Lemneck's statement of the first day, chamber officials believed that an overhaul of the 1906 act "would upset this situation by destroying precedents and creating confusion between Federal and State laws" if the federal laws were to change.[83]

After five long days of hearings on S 2800, and on S 1944 and S 2000 (its direct predecessors, and the versions with which many of the witnesses were familiar and had prepared remarks) as well as S 2858 (McCarran-Jenckes) and S 2355 (Stephens-Black), S 2800 was reported favorably out of the Senate Commerce Committee. The Senate as a whole also voted favorably, whereupon it went to the House. After one hour of discussion on the floor, the bill disappeared.[84]

Inspired by this near success, rather than daunted by failure, Copeland introduced a very similar piece of legislation at the beginning of the 74th Congress, in January 1935. In response, Senator McCarran and Representative James Michael Mead also introduced "their" bills, drafted by Charles Dunn on behalf of his many clients, and the Proprietary Association, respectively. The 74th Congress seemed like it might be propitious. After the triumphs of New Deal legislation in the 73rd Congress (albeit almost wholly in the emergency session), other legislation might now get due consideration. Copeland's latest version of the bill, S 5, again reflected modifications made in response to challenges and criticisms. As they had in the 73rd Congress, the Senate subcommittee of the Commerce Committee held hearings.

With competing versions of a food and drugs bill submitted, it was obvious that no one measure would please everybody. Comments by two groups who testified encapsulated the dilemma of whom the bill was meant to protect. Robert Godefroy, counsel for the Institute of Medical Manufacturers and a representative of Strong, Cobb & Co., Inc., stated, "We are not opposed to a reasonable regulation of these industries in favor of the consuming public, but we are opposed to an unreasonable regulation of the industries in an unjust manner."[85] Many representatives of manufacturers and trade associations began their testimony in a similar vein. Consumer groups expressed similar sentiments, because they believed the bill went too far the other way, benefiting business at the expense of the consumer. For all his vitriol and personal attacks at the hearings in March 1934, Consumers' Research's Arthur Kallet was most articulate speaking on behalf of consumers when he sought to explain his discomfort with S 5. "It is necessary to make a choice whether our prime interest is the protection of the businessman in these industries or the protection of the public."[86]

The three days of hearings on S 5, on March 2, 8, and 9, 1935, were considerably less crowded, in terms of people testifying, than previous hearings had been. Only sixty-nine parties offered testimony or submitted briefs. In several instances, one person submitted briefs for multiple organizations.[87] From the outset, those who asked to testify were urged to say something new, rather than repeat what had been said at the December 1933 and March 1934 hearings. Senator Bennett Clark, chair of the subcommittee of the Committee on Commerce, made it clear that he would prefer comments or changes on the bill at hand, rather than a reiteration of tired arguments already aired.[88]

The injunction against rehashing old arguments was mostly adhered to throughout the March 1935 hearings. FDA Chief Walter Campbell did not appear but submitted a written brief on behalf of the agency. His argument in favor of the legislation, with the added work and responsibility for his department notwithstanding, remained unswerving. If he was troubled by some of the changes Copeland had made, changes others perceived as favorable to industry rather than the consumer, he did not voice these concerns. As Campbell perceived it, his mission was to convince Congress to support a position long advocated by the FDA: increasing the FDA's power and responsibilities in order to enhance protection for the American public.[89]

Some testimony at the third round of hearings was completely new, such as that by Seth Richardson, who, on behalf of the Association of Soap & Glycerine Producers, Inc., outlined the myriad reasons for soap's exclusion from the definition of cosmetics.[90] Some lobbyists added new pieces of information in the course of their testimony, perhaps to bolster their argument. Seeking to distance themselves from Consumers' Research and the 50,000 consumers it represented, while at the same time purporting also to speak on behalf of the American consumer, representatives of women's organizations offered membership figures. Although an aggregate number is misleading, as many women had multiple memberships, 4,785,500 women were represented by the GFWC, National Congress of Parents and Teachers, American Association of University Women (AAUW), American Dietetic Association, American Nurses Association, YWCA, Girls Friendly Society, and the National Women's Trade Union League (NWTUL); this figure excluded members of the American Home Economic Association (AHEA), the Women's Christian Temperance Union and the Women's Homeopathic Medical Society, none of whom proffered numbers.[91]

Mrs. Mary Bannerman, on behalf of the National Congress of Parents and Teachers, explained the increase in interest. "By the last of February, 1934, when hearings were reopened, public sentiment had so developed that leaders of national organizations representing several millions of consumers appeared in support. As a result of careful study . . . several additional consumer groups have joined the growing army of supporters. The rapid growth in sentiment for this legislation," she added, "is due in large measure to the increasing distrust of the failure of products advertised to measure up to the sales recommendations made for it."[92] Subsequent women explained some of their particular concerns. "There is a question in our minds about 'injurious to health,'" Mrs. Harris T. Baldwin, first vice president of the National League of Women Voters, said. "We wondered if you would consider it injurious to health if a person used a cosmetic which had caustic properties and which had burned off the eyebrows. We wondered whether that would be injurious to the person or injurious to the beauty of the person. That thing has happened, and we are very anxious to see that we are protected from such happening again."[93] Similar sentiments were expressed on behalf of the AAUW and WTUL.[94] And, as a spokeswoman for the YWCA made clear, it was not only older women who were concerned. "The YWCA does not officially endorse the use of cosmetics, but it is part of the program of almost all women, I think you will agree that anything that adds beauty and color to life is a good thing," said Miss Elizabeth Eastman. "I think you would be interested to know of the report I have received from the girls in the association who were voluntarily asking for study clubs, in order to study this whole question as consumers, most of them with little money to spend, and they have asked me to give you this message from them, that they are looking to you and to their Government, to protect their lives."[95]

After the hearings, S 5 was again reported favorably out of the subcommittee. Guided by Copeland, several slight changes were made, and S 5 was reported out to the Senate as a whole. This time, for the first time, the hearings got some national press because President Roosevelt sent a message to Congress specifically about this bill. "It is time to make practical improvements," he urged. "A measure is needed which will extend the controls formerly applicable only to labels to advertising also, which will extend protection to the trade in cosmetics, which will provide for a cooperative method of setting standards and for a system of inspection and enforcement to reassure consumers grown hesitant and doubtful, and which will provide for a necessary flexibility in administration as products and conditions change. . . . [I]t is my hope that such legislation may be enacted in this session of Congress."[96] On April 1, 1935, following the president's injunction and Copeland's last-minute tinkering, S 5 reached the Senate floor, where it had "the most extended debate in either house in five years of consideration."[97]

Three issues threatened to derail S 5. The first was the power of the FDA to make multiple seizures of one product. Companies opposed to this included Vicks Chemical Company, based in North Carolina, and Lambert Pharmaceutical Company (makers of Listerine), based in Missouri. Senators Josiah Bailey of North Carolina and Bennett Clark of Missouri, both of whom were members of the Commerce Committee, opposed this provision in deference to their (business) constituents.[98] The second issue, and the one that would prove almost insurmountable, was whether the FDA or the FTC would control advertising. Although the FTC did monitor advertising, consensus slowly shifted to the FDA on the grounds that a single agency should have responsibility for the advertisements of products that it regulated. The problem was the reluctance of the FTC to cede power.[99] In addition to the support of the Proprietary Association, the United Medicine Manufacturers of America, and the Institute of Medical Manufacturers, the FTC also had the support of subcommittee chair Senator Clark, and Interstate and Foreign Commerce Committee chair Representative Clarence Lea. The unspoken basis for support for the FTC over the FDA monitoring advertising was the assumption that the FTC would less aggressively enforce any new provisions. The third and final issue was judicial review of the regulations by the secretary of agriculture. This provision would enable the USDA to establish acceptable tolerances and standards on their own.[100] In the past, the FDA needed to convince a jury that various amounts of lead or arsenic in foodstuffs were dangerous, regardless of existing scientific data. This new provision would allow the agency to establish standards without interference from juries and various affected trade groups.[101]

Josiah Bailey added three amendments, and the status of S 5 continued to be debated. Eventually, the first issue was resolved, in part by one of Bailey's suggestions: the power of seizure would be limited to one item only, thus giving proprietary drugs relief from multiple seizures. Although Copeland argued strenuously against this, fearing it too much compromised already weakened legislation, the modified version of S 5 passed 44 to 29 on May 28, 1935.[102] The legislation went to the

House Committee on Interstate and Foreign Commerce. The subcommittee, chaired by Virgil Chapman of Kentucky, decided also to hold hearings in late July and early August of 1935.

Unlike earlier hearings, Chapman asked specific and pointed questions to many of the witnesses about the organizations or products they represented.[103] Also, unlike the Senate hearings, these hearings generated some (minor) press coverage: the *New York Times* carried brief notices about the hearings on July 23, 25, 26, and 30 and August 9 and 11; these six stories combined, however, amounted to less than three columns.[104] The bills under consideration in the House committee hearings included Copeland's original bill, S 5; a bill (HR 6906) submitted by Representative Mead, drafted by the Proprietary Association; a bill (HR 8805) submitted by Representative William Sirovich; and a bill (HR 8941) submitted by Representative Virginia Jenckes, drafted by Charles Dunn.

This final set of hearings had almost the same number of witnesses as the first set of hearings two years earlier, but these final hearings lasted five times as long. Each bill under discussion had evolved from previous hearings: Copeland's bill incorporated suggestions and changes based on the three earlier rounds of hearings, and the trade-sponsored legislation did likewise. What previously had merely been rumblings of discontent regarding who regulated advertising, and the separate proposed increase in power for the secretary of agriculture, emerged as a serious contretemps. The most visible difference between the various bills was these two issues and the definition of cosmetics, a hitherto unregulated product.

Once again, Campbell testified first. He began by reciting the known limitations of the 1906 act, including loopholes of which the agency had been cognizant almost as soon as it had been signed into law.[105] "The more general, and apparently the more generous, use of cosmetics has created a condition that calls for a modification of an antiquated law that at the present time in nowise provides for the regulation of cosmetics."[106] Unlike the committee hearings in the Senate several months earlier, when witnesses had been asked to not repeat information already in the record and address only the current version of legislation, no such caveat was issued in the House. And so Campbell discussed various problems with the 1906 act and repeated what the FDA could and could not do as per restrictions on its activities. As he had done previously, Campbell brought examples of products that were fraudulent but perfectly legal.[107] And he again discussed Mrs. Musser:

As an illustration of the necessity for some such provision, let me submit to you a photograph of an unfortunate gentlewoman of Dayton, Ohio, who has been in Washington in the interest of this bill. She has suffered a deplorable injury. While she would prefer to avoid the publicity incident to appearance in support of this measure, she has said to us and has said to some Members of Congress whom she saw while in Washington that she was perfectly willing to devote herself to undertaking to do those things which might prevent a recurrent of just such accidents. Here is a product called "Lash-Lure." It is an eyelash dye containing a coal tar derivative, which with some people is quite harmless. In this individual, it resulted in the corroding of her eyeballs. There is a photograph immediately before it was applied and a photograph shortly afterward.

That is one instance—and they are being multiplied repeatedly—not as cases of blindness but as other serious damage to health which we can show by exhibits that I am not going to take time to produce now, but will later, if the Committee wishes.[108]

On his second day of testimony, Campbell proposed to "address myself merely to the outstanding contribution of the Copeland bill over the present law for public protection."[109] When the chair, Senator Chapman, aggressively questioned the motives of the FDA for wanting to assume some of the FTC's advertising enforcement responsibilities, Campbell demurred. "I deplore any controversy between us and the Federal Trade Commission about the enforcement agencies of this law." [110]

Those who represented women's groups and, by extension, consumer interests, with a single exception, did not appear before the subcommittee until the end of the hearings. Their testimony revealed a weakness in organizational life, and, conversely, a strength of lobbying groups. Most of the organizations to which these women belonged had at most an annual meeting for the full membership; others, such as the GFWC, held biennial meetings for members and annual board meetings. The representatives of the National Congress of Parents and Teachers and the National League of Women Voters, for example, began their testimony by recounting their organizations' resolutions at the 1934 meeting to support this legislation.[111] In a point-by-point analysis of the bill, the former noted: "Cosmetics: women especially recognize the necessity for guarding cosmetics against adulteration and misbranding since they must depend on manufacturers and the protection of the Government for the quality of these goods. . . . We believe," Mrs. Harris

Baldwin said, "that prompt passage of the bill is essential to protect the public from dangerous cosmetics. We hope that at some future time it will be possible to provide for the listing of ingredients of cosmetics on the label, so that we may have some means of judging to what extent the contents warrant the price charged."[112] Alas, the specific measure the groups had endorsed was no longer the legislation under discussion. Most damning of all, though, in highlighting gaps in the current law, may have been the testimony of Mrs. Alvin Barber, for the AAUW:

> Mrs. BARBER: I am late, Mr. Chairman, because I tried today, between the two sessions of these hearings, to get evidence which I thought would be of value to you, and I was successful, although it took me some time.
>
> I purchased in two shops in this city, packages of "Lash-Lure," that dye for eyelashes which has had such disastrous effect, resulting in blindness and death, not only before but after the hearings in the Senate committee on this bill were started.
>
> I found four shops in an area of less than six blocks on a single street where this "Lash-Lure" is being used. At two of these shops I purchased a package of Lash-Lure, which I should like to put in as an exhibit, with directions for use.
>
> Mr. CHAPMAN: The members of the committee will not be expected to use that, will they?
>
> Mrs. BARBER: I think I will leave that to the discretion of the committee.[113]

By contrast, trade organization representatives had specific and cogent comments on the bills. Most discussion focused on S 5, almost to the complete exclusion of the other three bills, which is striking given that people had spoken about bills not technically under discussion in earlier hearings, and now almost ignored the other bills on the table. A significant amount of time and attention also focused on cosmetics. Only one of the four definitions of cosmetics, that in HR 8941, excluded soap. The soap manufacturers argued against ostensibly taxing health by taxing cleanliness. Cosmetic chemists, the National Hairdressers and Cosmetologists Association (NHCA), and cosmetic manufacturers argued strenuously that cosmetics did need government regulations, for the protection of both consumers and manufacturers.[114]

At the same time that these rounds of hearing occurred, and the FDA received many queries about consumer protection on top of the normal mail volume, Ruth Lamb, FDA information officer, was privately working on a guinea pig book of her own on the inadequacies of the current food and drug law. Some the information in the book was available to any interested consumer or researcher, including articles from medical journals and advertising industry periodicals. Other information, including Hazel Fay Musser's letter to the president, was not public currency. In fact, Lamb ended the book with Hazel Fay "Brown"'s letter, in a sense flaunting her insider status.[115] In the preface, in which "the author ventures an explanation," Lamb acknowledged her "privilege to have access to official records—to observe impartially and at first hand the facts behind the Copeland Bill."[116] Presented as a book to educate consumers, it offered reasons why a new law was necessary and suggested what consumers could do to participate in or expedite the process. Uncannily echoing Mary Catherine Phillips's dedication in *Skin Deep, American Chamber of Horrors* was "dedicated to that gallant group of women who have been holding the front-line trenches in the consumers' war for pure foods, drugs and cosmetics."[117]

Not everyone was convinced that Lamb wrote the book on her own time, under her own auspices. One problem was that a 1919 congressional statute, 41 Stat. 68, prohibited any agency or its members from lobbying Congress on legislative matters affecting their agency. Her protestations that she had no official sanction for the book met disbelief in some quarters. "The numerous releases to the press . . . were bad enough, but the 'American Chamber of Horrors,' written by Ruth Lamb, Chief Education Officer of the Administration, indicates without question where the Administration stands," an editorial in *Drug and Cosmetic Industry* stated. "We know that the book is not an official response from the Department of Agriculture, but we well know that the job could not have been done outside the Department, and could not be done within the Department without approval of Miss Lamb's superiors." Further, the publication of the book seemed to spur industry (of all stripes) to greater action. "[I]t is time for the industry to discontinue its meek attitude of the past year and strike back at the Department . . . it is time for the industry again to point out to the public just where the Department's ideas of a bill would lead them."[118] An unsigned article a page later labeled the book "particularly nasty and replete with innuendos."[119] Imagine the dismay in certain quarters, then, when reports surfaced in the *New York Times* that director B. P. Sulzberger had acquired the movie rights.[120]

Meanwhile, on Capitol Hill, the four bills, recently the subject of the longest hearings to date on food and drug laws, sat in the House Commerce Committee until late in the second session of the 74th Congress.

When a bill was finally reported out (essentially S 5), various amendments were added that strengthened the multiple-seizure provisions and ceded little advertising control to the FDA. On June 19, 1936, the bill was placed before the House as a whole, albeit with a motion to suspend rules, thus limiting debate to only twenty minutes per side. The modified version passed 151 to 27.[121]

The Senate did not wholly agree with the House version, and the bill went to conference. On June 20, 1936, both sides quickly reached agreement on all points except enforcement of advertising. Copeland worked out a compromise in which the FDA only regulated advertisements relating to health. This successfully carried the measure forward and sent it to the House. In the House, discussion was more difficult because Ewin Davis, FTC commissioner, had previously served in the Senate.[122] In the moments leading up to the floor vote, representatives reminded each other of their role in creating the FTC and Davis's political origins. Representative Samuel McReynolds of Tennessee asked, "Now, Members of the House, what are you going to do about it? Are you going to turn this over to Tugwell for enforcement or are you going to leave it with the FTC with such men as Judge Davis and other men from this House or that Commission?"[123] The measure failed 70 to 190.[124]

Copeland was not discouraged by this latest failure. At the beginning of the first session of the 75th Congress, in March 1937, he introduced another, similar measure and managed to get the same designation—S 5—for it. S 5 was referred to the Committee on Commerce. There were no hearings, and several amendments were added, such as those supporting multiple seizures, in an attempt to make it more favorable to consumers than earlier versions had been. The bill was reported out of committee on February 15, 1937, and onto the floor for discussion and vote on March 8.[125] S 5, which was essentially what the Senate had approved in the 74th Congress, passed easily with little debate.[126]

Not everyone was pleased with this development. Many people interpreted this as putting industry needs and desires ahead of concern for the consumer. Senator Copeland entered into the record a vigorous criticism from four women's organizations which enumerated the many ways in which the bill failed to adequately protect consumers.[127] Supporters of the FTC, especially in the House, disliked the diminution of FTC power. As a result, when S 5 arrived in the House and was shuttled to the Committee on Interstate and Foreign Commerce, it was ignored for the remainder of the first session, including the special fall session in 1937. To address the FTC-FDA issue, the Senate had passed legislation proposed by Senator Burton Wheeler that strengthened the

FTC. This bill, too, was sent to the Interstate and Foreign Commerce Committee. Chairman Lea thought the solution to the dilemma of advertising lay with Wheeler's, rather than with Copeland's, measure. Towards that end, Lea also proposed amending the FTC act, specifically enjoining the commission to regulate food, drug, and cosmetic advertising.[128]

While this interagency squabbling consumed time in the halls of Congress, the FDA continued to fulfill its mandate to protect the public against unsafe products and unscrupulous claims. All the power of the agency and even the proposed new powers, however, were helpless to prevent what happened next.[129] Since the advent of sulfa drugs in Germany, pharmaceutical houses in the United States had been working to develop a product to deliver this miracle drug to an eager public.[130] A chemist at the Massengill Company in Tennessee realized that sulfa could be successfully suspended in diethylene glycol. What he failed to anticipate, though, was the toxicity of this combination. No law required premarket testing to prove the safety or efficacy of a new drug. The Massengill Company began production of its Sulfanilamide Elixir on August 28, 1937; distribution began September 4.

Word of the first deaths reached the FDA on October 14. Distribution of the elixir halted on the 15th, and the FDA ordered seizure of all sulfanilamide the following day. How could the FDA do this? On a mere technicality, as it turned out. According to the U.S. Pharmacopoeia, an "elixir" must contain alcohol, which Massengill's product did not. Had Massengill labeled its elixir a "solution," the FDA would have been helpless. The FDA response betrayed the severity of the case. Their single-minded goal was to prevent any unnecessary deaths. Towards that end, the FDA recruited officers from other field stations to track down as much of the 240 gallons produced as possible.[131] The elixir had been distributed in 633 shipments, not including 484 one-ounce doctor's samples and 187 two-ounce salesman's samples. All told, 228 gallons and two pints were seized, destroyed, collected as lab samples or wasted by spillage and breakage. Eleven gallons and six pints had been given by prescription or over-the-counter. Half of this had been consumed (causing death), and the other half was "retrieved before consumption."[132] In many ways, sulfanilamide was to the 1938 law what *The Jungle* was to the 1906 act, a spur to and an increase of widespread consumer outrage exerting more pressure on Washington.

Nothing in S 5, nor any of the other bills under consideration, would have prevented this tragedy.[133] A modification of S 5 submitted by Chapman, HR 9341, added a "new drug" section. Copeland introduced

S 3073 to forbid the introduction in interstate commerce of "any drug
. . . not generally recommended as safe for general use," legislation
remarkably similar to Chapman's. A second new section was added,
providing for extensive judicial review if one person objected to a
product on the market. Many people opposed this second clause,
including women's organizations, Consumers Union (the offshoot of
CR), and the American Medical Association. A minority on the House
Committee on Interstate and Foreign Commerce, composed of Representatives Virgil Chapman, John O'Connell, Carl Mapes, Charles
Wolverton, James Wolfenden, and Pehr Holmes, filed a report against
this second clause as well, arguing that it "assumed judges were experts
in chemistry, medicine, dietetics, pharmacy, and biology."

Politics being what they were, the pace of the legislation, although
quickened because of the national attention to the FDA shortcomings in
the sulfanilamide episode, was held back by FTC supporters in the
House. The floor debate on S 5 in the House, on January 12, 1938, hinged
primarily on giving the FTC deterrent efforts that in the proposed bill
had been earmarked for the FDA.[134] In the House, Representative Lea,
chair of the Interstate and Foreign Commerce Committee, delayed
approving S 5 until Wheeler's bill broadening FTC powers passed. In
the Senate, meanwhile, Copeland's bill (the new version) passed
without debate on May 5, 1938.[135]

Once reported out of committee, the House version contained two
amendments. Many groups were opposed to the House version. Consumer groups deluged the president and their congressional representatives with mail, protesting the weakened provisions.[136] The AMA
railed against the latest version as well.[137] The bill went to the floor of the
House on May 31 and was debated that and the following day.[138] The bill
finally passed 107 to 10 on June 1, 1938.[139] The Senate disagreed with the
House version and asked for a conference. Senators Copeland, Bailey,
Clark, Caraway, McNary, Arthur Vandenberg, and Ernest Gibson met
with Representatives Lea, Chapman, William Cole, Samuel Pettengill,
Herron Pearson, Mapes, Brazilla Reece, and Charles Halleck, on June 2
and 3. They issued a report on June 11. The compromise version
removed the advertising controls in the Senate version, now no longer
necessary because of Wheeler-Lea, altered judicial review provisions in
the House version, and compromised on the multiple seizures section.[140]
In the opinion of David Cavers, chief architect of the original Tugwell
bill, with few exceptions the changes made for a stronger law.[141] The
Senate agreed to the conference report without debate and approved the
compromise bill that same day. Three days later, after the apple growers

had voiced their concerns (again) over judicial review, the House also agreed with the compromise bill.[142] And the bill was sent to the president for his signature.

A little more than five years after Senator Copeland had first submitted a bill to Congress to revise the 1906 Food and Drugs Act, the president signed the bill into law. Unfortunately, Senator Copeland did not witness this final triumph. He had died in the intervening weeks between House and Senate approval and that of the president.[143] Unfortunately, too, many consumers were unhappy with this bill and believed that they had been cast aside in obeisance to the demands of business. The FDA, however, was pleased with the ultimate law. "I am convinced that the new law represents a vast improvement over the old one," said Walter Campbell, "a gain well worth five years of unremitting effort on the part of its Congressional champions of the Food and Drugs Act, and of the women's organizations which were its most active public supporters."[144]

• • •

What did the new bill offer consumers? Among other provisions, it offered judicial and administrative procedures for (FDA) enforcement, per the 1906 act, plus an extension of the agency's purview to include cosmetics and therapeutic devices and increased penalties for those who violated the law. As with most laws, the Food, Drug, and Cosmetic Act did not go into effect immediately. Instead, the law would take effect on July 1, 1939, after a year of decisions about how to implement and enforce the bill. The sole exception to this delay in enforcement was a provision relating to coal tar dyes, specifically those in eyelash and eyebrow dyes. According to the new law, cosmetics with coal tar dyes (primarily hair dyes and mascaras) needed to add a specific warning on their label. As these products, particularly Lash Lure, had caused problems earlier and gone unchallenged, the FDA desired to quash this problem immediately.

Ultimately, as with any piece of consumer legislation, most of the responsibility for safety lay with the consumer. As Walter Campbell reflected, "A perfect law had not been achieved. That must wait upon the education of the consumer, the spreading sense of public responsibility within the reach of those who now rely upon the radio and advertising pages for diagnosis and prescription. Progress along all three lines is evident."[145]

chapter five

"The big cosmetic houses aren't sorry that the regulation has come"

WHAT HAPPENED after President Franklin Roosevelt signed the Food, Drug, and Cosmetic Act into law? In this chapter, I will examine the Food and Drug Administration's (FDA) attempts to enforce this law. What emerged in the first years of enforcement was a loose collaboration between physicians, manufacturers, and the FDA. As the country entered a second world war, problems continued to crop up, but the FDA and manufacturers responded much more quickly than previously. By 1945, most of the fine-tuning in enforcement and manufacturing had been worked out, and, as had been the case prior to the 1938 law, most cosmetics on the market were completely safe.

As per standard practice, the 1938 Food, Drug, and Cosmetics Act would not go into effect until June 1939. This year's grace period benefited the FDA as well as food, drug, and cosmetic manufacturers, purveyors, and advertisers. Manufacturers had time to reformulate their products, important if they formerly had used ingredients now forbidden. Packaging could be redesigned so that all necessary and required information was clearly visible. Advertising firms designed new campaigns, carefully omitting questionable phrases.[1] "Interested parties" (mostly trade associations) met with FDA officials to hammer out specifics not detailed in the law, such as which coal tar dyes would be acceptable, and whether all formulas, including company secrets, needed to be explicitly detailed on the ingredients list. Perhaps most important of all, the year gave the FDA and Federal Trade Commission (FTC) time to organize and reorient themselves, and devise procedures and standards for enforcement.[2]

In the year of breathing space allotted to work out the myriad details, several things occurred. First, the FDA received permission and began (limited) enforcement almost immediately. Rather than quietly remove products from shelves, the FDA ballyhooed its accomplishments in print and on the air.[3] Second, implementation and enforcement of the bulk of the law was delayed another year (1940, rather than 1939). Most cosmetic and drug manufacturers in the early months of 1938 had supported the proposed Copeland bill. "Before the present year is over," an editorial in *Drug and Cosmetic Industry* theorized in January 1938, "this increased public interest in the products will likely make itself felt in the enactment of a new Federal Food and Drug Act. But if it does not happen this year, it will happen within the next few years. And every year that the matter is delayed, the greater will be the public interest, and the more stringent will be the law."[4] The combination of the drug and cosmetic industry's enthusiasm for the bill coupled with FDA desire to "catch the bad guys" suggested agreement and speedy resolve to begin enforcement.

When enforcement did begin, it brought more surprises: the actions of the FDA and those of the FTC. The FDA requested, and was granted, one exemption to the year's delay in enforcement. The agency was particularly keen to get known dangerous products out of the hands of consumers. Within the first year, the FDA targeted several specific cosmetics with dangerous ingredients. After the first few months, however, enforcement declined. This may be attributed to cosmetic companies withdrawing products from the market or to discussion with the FDA prior to releasing product to ensure compliance with every aspect of the new law, from packaging to labeling, advertising to ingredients. The FTC vigorously enforced and prosecuted "their" law, to the chagrin, if not disappointment, of those industries that had hoped for weaker enforcement at the hands of the FTC, an agency formerly considered friendlier to business and therefore preferable to monitor advertising for food, drugs, and cosmetics (hence the Wheeler-Lea Act). By the time the country turned its attention to the war in Europe, few companies violated either law, which supported the industry's 1938 contention that they wanted, and would benefit from, some formal governmental oversight.

● ● ●

Barely one week after President Roosevelt had signed the Food, Drug, and Cosmetic Act into law, the FDA made its first seizure—Lash Lure. The problems caused by Lash Lure had been a source of embarrassment for the FDA in 1933: although the administration knew that paraphenylenediamine (PPD), the dye in Lash Lure, was dangerous, it had been helpless to prevent injury. Short of warning women to be careful and avoid Lash Lure and other, similar mascaras, the agency had no power. Furthermore, PPD was cited in *100,000,000 Guinea Pigs* as an example of the FDA's inept protection of consumers from known dangers, and had been mentioned repeatedly at the congressional hearings.[5] Reputable mascara manufacturers also suffered from Lash Lure's taint: following well-publicized injuries, a panel in the "Chamber of Horrors," and a feature in a newsreel, eyelash dye sales slumped because worried consumers knew neither which mascara caused the problem nor what made a product safe or dangerous. The FDA's justification for immediate action against Lash Lure in June 1938, indeed the basis of its request for permission to selectively begin enforcement, was that PPD posed a serious threat, and Lash Lure's manufacturers, who were aware of the dangers, were knowingly causing injury.

The first court actions the FDA pressed under the new law were to issue notices of judgments (NJ) for Lash Lure and similar, almost identical, products: Magic-Di-Stik, Hollywood Lash & Brow Dye, Mary Luckie Lash & Brow Dye, Dark Eyes, and Roux.[6] Many of these mascaras were manufactured by the same firm but carried different labels. Those made by other companies contained the same key (and dangerous) ingredient. The FDA very publicly trumpeted this vigorous and early enforcement. "The Product against which the government has proceeded has an unenviable history, say Department [of Agriculture] officials," read one FDA press release. "Numerous instances of severe eye injury to women who have used the product are on record, including a number of cases of total blindness. Until the passage of the new Food, Drug and Cosmetics Act, the Government has been powerless to prevent continued traffic in this article."[7] The FDA's vigilance and determination to remove products that contained PPD strongly suggests that consumer protection was one motivation for the agency's enforcement policy.[8] FDA officials were taken aback at the audacity of the company not only to put the same product back on the market, but also to keep the name. In a 1933 Bureau of Investigation column in *Journal of the American Medical Association*, Arthur Cramp had charitably suggested that perhaps the creator of Lash Lure did not understand the toxicity of PPD.[9] A January 1939 interview with one of the owners of the company manufacturing Lash Lure undermined this assumption: Miss Charlotte Kolmitz admitted that she was well aware of the medical and scientific literature on PPD (including its dangers) but opted to use the aniline derivative anyway, in no small measure because of its "staying power."[10]

The quick enforcement and seizure of Lash Lure was repeated. Magic-Di-Stik's seizure illustrates how the FDA proceeded when confronted with a product in violation of the new 1938 law. The third and fourth NJs issued by the FDA were to Magic-Di-Stik, on grounds that it was adulterated because of the presence of PPD. After filing these charges, as per regulatory procedure, the FDA supplied its in-house counsel with a label and directions for application of Magic-Di-Stik. Neither complied with the new law. Shortly after the seizure, the Western District chief articulated in an internal memorandum why they were going to prosecute this case, the first under the new law. "Our position, that Magic-Di-Stik may cause blindness and other serious eye injury, is believed to be entirely sound. This case in nearly every respect seems to be on all fours with the Lash-Lure case."[11] When filing suit against Isaac Dellar and S. Meyer Kolmitz, trading as Magic-Di-Stik, the U.S. attorney for Southern California also listed claims filed by the U.S. attorneys of South Carolina, Texas, New York, Michigan, Indiana, Ohio, Tennessee, Arkansas, Missouri, Washington, Kansas, Louisiana, Mississippi, and Alabama.[12] The record also included transcripts of interviews of three women injured by Magic-Di-Stik, submitted by Harold Allen, chief of the New Orleans station.[13] Assistant FDA Chief Paul Dunbar sent the Los Angeles station a copy of a recent study that included the (highlighted) statement that "no coal tar dye can, without possibility of harm, be introduced close to the eyes."[14]

The summary and record of the case contained samples of Magic-Di-Stik; dates of shipment, approximately July 14, 1938; the seizures, each initially garnering its own NJ; witness affidavits confirming inspection and analysis of the dye by FDA chemists; a recommendation for prosecution; and the rationale: the presence of PPD constituted adulteration within the meaning of Section 601(a) of the Food, Drug, and Cosmetic Act of 1938.[15] The official record contained two additional statements. The first statement contained testimony from a respondent, in support of the Magic-Di-Stik company, who noted that the Department of Agriculture had not yet issued a list of permissible coal tar dyes; therefore the company was not violating 601(e). Also, the company's counsel argued that any injury incurred was likely the result of beauty operators neglecting to perform the necessary skin (patch) test, as per the product's packaging and label warning.[16] In the second statement, an unnamed FDA official noticed that the Dependable Concentrated Cosmetics Company officer list was identical to that of Magic-Di-Stik and recommended prosecution of that company as well.[17] Ultimately, in September 1939, Dellar and Kolmitz entered a plea of *nolo contendere* and were sentenced to one year probation concurrent with each of the nineteen counts.[18]

The second big case under the as-not-yet-totally-in-place law occurred almost a year later, in June 1939. June should have seen implementation of the 1938 law. For any number of reasons, however, enforcement of the law was delayed.[19] So the FDA continued to use provisional powers to tackle cosmetics, medical devices, and advertisements that posed an immediate threat to the health and welfare of consumers. The seizure that led to a prolonged and lengthy battle, both in and out of the federal and civil court systems, was NJ #16, the seizure of Guerlain lipstick.

Guerlain was manufactured in France and widely distributed in the United States at upscale department stores and retailers. At issue was the presence of cadmium and selenium in the lipstick: cadmium imparted a strong (or "true") red, and selenium prevented cadmium red from turning yellow. A random and routine analysis of lipstick at the FDA's New York field station revealed the presence of these chemicals in Guerlain lipsticks. These findings were independently corroborated by Dr. Ephraim Freedman, of R. H. Macy's Bureau of Standards. In his analysis of five lipsticks sold at Macy's, three were negative for selenium; the two that contained selenium were different shades from the same manufacturer, Guerlain. Macy's removed Guerlain lipsticks from display cases and returned the remaining stock to the company for credit towards exchange.[20]

In an interview, Mr. d'Escayrac, vice president of Guerlain, showed FDA inspectors a cable from company headquarters in France regarding the use of cadmium and selenium.[21] The issue was quite serious for U.S. distributors: Macy's had removed *all* Guerlain lipstick from its shelves, not just the two shades in question. In a second communiqué from France, company chemists confirmed that the "color in question" was found in light and medium shades, those already in the seized lots of 60146D and 60142D. A third shade, "Mandarin," also contained cadmium and selenium, but it was mostly off the market, a remnant of the previous year's fashion palette.[22]

A week later, d'Escayrac called the New York station chief to report (or complain) that an FDA inspector had been checking the firm's books for other possible violations. In the spirit of cooperation and compliance with regulatory authorities, d'Escayrac detailed Guerlain's response to the cadmium-selenium lipstick problem. In New York City, where product was distributed primarily to large department stores, all dealers would be alerted and ordered to retrieve the lipsticks and credit them against future purchases. The company would directly contact all drug-stores, large and small. Outside the New York metropolitan area, the company planned to mail letters to all distributors, in which Guerlain would note that some lipsticks were not in conformity with the Food, Drug, and Cosmetic Act, and as such, these items should be returned at once (again, for credit). D'Escayrac estimated that 3,000 letters would be mailed.[23]

Up to this point, Guerlain acted expeditiously and kept the govern-ment apprised of its actions. In fact, d'Escayrac repeatedly received reas-surance from the FDA that there would be no publicity precisely because the company was cooperating so completely with the govern-ment. Together, personnel from Guerlain and the FDA conceived of the appropriate steps for destroying the dangerous product following the recall of lipstick, including plans for ruining the canisters, melting down the tubes of lipstick, and shipping the resultant molten wax back to Paris.[24] At 10 A.M. on June 16, however, an assistant U.S. attorney called the public relations contact at the FDA's New York branch office, noti-fying him that the U.S. attorney's office planned on giving the seizure much attention. To improve the press release from the attorney general's office, the lawyer wanted to know what exactly cadmium and selenium were, and what effect they might have on the human body. The reply from the FDA was noninformative and curt. Until copies of the FDA's letter detailing the NJ and subsequent actions were formally sent to the FDA solicitor, and the solicitor's letter sent to the U.S. attorney's office, the U.S. attorney effectively (and officially) knew nothing. The memo-randum recapitulating this conversation concluded, "She [Miss Faconti, the assistant U.S. attorney] got no encouragement for publicity."[25]

Despite this rebuff, the U.S. attorney's office was not deterred. That became abundantly clear at 5 P.M. that same day, when Harold Whitman, a reporter with the *Daily News,* called the FDA branch office to find out whether any goods had been seized. No, replied Mr. Hill, the public relations officer; there had been routine delays in filing papers and so forth. Whitman was told that the FDA declined to make a state-ment, as the situation was very much "in progress," given a list of pub-lications in which NJs regularly appeared, and directed to the U.S. attorney's office.[26] The U.S. attorney's office subsequently advised both the FDA and d'Escayrac that publicity was imminent, even though the latter had been assured by the former that none would appear because of Guerlain's cooperation.[27]

With all parties duly warned, the U.S. attorney filed suit against Guerlain and unleashed a publicity blitz. Very similar articles appeared in the *Baltimore Sun* and the *New York Times* on June 17, 1939. "The lip-sticks, imported from France and of varying shades, were described in the libel as adulterated in violation of the law," according to the *Sun*.[28] The *New York Times* story read as if the U.S. attorney, not the FDA, enforced the law prohibiting poisonous and deleterious substances in cosmetics items. The *Times* reporter had also learned, from sources at the New York Academy of Medicine, that cadmium and selenium "had been known to exist" in lipstick in the past, but the Agriculture Depart-ment now specifically enjoined their use in cosmetics.[29] Five days later, the *Washington Post* joined the fray, properly crediting the FDA with enforcement. "With the eye-dye situation well in hand, the Food and Drug Administration—provoked by the Lea Amendment which went to the White House yesterday—has come into a job that suits its fighting spirit exactly. It has found a poisonous lipstick!" As the author of the story astutely noted, most provisions of the Food, Drug, and Cosmetic Act were not yet effective, although they should have been three days hence in July 1939. "The cosmetic drives, which have included a com-plete clean-up of the dangerous eyelash paint market, and most of the other teeth of the bill, will clamp down with relentless speed."[30]

Guerlain representatives were quite displeased with the negative publicity. Mr. d'Escayrac was upset about the product seizure. He feared that decreasing lipstick sales would cause many American employees of the company to lose their jobs in already difficult economic times.[31] Although FDA representatives repeatedly assured d'Escayrac that all the radio and newspaper publicity had not originated with their office, d'Escayrac hinted that Guerlain, which earlier had been cooperative, now intended to contest the seizures in court.[32] Bad press courtesy of the U.S. attorney's office to the contrary, FDA inspectors investigating Guer-lain's response found ample evidence that the company was acting in good faith, from letters sent to jobbers regarding retrieval to tracking returned goods.[33] Meanwhile, at a meeting in Washington between the attorney representing Guerlain, FDA Chief Walter Campbell, and Eastern District Chief George Larrick, the company's attorney noted that Guerlain was cooperating fully with the government by removing lipsticks from stores, even if it did not understand why, and was, there-fore, dismayed by the publicity. When Campbell (re)assured attorney Louis Bernstein that none of it had come from the FDA and stated his desire for continued cooperation between the agency and the company, Bernstein hedged as to whether the company would contest the seizure action.[34] However, two days prior to this meeting, an FDA inspector on a routine visit to check lipstick returns had been told that the company had, as per d'Escayrac's earlier hints, decided to "fight the case" because of the damage to the firm's reputation. In the letter from Guerlain in Paris that the FDA official was permitted to read (but not given a copy of), the FDA was mentioned twice: the list of permissible and certified colors was not available, and the NJ was issued. The case report stated, "Inspector Woods, noting that the publicity surrounding the seizure had shaken up the lipstick industry, felt that the entire situation cast the administration in a bad light."[35] Repeat visits by FDA officials, coupled with reports from Guerlain officials, confirmed that the lipstick recall was working.[36] A day before the June 27 deadline, the company was in receipt of 30,757 tubes of lip lacquer. The New York station chief believed that there would be no need to "file a new libel suit because the company was clearly complying with the FDA."[37]

The same day that an FDA inspector visited Guerlain to monitor its (recall) success, a New York University chemist visited the New York station. Dr. Leonard Goldwater had been approached by Guerlain to determine the toxicity of cadmium and selenium. He planned to test the absorption of cadmium using volunteers; based on the medical literature, he did not believe that this experiment would jeopardize anyone's health. He came to request information from the FDA on cadmium and selenium, inform FDA officials of his actions as it related to the Guerlain seizures, and solicit expert opinion, as he did not want to antagonize the FDA.[38] Subsequent to his visit, Goldwater again surveyed the literature and concluded that the amounts of cadmium and selenium present in the lipsticks were not poisonous. In a second interview with FDA officials, he admitted that he had not yet performed a series of toxicological tests. FDA drug inspectors offered Goldwater the agency's interpretation of "deleterious" ingredients, discussed public welfare versus public protection, and proffered recent FDA studies suggesting that cadmium and selenium might be toxic in amounts far smaller than previously thought. The FDA agenda at this follow-up interview was transparent: to affect how and what Goldwater would (decide to) report to Guerlain regarding toxicity levels.[39]

Two days later, on June 28, there was yet another development. A Guerlain advertisement in the New York Times stated that Dr. Alexander Gettler, a city toxicologist and NYU professor of toxicology, had been retained by the company. The reason for this advertisement-testimonial? An interview with Dr. Gettler illuminated the answer. An FDA official charged with investigating the matter expressed surprise at the lengthy signed statement prominently featured in the advertisement stating that the Guerlain lipsticks were not dangerous. In his professional opinion,

Gettler explained to the visiting officer, lipstick containing cadmium and selenium, as Guerlain's did, was not likely to produce injury. He had written as much to the company but had not given them permission to publish this private communication. As with Dr. Goldwater, the FDA official, a medical officer, explained the agency's interpretation of Section 601(a) of the Food, Drug, and Cosmetic Act regarding adulterated and misbranded cosmetics. Gettler understood and agreed with the FDA interpretation and suggested the administration spend more time concentrating on lead in products.[40]

In addition, a phone call from the U.S. attorney's office confirmed an injury (and lawsuit) caused by a Guerlain lipstick, on the heels of the FDA seizures.[41] The suit meant more interviews.[42] The physician who treated Mrs. Kelley, the injured party, told FDA officials that he had already spoken with USDA staff. Initially, the patient complained of a sore throat and mouth and then suffered epigastric pain, a distended abdomen, peeling of the lips, fatigue, and sore throat. All of this began when she changed lipsticks. As her condition worsened, she experienced nervousness, insomnia, a metallic taste in her mouth, blurred vision, numbness of the nose, and vomiting at bedtime, and she became paler and paler, which in turn led to increased use of cosmetics, including lipstick. Analysis of the lipstick revealed the presence of cadmium and selenium; analysis of the patient's urine revealed the presence of selenium. Kelley's physician expressed a willingness to cooperate with the government, in part to prevent future injury from this and similar products.[43]

On August 18, 1939, a decree was entered by consent in the Southern District of New York between the FDA and Guerlain. The company agreed to remove the contents of the (lipstick) containers, melt down the cylinders, put the contents in mass form (to avoid reuse), and ship said mass to Parfums Guerlain in Paris, all under careful supervision of the FDA.[44] One niggling problem, which took almost a year to resolve, was how much import duty should be refunded to Guerlain. In this matter, the company received little help or guidance from the FDA, despite the agency's insistence on shipping the wax back in this unusable form, and despite the increasing difficulties in shipping and the precarious situation in Europe. As the French company repeatedly explained to U.S. Customs Service, it was unfair to pay duty on a product not to be sold in this country—approximately 40,000 lipsticks—and more so on a product that the company had to ship back to France.[45] By mid-March 1940, the situation was (almost) resolved.[46]

The consent decree signaled the resolution of the FDA's case against

Guerlain. In early September 1939, Rachel Palmer of Consumers Union wrote to the New York station for information on the proceedings: she was writing a story on enforcement of the 1938 law.[47] Several weeks later, Palmer sent a draft of the article on government seizures, slated for the October issue of *Consumer Reports*. The article supported the FDA's action on behalf of consumers and criticized the toxicologists who (inadvertently, she had learned) supported Guerlain in print. The FDA's only comment on the draft was to reiterate that the product had, technically, been seized under Section 601(a), which meant that cadmium and selenium were classified as harmful, poisonous, or deleterious substances.[48]

The last time Guerlain appeared on the FDA radar was in regard to the civil lawsuit filed by Mrs. Hazel Allan Kelley. Lawyers representing the plaintiff wanted testimony from FDA personnel who had examined the original samples.[49] According to FDA regulations, information from analytical findings could not be given out, but information contained within the official seizure record was public record.[50] Ultimately, FDA Chief Walter Campbell allowed the appropriate personnel to testify. Since one of the analysts had moved to the Philadelphia station, and the other had recently been inducted into the army at Fort Dix, New Jersey, it was incumbent upon Kelley's lawyers to take depositions at the agents' current locations, rather than require that both men return to New York City.[51]

Each of these early enforcement cases took some time to resolve, in part because there were government interests and civil suits. The FDA justified their early intervention and quick action against certain products on grounds of consumer protection. As Campbell explained, "Some things had such bad histories, and there was so much clinical evidence against them that we immediately made laboratory tests."[52] In the Lash Lure seizure, for example, PPD was a clear danger, and the product had been on the market earlier (1931) with consequences so disastrous that the FDA complained at the time about their inability to seize it. As manufacturers rightly argued in contesting the 1938 seizures, the law was selectively enforced against targeted products or companies and against certain ingredients whose "standards" had yet to be delineated by the FDA. The seizure of Guerlain lipsticks fell in to this category: cadmium and selenium had not previously been the focus of FDA or medical literature, yet suddenly—and abruptly—the government seized the lipsticks.

And then there was Roux, an eyelash and eyebrow dye that combined elements of both the Lash Lure and Guerlain seizures. Roux contained two questionable ingredients, pyrogallol and silver nitrate. Both were strong, which increased the dye's "staying power" and increased the chances of (allergic) reaction. The FDA seized Roux under Section 601(c), a poisonous or dangerous substance. To slightly complicate matters, three cities—New York City, Chicago, and San Francisco—had laws more stringent than the 1938 act regarding the "safe" percentage of silver nitrate in cosmetics. The laws in Chicago and San Francisco were less stringent than those in New York City, where the FDA pursued its case.[53] As matters evolved, the New York City regulations had been written, in part, by Charles Barban, a chemist employed by Roux: if Barban had aided in determining "acceptable limits for silver nitrate and silver sulphate," it suggested an awareness of possible dangers from these components.[54]

The FDA carefully planned its legal argument against Roux. Wholesale cosmetic dealers and FDA inspectors discussed warning labels (or lack thereof) on the product. Pharmacologists explained the effects of silver nitrate, ammonia, and ammoniacal silver nitrate to the jury. Ophthalmologists analyzed experiments of the dyes on rabbits' eyes and testified about the injuries; the similarities between human and rabbit eyes heightened the impact of the scarring of the corneas and blindness in these laboratory animals.[55] And an FDA physician offered case reports—testimony from each injured party, the operator who applied the dye, and the physician who treated the injury—of Mrs. I. Reiss, Mrs. Bette Jablon, Miss Betty Needleman, Miss Pauline Cohen, and Mrs. Lucille Jones, each of whom had been injured using Roux.[56]

In spite of the FDA's seemingly infallible argument and their armamentarium of witnesses, the case deadlocked in April 1939. After the "success" of a hung jury, Roux continued to manufacture and sell its lash and brow dye, albeit one substantially altered: the silver salts were reduced by 50 percent.[57] The FDA refused to concede and accept defeat, as it had been forced to do in the early 1930s, without the law on its side, so the agency avidly sought additional medical case reports of women injured by Roux.[58] Happily for the FDA, with its zeal to get Roux off the market, several injured women pressed civil suits against the company. Even if a second government case dragged on, as many FDA officials feared it might, the time and the civil cases would be to the FDA's advantage.[59] Inspectors could attend the civil suits as spectators, noting weaknesses in the case, thus preempting these issues during the government retrial. Also, the FDA hoped to learn Roux's strategy, which would help the agency counter Roux's challenges more effectively.[60]

The real question for the FDA was, how involved should the agency be in the numerous civil suits? Should inspectors attend trials, posing as innocent and interested bystanders? Should they testify? Should they share their information—records, cases of injury, toxicity reports—with attorneys for the plaintiff?[61] Campbell's decision in the Guerlain civil suit set precedence. On the whole, the FDA willingly cooperated, with caveats about who could and could not help.[62] In one civil suit, FDA officials testified that they had analyzed the dye alleged to have caused the injury. In this particular case, the FDA chemist and pharmacist who testified were enjoined by Campbell to pay attention to Roux's case, and take notes if necessary, as Roux's argument in the civil suit would likely also be their strategy against the government.[63] The FDA officials' testimony had the potential to be extremely damaging. One FDA witness was prepared to discuss the collection report (when the organization initially seized Roux), samples received from Miss Taylor (the plaintiff), a sample received with the seal intact, and analysis of these and other samples.[64]

The civil suits against Roux dragged on: one trial scheduled for early November 1941 did not commence until December. As this case proceeded, the FDA continued to strengthen its case against Roux. In preparation for the retrial necessitated by the hung jury, the FDA gathered more names and case histories of women injured by Roux, and performed more chemical analyses on rabbit eyes to demonstrate toxicity of the various silver salts.[65] By March 1942, the government was ready. FDA counsel knew that Roux's argument—that the salts were neither universally harmful, nor were they dangerous—did not differ much from the claims at the original trial. A key element of the government's strategy would be to demonstrate what passed for common knowledge about dyes and dyeing among those who did it on a regular basis: beauty parlor operators. In pretrial interviews, beauty school instructors acknowledged the dangers of eyelash tinting. Operators whose customers were injured following routine application of Roux were questioned as well. Finally, owners of beauty shops explained why they discontinued use of lash and brow tints and dyes in their salons.[66] After the government's hung jury in 1939, the civil suits in 1940 and 1941, and the FDA's preparation for retrial, it did not occur. In the interim, between the first FDA trial and the scheduled retrial, the company independently changed the formulation of its tint and lash dye and lost several civil suits, all of which seemed to support the government's contention that the 1938 version of Roux with silver nitrate and pyrogallol was a harmful and dangerous substance.

As the above cases demonstrate, the FDA vigilantly enforced the law to ensure the public's well-being. With each seizure, the rationale had been the presence of a harmful or deleterious substance. But the FDA's enforcement extended beyond simply scrutinizing ingredients in products. In the year between passage and implementation of the 1938 law, the agency was involved in protracted discussions with the Toilet Goods Association (TGA) to work out specifics for the new labeling requirements so that everyone was happy with the final product. The TGA also aided the FDA by collecting samples of colors, each of which had to be certified.[67] Although every cosmetic company had different shades of lipstick, nail polish, powders and other products, most dealers did not manufacture their own product or their own dyes but instead bought them from one of several manufacturers. Initially, TGA counsel believed that fifteen or twenty dye lots, certified, would be sufficient to meet the needs of most cosmetic companies.[68] At the request of Albert Pacini, secretary of the TGA Manufacturers Color Committee, thirty-six coal tar dyes were also made available for FDA analysis and approval.[69] The cooperation of the TGA and other food, drug, and cosmetic associations was, some felt, indicative of the broad support the new law enjoyed.[70] "Really, the big cosmetic houses aren't sorry that the regulation has come," FDA Chief Walter Campbell wrote to W. Wharton, the Eastern chief, on the eve of the law's implementation in January 1940. "One spokesman for the industry said that they realized for some time that they were being driven too far by the 'lunatic fringe.' When some fly-by-night put out a paste and promised that one application would make a hag into a candidate for the front row of the chorus, more reputable houses felt pushed into making some assertions or suggestions which were on the inflated side."[71]

The "inflated claims" lay in the gray area between FDA and FTC jurisdiction. The Wheeler-Lea Amendment gave the FTC control over advertising and gave the FDA label-watching responsibilities. One consequence of this split in enforcement was that many companies sent their labels to the FDA for premarket approval, even though industry trade organizations provided this service for their members.[72] Companies hoped that this extra precaution would prevent product seizure or fines. Instead, it merely increased the workload of the FDA. Two examples will suffice. Early in the design process, the National Mineral Co. submitted its mockup of a label for Helene Curtis Vinegar Rinse to the FDA's Chicago field office for suggestions and comments. FDA officials made at least three suggestions: the font for "poison" was too small, especially compared with the font size of "Helene Curtis"; the phrase "As required by the Department of Agriculture" was misleading and as such ought to be deleted; because the product was technically a cosmetic, under Section 201(i), the label needed to be revised to conform with that statute, possibly by deleting the phrase "vinegar rinse," given the minute quantity of vinegar present.[73] Another product, Chen Yu Nail Lacquer, manufactured by Revlon, raised two flags. The azo dye, especially for Mandarin (a shade), was not a certified color, nor had Revlon submitted information on the coloring materials to either the TGA or FDA.[74] Second, the packaging and labeling implied a Chinese product: "the use of Chinese characters [on the label] gave the impression it was produced in China or of Chinese materials."[75]

FTC activity, particularly in regard to cosmetic advertisements, surpassed everyone's expectations. In the spring of 1938, many assumed that the FTC would be far less vigilant than would the FDA. Therefore, most (if not all) industry and trade organizations preferred that drug and cosmetic advertising be specifically the realm of the FTC. In this assumption, however, they were sadly mistaken. The FTC actively enforced Wheeler-Lea; a February 1939 press release noted that legal actions were "mounting steadily." Without many of its particulars determined, in January 1939 the FDA and FTC, acting in concert, seized two hair dyes with PPD and without warning labels, removed drugs with aminopyrine and ampules of glucose marked "sterile" but containing live bacteria, seized dangerous devices including nasal irrigants and nipple shields with lead, seized food with insects and filth, and removed butter from shelves that had less butterfat than allowed by law (an economic violation).[76]

Just when manufacturers and the FDA had tweaked the new laws and began enforcement in earnest in January 1940, the playing field changed. Embargoes on dyes, chemical constituents, and other essential ingredients because of World War II forced companies in the United States to alter recipes. Enterprising chemical companies created or produced substitutes. The FDA addressed this possible safety issue in a July 1942 radio broadcast of "Here's Your Answer." A listener questioned whether the new drugs and cosmetics were safe to use, fearing "lurking dangers" in part because of the war. Despite some changes, Fred B. Linton, author of the broadcast script, assured his audience that all products on the market met FDA standards; if anything, the war heightened FDA vigilance, rather than made for more lax enforcement.[77]

The FDA (and the FTC) relied in no small measure on the American public and physicians to alert the agency about possible problem products. "Congress had not provided us with facilities nor the personnel to make clinical tests of drugs, devices or cosmetics, ourselves," wrote Theodore Klumpp, chief of the FDA Drug Division, in *Wisconsin Medicine* in 1940. "We are dependent upon the reports of your experiences. . . . When you see injury resulting from dangerous articles, we hope that you will report them in the literature or directly to us."[78] Physicians were an important element in this system. As they had in the past, physicians were often a person's first line of defense when untoward or uncomfortable reactions occurred. Also, case reports continued to appear in the medical literature. The problems that occurred during World War II were due to ingredient substitutions, as many chemicals were unavailable or requisitioned by the government for war materiel.

One ongoing blemish in many a woman's beauty routine was problems associated with nail polish. Nail polish dermatitis was often tricky to diagnose, because the itching, redness, and swelling was not confined solely to the hands and fingers—the obvious location—but also manifested on eyelids, face, neck, or arms.[79] In one case, the lesions were limited to one ear. "The husband of the patient snored so loudly that she slept with one ear on the pillow, and in the other, she placed the tip of one finger."[80]

The common allergen, dermatologists eventually concluded, was the lacquer base. Once a simple product, "modern" nail polish consisted of cellulose nitrate (pyroxylin) as a base, plus solvents, plasticizers, resins, coloring materials, and perfume. Although the percentage of cellulose varied from brand to brand, it was almost always the culprit, not the dyes and perfumes that often caused problems in lipsticks and rouges. Not everyone made the connection between wartime exigencies and increased cases of allergy. A physician in Montreal simply noted that in the previous year (1940), he had thirty-five cases of contact dermatitis, "most of them within the last few months."[81]

Some physicians, in trying to determine what, specifically, their patients were allergic to, wrote the cosmetic companies and manufacturers of nail polish, asking for sample product or an ingredient list, to enable them to conduct patch tests with the right substances. After many tests, one dermatologist concluded that the "real sensitizer" was not nitrocellulose, as previously believed, but the solvent; a synthetic resin would solve the problem.[82] By the end of 1944, the problem resin had been identified: toluene sulfonamide formaldehyde caused twenty-five of twenty-six reactions in patch tests of women who reacted to nail polish.[83]

Changes in cosmetic composition, and women's wartime needs, produced unanticipated cosmetics and unexpected results. Some products appeared as stopgap solutions, such as leg makeup. In an era of silk (or cotton) stockings, cosmetic stockings were laughable at best, a waste of money at worst. With silk suddenly in short supply, and rayon an expensive (and not durable) substitute, however, fashionable women were stuck. Leg makeup took its cue from facial foundations and powders, albeit with a few significant constraints: fashionable colors in clothing were a consideration; a way to create the illusion of texture (e.g., ribbing) was desired; the product could not streak but had to be applied smoothly; it needed to be water-resistant (not run or smear if the wearer got caught in the rain) but not impossible to remove; it needed to adhere to the wearer, not clothing or furniture.[84] In its first year, leg makeup was a remarkable failure, in part because it was a new product, and women were unfamiliar with it, in part because not all the kinks had been worked out.[85] A survey in the summer 1942, conducted by *Fawcett's* magazine, revealed that only 3 percent of all women used any leg cosmetic regularly.[86] Manufacturers pinned their 1943 sales hopes on "many gals not being so fussy this year," rather than an improved product.[87] Manufacturers did, in fact, improve leg makeup, saleswomen at department store cosmetic counters improved their sales pitch, and women were willing to try it once more.[88] The "new" and "improved" versions of cosmetic stockings met with approval: more women bought more leg makeup in 1943 than in 1942. Sales for depilatory services or products at salons, for ease of application of creams, also increased.[89] More women wearing cosmetics meant that more women might have allergic reactions, a fact of which cosmetic companies were well aware. One leg makeup manufacturer concluded, "Inasmuch as this is the second case amongst users of several thousand bottles sold this summer, we are planning to eliminate this particular ingredient."[90]

The dermatitis caused by nail polish and leg makeup gradually appeared in the medical literature.[91] In contrast, "hair lacquers" caused so many problems in such a brief period of time that they were quickly removed from the market by the manufacturers themselves. Hair lacquer, a precursor to hair spray or hair gel, kept hair in place. "The new type of upswept hair dress, the shortage of hairpins, and the lack of time of women doing industry work have recently led to wide use of hair lacquer."[92] The demands of war work meant that many women adopted the "upsweep" to prevent their hair from getting caught in machinery, and applied the lacquer themselves, as time for beauty appointments was at a premium.[93] Sold for both salon and home use, "powder puffs" were soaked with lacquer for ease of application. Beauticians noted that the fluid of lacquers sold for home consumption was more "gluey" than that used in the salons.[94]

An initial report in the medical literature, in October 1943, noted "only" fifteen cases, eleven involving reaction to the pads, and four the lacquer itself. "Dr. Louis Schwartz, chief of the Dermatoses Investigation Section [Public Health Service], to whom I reported my observation," the first article noted, "informed me that he had received complaints of dermatitis caused by hair lacquer pads . . . from Baltimore . . . Houston, Texas . . . and Scranton, Pennsylvania."[95] By the end of the month, Schwartz received fifty-one more letters. "These letters," Schwartz noted in a separate article, "represent many times 51 cases because most of the letters represent several cases of dermatitis. About 100,000 packages of this particular hair lacquer were sold to stores before the manufacturer became alarmed and called back all the unsold packages from the dealers."[96] One reason for the hasty product removal was the clear (negative) impact the product and ingredient substitution had had. "Approximately four weeks ago, a new method of application with special lacquer pads was introduced into this vicinity," wrote J. Howell in a case report. "During the last week, nine additional cases of hair lacquer dermatitis were proved to be due to the use of these pads." Discussion with other dermatologists in his Texas town revealed fourteen similar cases within two weeks, a veritable rash of reactions.[97] The only drawback to the manufacturer withdrawing the product from the market was lack of a public announcement about the recall, so that women who had already purchased it for home use continued to use it after it had disappeared from store shelves.[98]

Much of the FDA's attention was diverted elsewhere during the war, such as monitoring penicillin production.[99] As the incidents with hair lacquer demonstrated, physicians notified the FDA and manufacturers; the latter responded quickly. What is surprising during the war years, however, is how another cosmetic-related death went largely unnoticed. In 1931, the FDA had made dire predictions about cosmetics as a whole and Koremlu in particular. In 1933, Lash Lure and its victims were quite topical, prominently featured in the FDA's display at the Century of Progress Exposition in Chicago and subsequent Paramount newsreel, and dragged out at every congressional hearing leading to passage of the 1938 act. By contrast, the FDA and drug and cosmetics trade journals were almost conspicuously silent in 1941. The tragedy centered on a new and fairly revolutionary product, the heatless (or cold) permanent wave. Unlike old fashioned permanents, the "cold wave" relied on chemicals alone to break the hair structure, and then "set" the curls. The cold wave was advantageous for salons that were suffering a shortage of qualified beauty operators, and a temporary halt in production of the large and costly machinery necessary for regular permanents. The cold wave was also advantageous for women who could give themselves (or friends) this procedure at home.[100]

On March 19, 1941, a woman went to her Atlanta beauty parlor for her 10:30 A.M. appointment. At 2:30 P.M., after preparation, the treatment began: spraying the permanent wave solution through a closed circuit of tubes in a rubber cap four times a minute for three minutes. The patron soon asked, "Does this ever make one feel faint?" at which time the beauty operator stopped squirting the wave solution, applied a neutralizing solution, and summoned help. A physician and ambulance arrived, administered artificial respiration to the woman who was turning "dark purplish" and whisked her to the hospital. She was declared dead at 3 P.M. The postmortem autopsy revealed numerous small hemorrhagic abrasions covering almost the entire scalp in which the surface epithelium had been destroyed down to the dermis. The abrasions were arranged in parallel rows, each row associated with a curl.[101] The liver was "abnormal, with brownish discoloration;" the spleen was three times its normal size; and the blood was darker than normal. What had happened? According to her physicians, the hydrogen sulfide in the wave solution had been absorbed through the scalp into the circulating blood, where its presence effectively inhibited oxygenation of the blood.[102] The FDA, however, did not consider the cause of death acute hydrogen sulfide poisoning, nor did the FDA suggest an alternative. In newspapers and magazines, the press speculated on the dangerous nature of permanent waves and decreased salon traffic for this highly profitable process even more. The beauty industry, especially salon owners, simply reemphasized the need to be careful when working on body appendages and skin, along with continual reminders to patch test all clients.[103]

● ● ●

The FDA enforced the 1938 law and issued many notices of judgment against products that circumvented the finer points of the law. The single most recurring phrase in the notices was "unsafe or deleterious ingredients."[104] In addition, the FTC regulated advertising. Medical and other journals continued to publish FTC stipulations and FDA notices of judgment.[105] Despite the number of notices and stipulations issued, cosmetics, food, and drugs were much safer, and consumers benefited from the enforced 1938 law through better public health protection and safer products.

epilogue

WAS THE AMERICAN public better protected in 1945 than it had been in 1900? The 1938 Food, Drug, and Cosmetic Act broadened the scope of FDA enforcement far beyond that of the 1906 Pure Food and Drugs Act, further increasing public health and safety. One could argue that it is important for manufacturers to list ingredients of drugs, food, and cosmetics, as individuals can choose to avoid products with common allergens. It is more important—and more of a safety measure—to test the efficacy (and side effects) of drugs before the products land on the market. In increasing public safety, the FDA also increased, to some extent, the onus of individual responsibility: by listing ingredients, for example, the task of avoiding ingredients to which one is allergic rests squarely on the individual. The right to increased knowledge and information about products means increasing responsibility as well.

Have the changes over the last one hundred years been noticeable and beneficial for consumers? Yes. The combined forces of consumer activism, financial interests of manufacturers, and the concern of government officials have made the FDA the regulatory watchdog agency it is today.[1] Just as there were numerous amendments to the 1906 law before 1938, there have been numerous revisions to the 1938 law as well. The Delaney Committee began to investigate the safety of chemicals in food and cosmetics in 1950; the 1954 Miller Pesticide Amendment, 1958 Food Additive Amendment, and the 1960 Color Additive Amendment were direct results of the committee.[2] Thalidomide was to the 1962 Kefauver- Harris Drug Amendment what *The Jungle* had been to the 1906 act and what Elixir of Sulfanilamide had been to the 1938 act.[3]

Public health is not typically regarded as beginning with grassroots activism; instead, we usually view it as beginning on an organizational level, often spurred by government, medical, or public health officials, or reformers, then filtering down to the community. In the case of food and drug reform, however, the desire for more protection began with women and consumer activists, operating at a grassroots level. Women's organizations, concerned about what they were feeding their families, wanted reliability and standards; not coincidentally, this occurred as the locus for food, drug, and cosmetic production moved firmly outside the home and into manufacturing plants, and the production of these items became increasingly complex. Consumer organizations advocated customers getting honest product—and value—for their money. And government officials, particularly those charged with enforcing a law they believed to be outdated, wanted to close loopholes and offer consumers more protection.

The bottom line was the same: protecting the consumer. More important, perhaps, than how much the food and drugs were regulated was the public perception of how much safety they were being offered. In 1906, most consumers assumed that cosmetics were monitored and their safety regulated by the federal government. Only when FDA radio broadcasts in 1930 delineated the particulars of the 1906 law (highlighting the exemptions, as per the propaganda or public health campaign) did most women learn otherwise. When women were injured by Koremlu in 1931 and blinded by Lash Lure in 1933, the popular press and especially consumer organizations were outraged to discover that these products were completely unregulated. A five-year legislative battle ensued, to afford consumers more protection. Likewise, many consumers at the beginning of the twenty-first century assume that vitamins and nutritional supplements are regulated, thus protecting the public from specious claims.[4] Injury, sickness, and death from these products can only be laid at the door of the unwary consumer, as had been the case with cosmetics in the early 1930s. Indeed, some have argued that consumers themselves were responsible for keeping these products beyond FDA purview, unlike earlier consumer-driven regulatory successes.[5]

Was the 1938 revision of the 1906 law too weak, catering to too many industry concerns and interests, as some consumers believed? The 1938 Food, Drug, and Cosmetic Act did have weaknesses. Some consumer groups wanted complete protection, while others believed in the dictum "something is better than nothing." The 1938 bill, greatly improved over its 1906 predecessor, offered and served as a starting point for further revisions. The process of constructing a bill is always a cumbersome and highly charged political one; few bills can adequately meet all needs, nor anticipate all future problems. This was more than adequately demonstrated in 1937. Even as various versions of a food, drug, and cosmetic bill were still being debated, the deaths caused by the Elixir of Sulfanilamide pointed to a glaring weakness in every proposed version: none included premarket testing for efficacy and safety. Such provisions were hastily added, without dispute.

What no one could have foreseen was the change in American culture after 1938. The war clearly impacted cosmetic sales, albeit in a positive way: wearing cosmetics could almost be patriotic, to keep one's morale up. But even as companies were coping with rationing of ingredients, they were quietly gearing up to capture the next market: teenage girls. Perceptive marketers realized early in the 1940s the discretionary buying power of teenage babysitters. Despite a divergent opinion about this market—to create a brand-loyal customer for life versus a woman willing to splurge for a lipstick—consensus held that the sooner a young woman learned the wonders of makeup, the sooner she became a lifelong purchaser. To aid and abet cosmetic companies, or perhaps it was the other way around, a new genre of magazine appeared, aimed at this same audience.

This campaign was in place before the baby boom began. Add to this a new "ideal" woman of the 1950s, with an emphasis on looking fresh and cheerful for the returning husband. An increasing sense of sociability, with a prescribed "look" for women, meant standing appointments at beauty salons for many. And in all of this, one of the most successful advertising campaigns ever, Revlon's "Fire and Ice," was launched. Cosmetic sales continued to increase, even when they might have decreased in the late 1960s and 1970s with the return to a natural look.[6] There are still women (and men) who have allergic reactions of varying severity to cosmetics. There are still cosmetics that are dangerous, such as the coal tars in hair dyes (exempted from the 1938 law). And there are still women who will change their look, or at least how they feel, by buying another lipstick.

The message propagated by the cosmetic industry—that if one looks good, one feels good—has sustained sales and transcended gender. Men might not buy blush, but they will buy a bronzer or instant tan for many of the same reasons women will. And while eyeshadow might not have a male product equivalent, lipsticks and lip glosses disguised as lip balms have gone unisex. "Men's grooming," including but not limited to shaving products, is one of the fastest growing segments of the cosmetics industry. And injectable beauty, from permanent eyeliner to Botox, has changed the playing field. In all cases, the FDA is aware of problems and pressured to take action only when comments or complaints are officially registered. The onus and the responsibility for safe products and good health (still) rest, ultimately, with the consumer.

• • •

After the bill was signed into law, the FDA (and FTC) moved extraordinarily quickly to enforce specific provisions. Almost immediately the FDA pounced on a succession of eyelash and eyebrow dyes whose presence had long been an annoyance. Enforcement of the 1938 Food, Drug, and Cosmetic Act officially began in January 1940. Given wartime exigencies, one would have expected enforcement to slacken, in the face of the agency's increased demands. One would also have expected manufacturers to take advantage of possibly weaker enforcement. Remarkably, some manufacturers became more responsive to consumer, physician, and FDA complaints. Adverse reactions could quickly be pinpointed and resolved, often before or without the FDA issuing a notice of judgment, recall, or similar action.

Ultimately, the 1938 Food, Drug, and Cosmetic Act gave Americans a safer food, drug, and cosmetic supply than had existed previously. FDA Chief Walter Campbell dedicated the bill as a memorial to Senator Royal S. Copeland, to honor his five years of dedication and perseverance in shepherding this bill through committee after committee, revision after revision.[7] I wonder if Copeland, had he lived another week, would have echoed Harvey Wiley's words thirty-two years earlier, when he had dedicated the bill to the tireless efforts of women's organizations and activists.

notes

Notes to Introduction

1. A. W. McCally, A. G. Farmer, and E. C. Loomis, "Corneal Ulceration Following Use of Lash-Lure," *JAMA* 101, no. 20 (11 November 1933): 1561.

2. The others were Clyde E. Harner, "Dermato-Ophthalmitis Due to the Eyelash Dye Lash-Lure," *JAMA* 101, no. 20 (11 November 1933): 1558–59; Oliver P. Bourbon, "Severe Eye Symptoms Due to Dyeing the Eyelashes," *JAMA* 101, no. 20: 1559–60; and R. C. Jamieson, "Eyelash Dye (Lash-Lure) Dermatitis with Conjunctivitis," *JAMA* 101, no. 20: 1560.

3. Robert S. McElvaine, *The Great Depression: America, 1929–1941* (New York: Times Books, 1993), 175–76.

4. Hazel Fay Musser to President Franklin Roosevelt, 2 January 1934; Food and Drug Act, January, Proposed legislation (062), General correspondence, 1934, Record Group 88, National Archives, College Park.

5. Recent work on the history of cosmetics in the United States includes Kathy Peiss, *Hope in a Jar: The Making of America's Beauty Culture* (New York: Metropolitan Books, 1998); Noliwe Rooks, *Hair Raising: Beauty, Culture, and African-American Women* (New Brunswick, NJ: Rutgers University Press, 1996); Mary Lisa Gavenas, *Color Stories Behind the Scenes of America's Billion-Dollar Beauty Industry* (New York: Simon & Schuster, 2002); and A'Lelia Bundles, *On Her Own Ground: The Life and Times of Madam C. J. Walker* (New York: Scribner, 2001). Older work, such as Lois Banner, *American Beauty* (Chicago: University of Chicago Press, 1983); and Gilbert Vail, *A History of Cosmetics in America* (New York: Toilet Goods Association, 1947) also elide most accidents.

6. Karen Blair, *The Clubwoman as Feminist: True Womanhood Redefined, 1858–1914* (New York: Holmes & Meier Publications, 1980) and Anne Firor Scott, *Natural Allies: Women's Associations in American History* (Urbana: University of Illinois Press, 1991) discuss women's organizations in the community. For women's activism regarding food and drug laws, see Lorine Swainston Goodwin, *The Pure Food, Drink, and Drug Crusaders, 1879–1914* (Jefferson, NC: McFarland & Co., 1999).

7. On prostitution, see Barbara Hobson, *Uneasy Virtue: The Politics of Prostitution and the American Reform Tradition* (New York: Basic Books, 1987); Mark Connelly, *The Response to Prostitution in the Progressive Era* (Chapel Hill: University

of North Carolina Press, 1980); and David Pivar, *Purity and Hygiene: Women, Prostitution and the "American Plan," 1900–1930* (Westport, CT: Greenwood Press, 2002). On temperance, see Lori Ginzberg, *Women and the Work of Benevolence: Morality, Politics and Class in the Nineteenth-Century United States* (New Haven, CT: Yale University Press, 1990) and Catherine Gilbert Murdock, *Domesticating Drink: Women, Men, and Alcohol in America, 1870–1940* (Baltimore: Johns Hopkins University Press, 1998).

8. On the 1906 Pure Food and Drugs Act, and the activity and effort leading up to its passage, see Goodwin, *The Pure Food, Drink, and Drug Crusaders;* James Harvey Young, *Pure Food: Securing the Federal Food and Drugs Act of 1906* (Princeton, NJ: Princeton University Press, 1989); and Mitchell Okun, *Fair Play in the Market Place: The First Battle for Pure Food and Drugs* (DeKalb: Northern Illinois University Press, 1986).

Notes to Chapter 1

1. Frederick Accum, *A Treatise on the Adulteration of Food* (Philadelphia: 1820).

2. Mitchell Okun, *Fair Play in the Market Place: The First Battle for Pure Food and Drugs* (DeKalb: Northern Illinois University Press, 1986), 3–6.

3. Charles Rosenberg, "Medical Text and Social Context: Explaining William Buchan's *Domestic Medicine*," *Bulletin of the History of Medicine* 57, no. 1 (Spring 1983): 22–42; and Christopher J. Lawrence, "William Buchan: Medicine Laid Open," *Medical History* 19, no. 1 (1975): 20–35.

4. The different forms are solid, an emulsion suspension, and a semisolid. For typical "cosmetic recipe manuals," see Max Joseph, *A Short Handbook on Cosmetics*, English trans. (New York: E. B. Treat & Co., 1909); and George W. Askinson, *Perfumes and Cosmetics, Their Preparation and Manufacture* (New York: Norman W. Healey Publishing Co., 1915).

5. Arnold J. Cooley, *The Toilet and Cosmetic Arts in Ancient and Modern Times* (Philadelphia: Lindsay & Blakiston, 1866), 400.

6. Cooley, *Instructions and Cautions*, 429. Similar warnings appear in Askinson, *Perfumes and Cosmetics*.

7. Oscar Schisgall, *Eyes on Tomorrow: The Evolution of Procter & Gamble* (Chicago: J. G. Ferguson Publishing Co., 1981), especially 1–36.

8. See Nancy Tomes, *The Gospel of Germs: Men, Women, and the Microbe in American Life* (Cambridge, MA: Harvard University Press, 1998); Suellen Hoy, *Chasing Dirt: The American Pursuit of Cleanliness* (New York: Oxford University Press, 1995); and Vincent Vinikas, *Soft Soap, Hard Sell: American Hygiene in an Age of Advertisement* (Ames: Iowa State University Press, 1992).

9. On the interplay between production and consumerism shaping what is manufactured, see Regina Lee Blaszczyk, *Imagining Consumers: Design and Innovation from Wedgwood to Corning* (Baltimore: Johns Hopkins University Press, 2000).

10. Kathy Peiss, *Hope in a Jar: The Making of America's Beauty Culture* (New York: Metropolitan Books, 1998), 64. Accounts of Ayer's life include Margaret Hubbard Ayer and Isabell Taves, *The Three Lives of Harriet Hubbard Ayer* (Philadelphia: J. B Lippincott Co., 1957) and Bernard A. Weisberger, "Harriet

Hubbard Ayer," in *Notable American Women, 1607–1950*, vol. 1, ed. Edward T. James (Cambridge, MA: Harvard University Press, 1971), 72–74.

11. A similar episode concerning loans, stocks, and losing control over one's own company happened in the 1950s to Hazel Bishop. See Gwen Kay, "Hazel Bishop," *Chemical Heritage* 18, no. 1 (Spring 2000):57–59; and the Hazel Bishop Papers, Manuscripts and Archives, Arthur and Elizabeth Schlesinger Library on the History of Women in America, Radcliffe College, Cambridge, MA.

12. Harriet Hubbard Ayer, *Harriet Hubbard Ayer's Book of Health and Beauty* (New York: King-Richardson, 1902).

13. Karen Halttunen, *Confidence Men and Painted Ladies: A Study of Middle-Class Culture in America, 1830–1870* (New Haven, CT: Yale University Press, 1982); Peiss, *Hope in a Jar;* and Lois Banner, *American Beauty* (Chicago: University of Chicago Press, 1983).

14. Kathy Peiss, *Cheap Amusements: Working Women and Leisure in Turn-of-the-Century New York* (Philadelphia: Temple University Press, 1986); and Ruth Rosen, *The Lost Sisterhood: Prostitution in America, 1900–1918* (Baltimore: Johns Hopkins University Press, 1983).

15. Table 623, "Summary for the Industry and Its Branches, for the United States: 1849 to 1921," in *Biennial Census of Manufacturers 1921* (Washington, DC: U.S. Government Printing Office, 1924).

16. For a broader view of the expectations of Progressives vis-á-vis government, see George Mowry, *Theodore Roosevelt and the Progressive Movement* (Madison: University of Wisconsin Press, 1946); Robert Wiebe, *The Search for Order, 1877–1920* (New York: Hill & Wang, 1967); and Kevin Mattson, *Creating a Democratic Public: The Struggle for Urban Participatory Democracy During the Progressive Era* (University Park: Pennsylvania State University Press, 1998).

17. Judith Walzer Leavitt, *The Healthiest City: Milwaukee and the Politics of Health Reform* (Princeton, NJ: Princeton University Press, 1982); Tomes, *The Gospel of Germs;* Margaret Ripley Wolfe, *Lucius Polk Brown and Progressive Food and Drug Control: Tennessee and New York City, 1908–1920* (Lawrence: Regents Press of Kansas, 1978); and John Ettling, *The Germs of Laziness: Rockefeller Philanthropy and Public Health in the New South* (Cambridge, MA: Harvard University Press, 1981) for explicit connections between Progressive ideals and public health work.

18. Barbara Gutmann Rosenkrantz, "Cart before Horse: Theory, Practice and Professional Image in American Public Health, 1870–1920," *Journal of the History of Medicine and Allied Sciences* 29 (January 1974): 55–73.

19. For a description of state laws, see Lorine Swainston Goodwin, *The Pure Food, Drink, and Drug Crusaders, 1879–1914* (Jefferson, NC: McFarland & Co., 1999), 68.

20. Oscar Anderson's *The Health of the Nation: Harvey W. Wiley and the Fight for Pure Food* (Chicago: University of Chicago Press, 1958) provides a more balanced picture than Harvey Wiley, *The History of a Crime Against the Food Law: The Amazing Story of the National Food and Drugs Law Intended to Protect the Health of the People Perverted to Protect Adulteration of Foods and Drugs* (Washington, DC: Harvey Wiley, private publisher, 1929) and idem, *Harvey W. Wiley: An Autobiography* (Indianapolis: Bobbs-Merrill, 1930).

21. *Bulletin #13, Food and Food Adulterants* (Washington, DC: Department of Agriculture, Division of Chemistry): Part 1 (1887): physical and chemical properties

of butter and oleomargarine; Part 2 (1887): adulteration of spices and condiments; Part 3 (1887): alcoholic beverages (whiskey, malt liquor, wine, and cider); Part 4 (1889): adulteration of lard; Part 5 (1889): baking powders; Part 6 (1892): sugar, molasses, syrup, honey, and confections; Part 7 (1892): tea, coffee, and cocoa; Part 8 (1893): canned vegetables; Part 10 (1902): canned beef.

22. For more on home economics, see Sarah Stage and Virginia Vincenti, eds., *Rethinking Home Economics: Women and the History of a Profession* (Ithaca, NY: Cornell University Press, 1997); Sarah Leavitt, *From Catherine Beecher to Martha Stewart: A Cultural History of Domestic Advice* (Chapel Hill: University of North Carolina Press, 2002); Phyllis Palmer, *Domesticity and Dirt: Housewives and Domestic Servants in the United States, 1920–1945* (Philadelphia: Temple University Press, 1989), especially ch. 5; Ruth Schwartz Cowan, *More Work for Mother: The Ironies of Household Technology from the Open Hearth to the Microwave* (New York: Basic Books, 1983); Susan Strasser, *Never Done: A History of American Housework* (New York: Pantheon, 1982); Barbara Ehrenreich and Deirdre English, *For Her Own Good: 150 Years of the Experts' Advice to Women* (Garden City, NY: Anchor Press, 1978); *Lake Placid Conferences on Home Economics: Proceedings* (Essex County, New York: Lake Placid Club, n.d. [c.1910]); and Gwen Kay, "The Lake Placid Conferences and the American Home Economics Association," unpublished paper, May 1992.

23. At yearly meetings, educators and others discussed home economics as a discipline for women, particularly suited to state universities, which were mandated by the Morrill Act to educate all citizens of a state, male and female. The discipline itself did not form a professional association, the American Home Economics Association, until 1908. Despite the tardy formal organization, home economics courses were taught in universities in the 1890s. See Margaret Rossiter, *Women Scientists in America: Struggles and Strategies to 1940* (Baltimore: Johns Hopkins University Press, 1982), especially 68–70, 121, 200–203, 298–300.

24. Karen J. Blair, *The Clubwoman as Feminist, True Womanhood Redefined, 1868–1914* (New York: Holmes & Stiener, 1980), 5; and Anne Firor Scott, *Natural Allies: Women's Associations in American History* (Urbana: University of Illinois Press, 1991).

25. Charles O. Jackson, *Food and Drug Legislation in the New Deal* (Princeton, NJ: Princeton University Press, 1970), 4.

26. Goodwin, *Pure Food, Drink and Drug Crusaders*, ch. 4 and 5; and Jonathan Zimmerman, *Distilling Democracy: Alcohol Education in America's Public Schools, 1880–1925* (Lawrence: University Press of Kansas, 1999).

27. Goodwin, *Pure Food, Drink and Drug Crusaders*, 96–106.

28. Ibid., 129.

29. For more on the GFWC, see its internal histories: Jane Cunningham Croly, *The History of the Woman's Club Movement in America* (New York: Henry G. Allen, 1898); Mary I. Wood, *The History of the General Federation of Women's Clubs for the First Twenty-two Years of Its Organization* (New York: History Department of the GFWC, 1912); Mildred White Wells, *Unity in Diversity: The History of the General Federation of Women's Clubs* (Washington, DC: GFWC, 1953, 1975); and Mary Jean Houde, *Reaching Out: A Story of the General Federation of Women's Clubs* (Chicago: Mobium Press, 1989). For a superb "outsider" history, see Blair, *Clubwoman as Feminist*.

30. General Federation of Women's Clubs, Board of Directors, Record Group 1, p. 6; General Federation of Women's Clubs Archives, Washington, DC; Goodwin, *Pure Food, Drink and Drug Crusaders*, ch. 6, pays particular attention to the role of the GFWC.

31. Goodwin, *Pure Food, Drink and Drug Crusaders*, 146–47, 156–57.

32. Katherine Kish Sklar, *Florence Kelley and the Nation's Work: The Rise of Women's Political Culture, 1830–1900* (New Haven, CT: Yale University Press, 1995), 308–10.

33. Goodwin, *Pure Food, Drink and Drug Crusaders*, 152.

34. The NCL provided Louis Brandeis with information on working conditions for women in Germany, England, and France that became part of the Brandeis Brief in *Muller v. Oregon* (1908).

35. Sklar, *Florence Kelley and the Nation's Work*, 311.

36. The Meat Export Act, 26 U.S. Stat. 414, applied only to pork. As the name implies, the law benefited meat destined for export only. Any meat, including infected cattle and unwholesome meat, could be processed and shipped to American consumers. The law served to placate foreign markets and allowed for export of surplus meats. An 1891 amendment added inspection of all cattle, sheep, and hogs, as well as microscopic examination of hog flesh. James Harvey Young, *Pure Food: Securing the Federal Food and Drugs Act of 1906* (Princeton, NJ: Princeton University Press, 1989), 6; and Louise Carroll Wade, *Chicago's Pride: The Stockyards, Packingtown, and Environs in the Nineteenth Century* (Urbana: University of Illinois Press, 1987), 212.

37. Many soldiers got food poisoning from the tainted meat. Given the haste with which government contracts were awarded, it seemed reasonable to assume that corruption aided in securing the bid, and poor practices helped fill it. In *Pure Food*, Young notes that tests of the meat revealed no problems. The problem, a panel concluded, was the combination of poor handling, slow transport to Cuba, inadequate sanitation, and slow construction of cold-storage facilities in Cuba (132–33).

38. In St. Louis, the antitoxin had been made from the serum of a horse that had tetanus. Technically, both the horse and the serum should have been destroyed, but no controls were in place to enforce this policy. Young, *Pure Food*, 148.

39. Ramunas Kondratas, "The Biologics Control Act of 1902," in *The Early Years of Food and Drug Control*, ed. James Harvey Young (Madison, WI: American Institute for the History of Pharmacy, 1982).

40. *Bulletin #84, Department of Agriculture, Bureau of Chemistry, Influence of Food Preservatives and Artificial Colors on Digestion and Health* (Washington, DC: 1904–8).

41. Anderson, *Health of a Nation*, 148–52; Wiley, *The History of a Crime Against the Food Law*, 57–77; Mark Hamel, "Purity and Publicity: Nutrition Science, Government Regulation, and Welfare Corporatism in American Food Production, 1890–1930," History of Science Society Meeting, November 1996, Atlanta, GA.

42. Wiley said, "My poison squad laboratory became the most highly advertised boarding-house in the world. Comments on my method of determining the effects of adulterated foods ran the whole range from ridicule to satire to tearful and vigorous protests that the poisoning of fine young men, in the interests of science or otherwise, should cease." Quoted in Stephen Wilson, *Food and Drug*

Regulations (Washington, DC: American Council on Public Affairs, 1942), 21–22.

43. Goodwin, *Pure Food, Drink and Drug Crusaders*, 183.

44. For more on the AMA and its consolidation of power, see James G. Burrow, *AMA: Voice of American Medicine* (Baltimore: Johns Hopkins University Press, 1963); idem, *Organized Medicine in the Progressive Era: The Move Toward Monopoly* (Baltimore: Johns Hopkins University Press, 1977); Harris Coulter, *Science and Ethics in American Medicine, 1800 to 1914* (Richmond, CA: North Atlantic Books, 1982); Morris Fishbein, *A History of the American Medical Association, 1847 to 1947* (Philadelphia: Saunders, 1947); Oliver Garceau, *The Political Life of the AMA* (Hamden, CT: Archon Books, 1941); and Paul Starr, *The Social Transformation of American Medicine* (New York: Basic Books, 1982), book 1, ch. 3.

45. Young, *Pure Food*, 188–89; *Cong. Rec.*, 58th Cong., 3d sess., 128.

46. Burrow, *AMA*, 77.

47. Ibid., 80–81; Editorial, *JAMA* 46 (7 April 1906): 1036–37; Editorial, *JAMA* 46 (21 April 1906): 1209; and Anderson, *Health of a Nation*, 189–90.

48. Burrow, *AMA*, 83.

49. "The American Medical Association played a leading part in the movement that led to the adoption of the Food and Drug Act of 1906. It has been at the vanguard of every effort that has been made since that time to improve such legislation." Brief submitted, "Hearings before a Subcommittee of the Committee on Commerce, United States Senate, 73rd Congress, 2d session, on S 2800, A Bill to Prevent the Manufacture, Shipment and Sale of Adulterated or Misbranded Food, Drink, Drugs, and Cosmetics," 370.

50. Henry May, *The End of American Innocence: A Study of the First Years of Our Time, 1912–1917* (New York: Columbia University Press, 1957); Louis Filler, *The Muckrakers* (Stanford, CA: Stanford University Press, 1968), 29–30 and, on Hearst, 107–41; and Arthur and Lila Weinberg, *The Muckrakers: The Era in Journalism That Moved America to Reform—The Most Significant Articles of 1901–1912* (New York: Simon & Schuster, 1961), xiv–xv, xvi–xxi.

51. Jennifer Scanlon, *Inarticulate Longings: The* Ladies' Home Journal, *Gender and the Promises of Consumer Culture* (New York: Routledge, 1995). See also Helen Damon-Moore, *Magazines for the Millions: Gender and Commerce in the* Ladies' Home Journal *and the* Saturday Evening Post, *1880–1910* (Albany: SUNY Press, 1994) and Helen Woodward, *The Lady Persuaders* (New York: Ivan Obolensky, 1960).

52. Sarah Stage, *Female Complaints: Lydia Pinkham and the Business of Women's Medicine* (New York: W. W. Norton, 1979), especially 160–76.

53. James Harvey Young, *The Toadstool Millionaires: A Social History of Patent Medicines in America before Federal Regulation* (Princeton, NJ: Princeton University Press, 1961), 211–13.

54. Filler, *The Muckrakers*, 9, 13–15, 238.

55. Ronald Gottesman, ed., "Introduction to *The Jungle*" (New York, Penguin Classics, 1985), xxiv.

56. Samuel Hopkins Adams, "The Patent Medicine Conspiracy against Freedom of the Press," *Collier's* 36 (4 November 1905), 13–16, 25; the story is related in Mark Sullivan, *The Education of an American* (New York: Doubleday, 1938), 188–91.

57. Goodwin, *Pure Food, Drink, and Drug Crusaders*, 55, 218; Young, *Toadstool Millionaires*, 211, 214; and idem, *Medical Messiahs: A Social History of Health Quackery in Twentieth-Century America* (Princeton, NJ: Princeton University Press, 1967), 28.

58. Lincoln Steffens, Ida Tarbell, and Ida Barnett Wells covered the first three.

59. For a brief overview of "The Great American Fraud," see Young, *Pure Food*, 201–3. The articles included Samuel Hopkins Adams, "The Great American Fraud," *Collier's* 36 (7 October 1905); "The Nostrum Evil," *Collier's* 36 (14 October 1905); "Peruna and the 'Bracers,'" *Collier's* 36 (28 October 1905); "Liquizone," *Collier's* 36 (18 November 1905); "The Subtle Poisoners," *Collier's* 36 (2 December 1905); "Preying on the Incurables," *Collier's* 36 (13 January 1906); and "The Fundamental Fakes," *Collier's* 36 (17 February 1906); the series was printed in its entirety in Samuel Hopkins Adams, *The Great American Fraud* (New York: P. F. Collier & Son, 1907).

60. Young, *Toadstool Millionaires*, ch. 13 (especially 205, 216–22); Young, *Medical Messiahs*, 30–32; and Filler, *The Muckrakers*, 152–55.

61. Goodwin, *Pure Food, Drink, and Drug Crusaders*, 216–20.

62. Filler, *The Muckrakers*, 121–24, 157–59, and 162–70. For other books on Packingtown, see Margaret Walsh, *The Rise of the Midwestern Meat Packing Industry* (Lexington: University Press of Kentucky, 1982), with particular emphasis on hogs; Wade, *Chicago's Pride;* and Mary Yeager, *Competition and Regulation: The Development of Oligopoly in the Meat Packing Industry* (Greenwich, CT: Jai Press, 1981), especially 197–217.

63. *Cong. Rec.*, 59th Cong, 1st sess., 894–95.

64. *Cong. Rec.*, 59th Cong, 2d sess., 102.

65. Burrow, *AMA*, 79. On the controversy over the Committee of Experts, see 80–83. See also Mark Sullivan, *Our Times: The United States 1900–1925*, vol. 2 (New York: Charles Scribner's Sons, 1927), 533–34.

66. Many of those abstaining did so because of concerns about states' rights and the extension of interstate commerce powers by Congress. In almost every case, abstaining voters expressed their support of the law, or the idea of the law, even if they did not vote for it.

67. Given that Alice Lakey had, on behalf of the GFWC Pure Food Subcommittee, handwritten over 500 letters to legislators, that was saying something. Goodwin, *Pure Food, Drink, and Drug Crusaders*, 246.

68. *New York Times*, 5 June 1906, p. 1–2; *Conditions in the Stockyards*, 59th Cong. 1st sess., H. Doc. 873.

69. *New York Times*, 6 June 1906, p. 8. The packers were Armour & Company; Swift & Company; Nelson Morris & Company; G. H. Hammond Company; Omaha Packing Company; Anglo-American Provision Company; Libby, McNeil & Libby; and Schwarzschild, Sulsberger Company. Goodwin, *Pure Food, Drink and Drug Crusaders*, 251–53; and Young, *Pure Food*, 239–46.

70. Goodwin, *Pure Food, Drink and Drug Crusaders*, 247; Wood, *History of the General Federation of Women's Clubs*, 216; and General Federation of Women's Clubs, Board of Directors (RG1), vol. 5. Minutes, p. 105–8 (1904 meeting), General Federation of Women's Clubs Archives, Washington, DC.

71. Young, *Pure Food*, 204–7.

72. *Cong. Rec.*, 59th Cong, 1st sess., pp. 9068–9069, 9075–9076.

73. *Cong. Rec.*, 59th Cong, 1st sess., pp. 9655, 9740.

74. Robert M. Allen, *Popular Science Monthly* 34 (July 1906): 53, cited in Young, *Pure Food*, 264. For a discussion comparing intent of the two bills, see Young, *Pure Food*, 262–64.

75. The *United States Pharmacopoeia* was an attempt to standardize pharmacy. The book described drugs and chemicals, with information about "standard" composition, formulae, and related information. The book's contents are evaluated and updated by a committee of pharmacists and others. Physicians were involved in this process in the earliest versions in the 1820s. Okun, *Fair Play in the Market Place*, 25–26.

76. The 1912 Sherley Amendment (37 Stat. 416) tried to close the "mislabeling" loophole. The 1913 Kenyon Act (37 Stat. 732) required weights and measures on packaging and was in 1919 extended to include butter (41 Stat. 271). The 1930 McNary-Mapes Act or Canner's Bill (46 Stat. 1019) established canning standards. The 1934 Shrimp Amendment (48 Stat. 1204) provided for factory inspection of seafood.

77. Women's groups did not support several pure food bills proposed between 1889 and 1902 because they felt the bills offered too little protection for the general population. Goodwin, *Pure Food, Drink and Drug Crusaders*, 244.

78. Ibid., 266–88.

79. "Editorial: Woman and Her Work," *National Drug Clerk* 2, no. 2 (April 1914): 196–97.

80. Harvey Wiley acknowledged the help of others, noting that the law was "a victory of the women of this country." Cited in Goodwin, *Pure Food, Drink and Drugs Crusaders*, 260.

81. Oscar Anderson, "The Pure Food Issue: A Republican Dilemma," *American Historical Review* 51 (1956): 551; Young, *Medical Messiahs*, 41–66; Goodwin, *Pure Food, Drink, and Drug Crusaders*, 266–81; and Wiley, *An Autobiography*, 231–77.

82. The location of some offices changed, but they included Atlanta, Baltimore, Boston, Buffalo, New York City, and Philadelphia (Eastern Division); Chicago, Cincinnati, Kansas City, Minneapolis, New Orleans, and St. Louis (Central Division); and Denver, Los Angeles, San Francisco, and Seattle (Western Division). Gustavus Weber, *The Food, Drug and Insecticide Administration: Its History, Activities, and Organization* (Baltimore: Johns Hopkins University Press, 1928), 64.

83. Wiley's account, in his *Autobiography*, 278–93, is balanced by Anderson, "The Pure Food Issue," 568. Wiley married Anna Kelton. Some thirty years his junior, Kelton had been active in the fight for pure food with both the General Federation of Women's Clubs and the Pure Food League. See the Anna Kelton Wiley Papers, Manuscripts Collection, Library of Congress, Washington, DC.

84. "President Taft Appoints a Successor to Dr. Harvey Wiley," *National Drug Clerk* 1, no. 1 (January 1913): 21. As the journal wryly noted, "The position of Chief Chemist . . . is regarded . . . as a non-political position, regardless of the apparent political activity in behalf of some of the aspirants." A longer and more detailed profile of Alsberg appeared the following month, in the State Drug and Food Dep'ts [sic] column, "New Chief of the Bureau of Chemistry Department of Agriculture," *National Drug Clerk* 1, no. 2 (February 1913): 69.

85. On advertising in the late nineteenth and early twentieth centuries, see Pamela Laird, *Advertising Progress: American Business and the Rise of Consumer Marketing* (Baltimore: Johns Hopkins University Press, 1998); and Jackson Lears, *Fables of Abundance: A Cultural History of Advertising in America* (New York: Basic Books, 1994); on hygiene items in particular, see Vinikas, *Soft Soap, Hard Sell;* Hoy, *Chasing Dirt;* and Tomes, *Gospel of Germs.*

86. There are widely divergent assessments of Roosevelt as Progressive; see Gabriel Kolko, *The Triumph of Conservatism: A Reinterpretation of American History, 1900–1916* (New York: Free Press of Glencoe, 1963); Samuel P. Hayes, *Conservation and the Gospel of Efficiency: The Progressive Conservation Movement, 1890–1920* (Cambridge, MA: Harvard University Press, 1959); George E. Mowry, *Theodore Roosevelt and the Progressive Movement* (Madison: University of Wisconsin Press, 1946); Richard Hofstadter, *The Age of Reform: From Bryan to F.D.R.* (New York: Vintage, 1955); Steven Diner, *A Very Different Age: Americans of the Progressive Era* (New York: Hill & Wang, 1998); and Edmund Morris, *Theodore Rex* (New York: Random House, 2001).

87. Anderson, "Pure Food," 553–57.

88. Kolko argues that Roosevelt's three most significant pieces of legislation— meat inspection, the food and drug act, and railroad regulation—were passed because industry wanted government legislation, not because consumers wanted government legislation.

89. W. Stull Holt, *The Federal Trade Commission: Its History, Activities and Organizations* (New York: D. Appleton and Company, 1922), 3; 32 Stat. 827.

90. Holt, *Federal Trade Commission,* 5.

91. Gerald Henderson, *The Federal Trade Commission: A Study in Administrative Law and Practice* (New Haven, CT: Yale University Press, 1924), 12. Richard Posner, *Regulation of Advertising by the FTC* (Washington, DC: American Enterprise Institute for Public Policy Research, 1973), offers a broad overview of the commission.

92. Henderson, *Federal Trade Commission,* 12–22; and Holt, *Federal Trade Commission,* 6. A bill submitted by Newlands on 5 July 1911 was accepted, in amended form, on 21 August 1911; *Cong. Rec.* 62:1225. See "Control of Corporations," hearings before the Senate Committee on Interstate Commerce (1911) and "Trust Legislation," hearings before the House Judiciary Committee (1912).

93. *Cong. Rec.* 63 (20 January 1914):1963.

94. 38 Stat. 717. For more detail, see Holt, *Federal Trade Commission,* 7–8 and 32–47.

95. 38 Stat. 730.

Notes to Chapter 2

1. On the growth of cosmetics in the United States, see Kathy Peiss, *Hope in a Jar: The Making of America's Beauty Culture* (New York: Metropolitan Books, 1998) and Lois Banner, *American Beauty* (Chicago: University of Chicago Press, 1983).

2. For a much-needed corrective, see the varied contributions in Philip Scranton, ed., *Beauty and Business: Commerce, Gender, and Culture in Modern America* (New York: Routledge, 2000).

3. "What to Stock: Toilet Goods," *National Drug Clerk* 4, no. 1 (January 1918): 73.

4. "Effectively, the bill would ban cosmetic use altogether, because to plead an exemption, a woman must of necessity confess to more than forty-five years of age." "Beauty Aids Banned," *Weekly Drug Markets* 1, no. 23 (17 February 1915): 2. The proposed Kansas law was not new; similar laws had been passed in early modern Europe.

5. James Harvey Young, *The Medical Messiahs: A Social History of Health Quackery in Twentieth-Century America* (Princeton, NJ: Princeton University Press, 1992), 41.

6. For a succinct summary of this shift in perception, see Peiss, *Hope in a Jar,* 55–60.

7. Ibid., 146–51 and 188–89. On the beauty ideal for black women, see Noliwe Rooks, *Hair Raising: Beauty, Culture, and African American Women* (New Brunswick, NJ: Rutgers University Press, 1996); Julie Willett, *Permanent Waves: The Making of the American Beauty Shop* (New York: New York University Press, 2000); A'Lelia Bundles, *On Her Own Ground: The Life and Times of Madam C. J. Walker* (New York: Scribner, 2001); and Gwendolyn Robinson, "Class, Race, and Gender: A Transcultural Theoretical and Sociohistorical Analysis of Cosmetic Institutions and Practices to 1920" (Ph.D. diss., University of Illinois, Chicago, 1984).

8. Mary Douglas, *Purity and Danger: An Analysis of Concepts of Pollution and Taboo* (London: Routledge & Kegan Paul, 1966); Nancy Tomes, *The Gospel of Germs: Men, Women, and the Microbe in American Life* (Cambridge, MA: Harvard University Press, 1998); Peiss, *Hope in a Jar,* 42–43; Suellen Hoy, *Chasing Dirt: The American Pursuit of Cleanliness* (New York: Oxford University Press, 1995); and Vincent Vinikas, *Soft Soap, Hard Sell: American Hygiene in an Age of Advertisement* (Ames: Iowa State University Press, 1992).

9. See Karen Halttunen, *Confidence Men and Painted Women: A Story of Middle-Class Culture in America, 1830–1870* (New Haven, CT: Yale University Press, 1982); and Gilbert Vail, *A History of Cosmetics in America* (New York: Toilet Goods Association, 1947).

10. Banner, *American Beauty,* 5.

11. On women's health culture, see Martha Verbrugge, *Able-Bodied Womanhood: Personal Health and Social Change in Nineteenth-Century Boston* (New York: Oxford University Press, 1986); and Jan Todd, *Physical Culture and the Body Beautiful: Purposive Exercise in the Lives of American Women, 1800–1870* (Macon, GA: Mercer University Press, 1998); on women's bodies, see Joan Jacobs Brumberg, *Fasting Girls: The Emergence of Anorexia Nervosa as a Modern Disease* (Cambridge, MA: Harvard University Press, 1985) and idem, *The Body Project: An Intimate History of American Girls* (New York: Vintage Books, 1997).

12. See "A Personal Note," in Helena Rubinstein, *The Art of Feminine Beauty* (New York: Horace Liveright, 1930); idem, *My Life for Beauty* (New York: Simon & Schuster, 1964); Patrick O'Higgins, *Madame: An Intimate Biography of Helena Rubinstein* (New York: Viking Press, 1971); Maxene Fabe, *Beauty Millionaire: The Life of Helena Rubinstein* (New York: Thomas Y. Crowell, 1972); and Sarah Alpern, "Helena Rubinstein," in *Encyclopedia of American Jewish Women,* ed. Paula Hyman and Debra Dash Moore (New York: Routledge, 1997), 1188–91. Information about

both Rubinstein and Arden needs to be read with caution. Like many women in business, especially the beauty business, they dropped years and altered the past. Most versions of Rubinstein's beginnings, for instance, eliminate hardship and obscure the truth.

13. See Alfred Allan Lewis and Constance Woodworth, *Miss Elizabeth Arden* (New York: Coward, McCann and Geoghegan, 1972) and Albro Martin, "Elizabeth Arden," in *Notable American Women*, ed. James, vol. 1, 32–33.

14. Lewis and Woodworth, *Miss Elizabeth Arden*, 62, 75–77, 88, 147–48, 188, 225–33.

15. See Fred Basten, with Robert Salvatore and Paul Kaufman, *Max Factor's Hollywood: Glamour, Movies, Make-up* (Santa Monica, CA: General Publishing Group, 1995) and Marianne Marino, *Max Factor: The Man Who Changed the Face of the World* (Los Angeles: Tale Weaver, 1989).

16. According to legend, when he brought the first six puffs onto a movie set, all but one disappeared. The last remaining original powder puff, formerly at the Max Factor Museum, Los Angeles, California, is now at the Entertainment Museum, Hollywood, California. I thank Robin LeVan, formerly at the Museum of Cosmetology Arts and Sciences for this story, and Thomas La Porte for following the closure of the Max Factor Museum. Basten and Salvatore, *Max Factor's Hollywood*, 45–46, 55, 79, 147, 165.

17. Basten, *Max Factor's Hollywood*, 36.

18. In 1937, 10 to 15 percent of all cosmetic sales—between $20 million and $30 million wholesale—were made door-to-door. Avon and one other company accounted for $4 million to $5 million of business in 1937, and there were some twenty other, smaller firms making from $100,000 a day to $1.5 million a year. "House-to-House Cosmetics," *Drug and Cosmetic Industry* 43, no. 4 (October 1938): 413–14. See also Katina Lee Manko, "'Ding Dong! Avon Calling!' Gender, Business and Door-to-Door Selling, 1890–1955" (Ph.D. diss., University of Delaware, 2001).

19. "Information about Mr. McConnell, April 15, 1936," in Record Group II, Section 8, folder #125, Avon Collection, Hagley Museum and Library and Center for the History of Business, Technology, and Society, Wilmington, DE (hereafter Avon Collection).

20. "David H. McConnell," RGII, Section 8, box 125, Avon Collection.

21. New products included shampoo, cream, a cream balm, and tooth tablet (a solid to which one added water after scraping some off on a brush). "Mr. McConnell and the California Perfume Company," RGII, Section 8, box 125, Avon Collection.

22. Katina Manko, "'Now You Are in Business for Yourself:' The Independent Contractors of the California Perfume Company, 1886–1930," *Business & Economic History* 26, no. 1 (1997): 5–26.

23. "Avon Products, Inc., History," Lynn Catanes, in "Finding Aid and Guide to the Avon Collection," iii, Avon Collection.

24. In her diary, Louise Fogartie found the travel and day-to-day life difficult and, at times, demoralizing. "Diary of Louise Fogartie," Record Group II, Section 8, box 125, Avon Collection.

25. "Mr. McConnell and the California Perfume Company," 2, RGII, Section 8, box 125, Avon Collection.

26. The branch offices opened in 1895, 1898, and 1903 respectively. "Avon Products, Inc. History," iii, Avon Collection.

27. "CPC Chats," the daily encouraging letter, variously reminded supervisors of products to push, told uplifting or humorous stories, and cheered on the ranks with pep talks. Originally written (or ghostwritten) by McConnell, these epistles soon came from the Kansas City manager of the sales force.

28. See Bundles, *On Her Own Ground*; a fictionalized narrative, Tananarive Due, *The Black Rose* (New York: One World, 2000); Peiss, *Hope in a Jar*, 69–70 and 75–77; and Rooks, *Hair Raising*, 55–60. See also the Madam C. J. Walker Papers, Indiana Historical Society, Indianapolis.

29. "To Our Depot Managers," 7 October 1901. RGII, Section 8, box 125, Avon Collection.

30. By comparison, Rubinstein controlled her company until she died and had many women in key positions (but only in the New York office). Arden turned the day-to-day running of the company over to others (mostly men) to pursue horses. Max Factor was succeeded upon his death by his son; all company officers were male.

31. Paula Fass, *The Damned and the Beautiful: American Youth in the 1920s* (New York: Oxford University Press, 1977), 230–34, 247.

32. As late as 1929, some pharmacy owners recognized that the older generation was more reticent than the younger. "In the drug business," one owner wrote, "there are many things which pertain only to women, things which they hesitate to talk to male clerks about." S. I. Katz, "Women Waiting on Women," *Drug Topics* 45, no. 4 (April 1929): 70.

33. Cornelia Comer, "A Letter to the Rising Generation." *Atlantic Monthly* 107 (February 1911): 145.

34. On women and leisure, see Kathy Peiss, *Cheap Amusements: Working Women and Leisure in Turn-of-the-Century New York* (Philadelphia: Temple University Press, 1986); on single women in the city, see Joanne Meyerowitz, *Women Adrift: Independent Wage Earners in Chicago, 1880–1930* (Chicago: University of Chicago Press, 1988).

35. Two articles that exemplify this stance of innocence and proper behavior in the previous generation are A. Porritt, "When I was Young—" *Independent* 105 (25 June 1921): 660–661+ and J. E. Downey, "Is Modern Youth Going to the Devil?" *Sunset* 56 (March 1926): 3+.

36. The flapper's lifestyle was not a healthy one, according to C. F. Pabst. In "A Doctor's Warning to Flappers," *Literary Digest* 91 (30 October 1926): 21–22, he inveighed against cosmetics, listening and dancing to jazz, smoking, and riding in automobiles without a chaperone.

37. Frederick Allen, *Only Yesterday: An Informal History of the Nineteen-Twenties* (New York: Harper & Brothers, 1931), 88. Allen realized his limits as a historian or chronicler of a decade only just ended and was conscious that he was breaking new ground. "Further research will undoubtedly disclose errors and deficiencies in the book, and the passage of time will reveal the shortsightedness of many of my judgments and interpretations" (xiv). He justified such a history because he had "the special opportunity to recount the fads and fashions and follies of the time, the things which millions of people thought and talked about and became excited about"; he deliberately left political interpretation to future historians

(xiv). For different sensibilities about the 1920s, see Ann Douglas, *Terrible Honesty: Mongrel Manhattan in the 1920s* (New York: Farrar, Straus & Giroux, 1995); Lynn Dumenil, *Modern Temper: American Culture and Society in the 1920s* (New York: Hill & Wang, 1995); and Michael Parrish, *Anxious Decades: America in Prosperity and Depression, 1920–1941* (New York: W. W. Norton, 1992).

38. Quoted in Allen, *Only Yesterday*, 88.

39. Both articles cited in Banner, *American Beauty*, 182.

40. B. W. Currie, "The Cosmetic Age," *Ladies' Home Journal* 43 (February 1926): 30.

41. "The Matter of Beauty: What It Meant to This Girl," *Ladies' Home Journal* 29 (August 1912): 47.

42. "Wrinkles in the Wrinkle-Lotion Business," *Everybody's Magazine* 33 (December 1915): 770.

43. L. B. Allyn, "Good and Bad Toilet Preparations Examined in the Westfield-McClure Laboratory," *McClure's* 45 (August 1915): 40; emphasis added.

44. Toilet goods, as defined by the Department of Commerce, included cosmetics, baby powders, soaps, dentifrices, deodorants, shampoos, and hair dyes.

45. Frances Kaye, "The Cream of the Cream Matter," *Beautician* 1, no. 8 (April 1925): 22.

46. Mary Winslow, "Magic Preparations and Tragic," *Beautician* 2, no. 12 (May/June 1926): 74.

47. "War Revenue Tax Bill (Stamps Required for Proprietary Medicines, Cosmetics, Etc.)," *Weekly Drug Markets* 1, no. 5 (14 October 1914): 13.

48. "May Be Exemptions," *Weekly Drug Markets* 1, no. 7 (28 October 1914): 1.

49. By comparison, manufacturers of beer, wine, liquor, and oleomargarine paid more than $6.7 million in the same period. "Manufacturers of Cosmetics Paid $33,647 to U.S. in September," *Weekly Drug Market* 2, no. 8 (3 November 1915): 18.

50. "The Tax on Toilet Goods," *Drug and Chemical Markets* 9, no. 14 (5 October 1921): 678.

51. Max Factor believed that public reaction was critical, and that knowledgeable drug store clerks could help "sell" a product line. Before Max Factor and Company introduced the Society Line in 1920, top executives worked as clerks in drugstores to learn how and what cosmetics women bought. Basten, *Max Factor's Hollywood*, 79.

52. Women's jobs ranged from the conventional—secretary, teacher, nurse—to the more unusual—taxidermist, attorney, physician, chemist, pharmacist, public employment official. For more on women's employment at this time, see Joseph Hill, *Women in Gainful Occupations, 1870 to 1920* (Washington, DC: U.S. Bureau of Census, 1929); Julia Kirk Blackwelder, *Now Hiring: The Feminization of Work in the United States, 1900–1995* (College Station: Texas A&M University Press, 1997); Meyerowitz, *Women Adrift*; Susan Porter Benson, *Counter Culture: Saleswomen, Managers, and Customers in American Department Stores, 1890–1940* (Urbana: University of Illinois Press, 1986); Margery Davies, *Woman's Place Is at the Typewriter: Office Work and Office Workers, 1870–1930* (Philadelphia: Temple University Press, 1982); Alice Kessler Harris, *Out to Work: A History of America's Wage-Earning Women* (New York: Oxford University Press, 1982); and Leslie Tentler, *Wage-Earning Women: Industrial Work and Family Life in the United States, 1900–1930* (New York: Oxford University Press, 1979). On cosmetologists in par-

ticular, see Julie Willett, *Permanent Waves: The Making of the American Beauty Shop* (New York: New York University Press, 2000).

53. Everett G. McDonough, *The Truth about Cosmetics* (New York: Drug and Cosmetic Industry, 1937), 110. The Drug and Cosmetic Industry, a trade organization, published a journal by the same name.

54. Catherine Filene, ed., *Careers for Women: New Ideas, New Methods, New Opportunities—To Fit a Better World* (New York: Houghton Mifflin, 1920). Experts in various fields wrote appropriate chapters: Lillian Moller Gilbreth wrote about engineering, and Margaret Bourke White wrote about photography, for example.

55. Helena Rubinstein, "The Beauty Culturist," in ibid., 101.

56. On the struggle for professionalism in nursing, see Susan Reverby, *Ordered to Care: The Dilemma of American Nursing, 1850–1945* (New York: Cambridge University Press, 1987) and Darlene Clark Hine, *Black Women in White: Racial Conflict and Cooperation in Nursing, 1890–1950* (Bloomington: Indiana University Press, 1989). On professionalism, see Angel Kwolek-Folland, *Incorporating Women: A History of Women and Business in the United States* (New York: Twayne Publishers, 1998) and Barbara J. Harris, *Beyond Her Sphere: Women and the Professions in American History* (Westport, CT: Greenwood Press, 1978).

57. Rubinstein, "The Beauty Culturist," in *Careers for Women*, ed. Filene, 104.

58. Gwen Kay, "Licensed to Curl: Cosmetology Comes of Age," presented at Organization of American Historians annual meeting, April 1998.

59. "Beauty Industry at the Threshold of Amalgamation," *American Hairdresser* 54, no. 9 (September 1931): 39.

60. Standards varied widely. In 1931, Oregon enforced its law requiring an eighth grade education, or its equivalent, in addition to the beauty school education. "Strict enforcement of Oregon law," *American Hairdresser* 54, no. 2 (February 1931): 100. A beauty shop in San Francisco increased the academic standards required prior to training. "Beauty College Requires High School Education," *American Hairdresser* 54, no. 3 (March 1931): 97.

61. "Defeat Bill to Tax Chicago Beauty Shops," *American Hairdresser* 54, no. 7 (July 1931): 71. The bill failed.

62. McDonough, *Truth about Cosmetics*, 9.

63. "Busy Legislative Season for NHCA," *American Hairdresser* 54, no. 4 (April 1931): 108. In Oklahoma, state association delegates scheduled a meeting with the governor. A proposed bill in Tennessee permitted barbers to do everything. Similar bills were defeated in Alabama, Arkansas, Kansas, Maryland, Nebraska, and New Jersey.

64. "To Hold Mass Meeting on Pending Legislation," *American Hairdresser* 54, no. 1 (January 1931): 98.

65. "Pending Legislation Discussed at Schools' Convention," *American Hairdresser* 54, no. 5 (May 1931): 110.

66. Winifred Bryant, "Acne Treatment is a Beauty Service," *Beautician* 2, no. 11 (April 1926): 19–21+. Many salons retained a physician "on call" in case of injury to patron or employee.

67. Personal communication with Rose Juda, owner of a beauty shop in Fall River, MA.

68. G. Alexander Ward, "Acne Medicine is a Beauty Service, Rather than a Medical Service," *American Hairdresser* 55, no. 11 (November 1932): 74.

69. "Any face-peeling produced should be done with great caution and should be carefully supervised by a physician-dermatologist." Mary MacFadyen, *Beauty Plus: The Smart Woman's Key to Beauty, Health and Charm* (New York: Emerson Books, 1938), 35–36.

For more on face peeling, see Elizabeth Haiken, *Venus Envy: A History of Cosmetic Surgery* (Baltimore: Johns Hopkins University Press, 1997), 92, 97–99; and Banner, *American Beauty*, 211.

70. "Skin Peeling and Its Place in the Beauty Shop of Today and Tomorrow," *American Hairdresser* 55, no. 5 (May 1932): 47. In the medical literature, face peels gone awry were almost always blamed on beauticians.

71. William A. Ringel, "Patrons will sue! When are you liable?" *American Hairdresser* 56, no. 2 (February 1933): 28. Ringel's article was one of many on malpractice and how to avoid it. One complaint of the New York Women's Protective Committee was a lack of adequate insurance.

72. Oscar L. Levin, *Save Your Hair!* (New York: Greenberg Publishers, 1926), 53. Similar warnings appeared in Bernarr MacFadden, *Hair Culture: Rational Methods for Growing the Hair and for Developing Its Strength and Beauty* (New York: MacFadden Publishers, 1924), 165–71.

73. Accidents were infrequent, but dramatic enough to ruin individual shops and the larger industry. In "Insurance Statistics show serious over-dramatization of abuses in Cosmetic Industry and prove Fallacies in Tugwell Bill," George Mause provides tables of insurance liability to bolster his argument. *American Hairdresser* 57, no. 1 (January 1934): 26. These arguments pale in the light of the more than 100 court cases presented in Romeyn Sammons, *Cosmetology Jurisprudence* (Los Angeles: Parker & Baird Company, 1938).

74. Charles C. Merlet and Julian L. Deane, "Peggy in Uniform," *American Hairdresser* 56, no. 7 (July 1933): 22. I assume that the NHCA commissioned the article.

75. There were moral overtones as well: many clients were "fast." On Peggy's first day, another operator confided that "Rosalie's is always the first with the latest. We have to be; you see, dearie, our customers may not belong to the four hundred, but their money's just as good, and they're freer with it. With them," Ella continued, "vanity is the spice of life, and we teach them it's the same with beauty. They like it, too—you know, blond today, brunette tomorrow, and if she don't like it, then back to blond again, or maybe henna." Two serial episodes later, Peggy unburdened herself to friend. "You can't judge a book by its cover, you know, Alice. I happen to know that the dolled up customers who frequent Rosalie's, well, what does it matter?" *American Hairdresser* 56, no. 9 (September 1933): 38–39 and 56, no. 11 (November 1933): 37.

76. In "The Skin Game: About the Value of Cosmetics," *Forum* 91 (March 1934): 180–84, B. B. Eskil reinforces the necessity of beauty products, particularly those to make women look young (smooth skin, dark hair).

77. "Bargains Are No Better Than They Should Be," *Delineator* 121 (December 1932): 87.

78. "Gentlemen Prefer—," *Reader's Digest* 28 (April 1936): 18.

79. J. Beem, "Do's and Don'ts for Dates," *Woman's Home Companion* 64 (April 1937): 99.

80. G. W. Vanden, "It's Cosmetic Time in America," *American Hairdresser* 55, no. 7 (July 1932): 60.

81. Hazel L. Kozlay, "Reflections of Beauty and Blemishes," *American Hairdresser* 55, no. 3 (March 1932): 37.

82. Anne Kellogg, "Making the Toilet Goods Counter Work," *Beautician* 2, no. 3 (August 1925): 28.

83. Hager's emphasis, "Physician, Speaking before Chicago Association Meeting, Lauds Beauty Culture," *American Hairdresser* 55, no. 4 (April 1932): 94.

84. C. C. Concannon, "Drugs and Cosmetics in the Depression," *Drug and Cosmetic Industry* 32, no. 3 (March 1933): 209–10.

85. Campana had 31.4% of the market, Jergen's 11.9%, and Hind's 11.2%. "Cold cream," *Drug and Cosmetic Industry* 36, no. 5 (May 1935): 575.

86. This advertising campaign is assessed in Jennifer Scanlon, *Inarticulate Longings: The* Ladies' Home Journal, *Gender and the Promises of Consumer Culture* (New York: Routledge, 1995), ch. 5; Peiss, *Hope in a Jar,* 136–140; also idem, "Advertising Women: The J. Walter Thompson Company Women's Education Department," in *The Gender and Consumption Reader,* ed. Jennifer Scanlon (New York: New York University Press, 2000).

87. "Account Histories, 1923–1926," Account Files, J. Walter Thompson Archives, Hartmann Center for Sales, Advertising and Marketing History, Duke University, Durham, North Carolina (hereafter JWT Archives).

88. Cold cream cleanses the face; vanishing cream washes it. "Pond's History of Advertising," 1955, Account Files, JWT Archives.

89. "Accounts, Case studies, partial list JWT clients, 1920s," 10, Vertical Files, Information Center Records, JWT Archives.

90. "Pond's History of Advertising," 8, and "Account Histories," Account Files [n.d.], JWT Archives.

91. "Account Histories, 1923–1926," 4, JWT Archives (emphasis in original).

92. Representatives Meeting, April 9, 1928, #1, Staff Meeting Minutes, JWT Archives.

93. "Pond's History of Advertising," 9, JWT Archives. The agency carefully watched journal circulation and readership. In 1916, J. W. Young wrote that "we keep getting from various sources, opinions from women about their favorite magazines that seem to indicate that *Ladies' Home Journal* is not nearly as well-liked by some classes of women as it used to be. We hear of its stories being described as mushy and unreal, and its general attitude toward things in general as being old-maidish. Of late we have heard so many statements of this kind from so many different women that it seems to us worth asking ourselves whether the *Journal* is keeping abreast of the modern woman's needs." "Confidential Letter, 11 July 1916," News Bulletin, 6 June–25 July 1916, Newsletter #1, Newsletters Collection, JWT Archives.

94. "Pond's History of Advertising," 9, JWT Archives. Cold cream in general, and Pond's in particular, continued to enjoy steady sales. According to "Cleansing Creams," a news article in *Drug and Cosmetic Industry* (33, no 4: 336), Pond's was "leading all other creams in value of sales, cleansing cream is one of the most stable products of the trade." Through 1945, Pond's continued to be the most popular cream on the market, accounting for 35 percent of all creams sold.

95. Vincent Vinikas, in *Soft Soap, Hard Sell,* examines the advertising campaigns for other toiletry items, including mouthwash, soap, and toothpaste. See also Nancy Tomes, "Merchants of Health: Medicine and Consumer Culture in the

United States, 1900–1940," *Journal of American History* 88, no. 2 (2001): 519–548; Philip Scranton, ed., *Beauty and Business: Commerce, Gender, and Culture in Modern America* (New York: Routledge Press, 2000); and Suellen Hoy, *Chasing Dirt.*

96. In *Advertising the American Dream: Making Way for Modernity, 1920–1940* (Berkeley: University of California Press, 1985), Roland Marchand argues that advertisements were couched in language to make women feel scientifically up-to-the-minute and socially correct. For more on this transformation in advertising and how campaigns were marketed towards women, see T. J. Jackson Lears, *Fables of Abundance: A Cultural History of Advertising in America* (New York: Basic Books, 1994); James Norris, *Advertising and the Transformation of American Society, 1865–1920* (Westport, CT: Greenwood Press, 1990); Vinikas, *Soft Soap, Hard Sell.* The demographics from advertising firms illustrate their understanding of the consumer; see, for instance, J. Walter Thompson Co., *Population and Its Distribution* (New York: McGraw-Hill, 1952).

97. For more on advertising in the 1920s, see Marchand, *Advertising the American Dream;* Lears, *Fables of Abundance;* Stuart Ewen, *Captains of Consciousness: Advertising and the Social Roots of the Consumer Culture* (New York: McGraw-Hill, 1976); and, for the "health" rationale, see Tomes, *Gospel of Germs.*

98. How and where purchases were made changed as society and marketing strategies became more sophisticated. For more on consumption and where it occurred, see Regina Blaszczyk, *Imagining Consumers: Design and Innovation from Wedgwood to Corning* (Baltimore: Johns Hopkins University Press, 2000); Susan Strasser, *Satisfaction Guaranteed: The Making of America's Mass Market* (Washington, DC: Smithsonian Institution Press, 1995); William Leach, *Land of Desire: From the Department Store to the Department of Commerce, the Rise of America's Commercial Culture* (New York: Pantheon Books, 1993).

99. The role of women's magazines in shaping culture has been examined by Jennifer Scanlon, *Inarticulate Longings;* Ellen Gruber Harvey, *The Adman in the Parlor: Magazines and the Gendering of Consumer Culture, 1880s to 1910s* (New York: Oxford University Press, 1996); and Helen Damon-Moore, *Magazines for the Millions: Gender and Commerce in the* Ladies' Home Journal *and the* Saturday Evening Post, *1880–1910* (Albany: SUNY Press, 1994).

100. Allen, *Only Yesterday,* 71.

101. For more on literary tastes in this country, particularly in books, see Janice Radway, *A Feeling for the Book: The Book-of-the-Month Club, Literary Taste, and Middle-Class Desire* (Chapel Hill: University of North Carolina Press, 1997); Joan Shelley Rubin, *The Making of Middlebrow Culture* (Chapel Hill: University of North Carolina Press, 1992); and Lawrence Levine, *Highbrow/Lowbrow: The Emergence of Cultural Hierarchy in America* (Cambridge, MA: Harvard University Press, 1988).

102. Between 1919 and 1929, the number of periodicals jumped from 4,796 to 5,157. Bureau of the Census, U.S. Department of Commerce, *Historical Statistics in the United States, Colonial Times to 1970, Part 2* (Washington, DC, 1975), R 232–43 and R 244–57.

103. In 1926, Robert Lynd and Helen Merrell Lynd undertook a sociology project of daunting proportions. Funded by the Rockefeller Committee on Social and Religious Surveys, they were to study every aspect of life in a typical American community. They chose Muncie, Indiana, and renamed it Middletown for publication purposes. Robert S. Lynd and Helen Merrell Lynd, *Middletown: A Study in*

Modern American Culture (New York: Harcourt Brace Jovanovich), 158, 231, and 230–40. For an analysis of the Lynds' work in Middletown, see Richard Wightman Fox, "Epitaph for Middletown: Robert S. Lynd and the Analysis of Consumer Culture" in Richard Wightman Fox and T. Jackson Lears, eds., *The Culture of Consumption: Critical Essays in American History, 1880–1980* (New York: Pantheon Books, 1983).

The reading material of choice for the younger generation roughly corresponded with household subscriptions, with greater emphasis on humor. College students typically read *Saturday Evening Post, Life, Ladies' Home Journal, True Romance,* and *Cosmopolitan;* occasionally read *Atlantic Monthly* or *Scribner's Magazine;* sometimes read the *New Republic* or the *Nation;* and only rarely read the *American Mercury.* Fass, *The Damned and the Beautiful,* 365.

104. For a modern take on how beauty columns work, see Mary Lisa Gavenas, *Color Stories: Behind the Scenes of America's Billion-Dollar Beauty Industry* (New York: Simon & Schuster, 2002).

105. Helen Rawson Cades took over the *Woman's Home Companion* position in 1923. *Parents' Magazine* began publication in 1929, and Eaton's column started in 1933.

106. Although advertisements for cosmetics appear throughout the magazines, they are especially noteworthy on the page of, and opposite, the beauty column. Often the very products touted on one page are derided as unhealthful or useless on the page opposite.

107. Mary Pickford was one of the first stars to introduce a line of makeup bearing her name. On rare occasions, the name and knowledge were unsurpassed, as with the cosmetic line offered by Max Factor. For the consuming public, however, there was no way to distinguish an innovative product from a tired one.

108. William A. Woodbury, *Beauty Culture: A Practical Handbook on the Care of the Person, Designed for Both Profit and Private Use* (New York: G. W. Dillingham Co., 1910), 15. Woodbury invented, or created, Camay soap; another dermatologist, William Pusey, promoted the soap in 1921.

Notes to Chapter 3

1. Ruth Lamb to Stephen Early, 6 January 1934; Food and Drug Act, January, Proposed legislation (062), General correspondence, 1933, Record Group 88, National Archives, College Park (hereafter NACP 88).

2. "Tugwell Bill Is Revised," *Oil, Paint & Drug Reporter,* 1125, no. 2 (8 January 1934): 15.

3. For different views of the Progressive Era, and different endpoints for that age, see Steven Diner, *A Very Different Age: America of the Progressive Era* (New York: Hill & Wang, 1998); Robert Wiebe, *The Search for Order, 1877–1920* (New York: Hill & Wang, 1967); Gabriel Kolko, *The Triumph of Conservatism A Reinterpretation of American History, 1900–1916* (New York: Free Press of Glencoe, 1963); and Richard Hofstadter, *Age of Reform: From Bryan to F.D.R.* (New York: Vintage, 1955).

4. For a refutation of this argument, see Nancy Cott, *The Grounding of Modern Feminism* (New Haven, CT: Yale University Press, 1987); Kristi Andersen, *After*

Suffrage: Women in Partisan and Elected Politics Before the New Deal (Chicago: University of Chicago Press, 1995); and Jan Doolittle, "'Organized and Under Attack': The Women's Joint Congressional Committee and Its Legislative Campaigns for Mothers and Children, 1920–1930" (Ph.D. diss., Binghamton University, 2000).

5. On women and activism prior to suffrage, see Noralee Frankel and Nancy S. Dye, eds., *Gender, Class, Race and Reform in the Progressive Era* (Lexington: University Press of Kentucky, 1991); Lori Ginzburg, *Women and the Work of Benevolence: Morality, Politics and Class in the Nineteenth-Century United States* (New Haven, CT: Yale University Press, 1990); Paula Baker, "The Domestication of Politics: Women and American Political Society, 1780–1920," *Reviews in American History* 89, no. 3: 620–47; and Karen Blair, *The Clubwoman as Feminist: True Womanhood Redefined, 1868 to 1914* (New York: Holmes & Meier, 1980).

6. The charter members of the WJCC were the LWV, the General Federation of Women's Clubs (GFWC), the Women's Trade Union League, the National Consumers League, and the National Federation of Business and Professional Women (NFBPW). Other members included the American Association of University Women, the National Parent-Teachers Association, the National Council of Jewish Women, and the American Home Economics Association. These organizations, and others that joined the WJCC, represented thousands of women: the GFWC membership stood at one million in 1910, the NFBPW had 30,000 members in its first three years, the PTA had 1.5 million members in the mid-1920s. Cott, *Grounding of Modern Feminism*, 86–97.

7. In the Senate, the bill passed by a margin of nine to one; in the House, seven to one. As Cott pointedly notes, this generous margin stood in sharp contrast to the Nineteenth Amendment, which barely squeaked by. Ibid., 98.

8. Ibid., 98–99.

9. The Section on Pediatrics supported Sheppard-Towner, but was overruled by the House of Delegates. Rosemary Stevens, *American Medicine and the Public Interest* (Berkeley: University of California Press, 1998), 143–45; and James Burrow, *AMA: Voice of American Medicine* (Baltimore: Johns Hopkins University Press, 1963), 161–63. For an alternative interpretation, see Johanne Harrigan, "The Making of a Contender: The political awakening of the American Medical Association and its impact on the Sheppard-Towner Act" (M.A. Thesis, Oswego State University).

10. Burrow, *AMA*, 383; and "Editorial," *JAMA* 76 (28 February 1927): 1504. See also Sydney Halpern, *American Pediatrics: The Social Dynamics of Professionalism, 1880–1980* (Berkeley: University of California Press, 1988) and Richard Meckel, *"Save the Babies:" American Public Health Reform and the Prevention of Infant Mortality, 1850–1929* (Baltimore: Johns Hopkins University Press, 1990). On the Children's Bureau, see Kriste Lindenmeyer, *A Right to Childhood: The U.S. Children's Bureau and Child Welfare, 1912–46* (Urbana: University of Illinois Press, 1997); Molly Ladd-Taylor, *Mother-Work: Women, Child Welfare and the State, 1890–1930* (Urbana: University of Illinois Press, 1994); and James Tobey, *The Children's Bureau: Its History, Activities and Organization* (Baltimore: Johns Hopkins University Press, 1925).

11. *JAMA* 86 (February 6, 1926): 421.

12. Elizabeth Arden resigned from the New York Federation of Women's

Clubs after this investigation. Although the standards in her salons were beyond reproach, she resigned on principle. "'You don't know enough to judge what's right or wrong in my business,' she told club women who questioned her." Alfred Allan Lewis and Constance Woodworth, *Miss Elizabeth Arden* (New York: Coward, McCann & Geoghegan, Inc., 1972), 167.

13. Gertrude M. Duncan, "Women's Protective Committee Investigates Beauty Shops and Schools and Berates Trade Conditions," *American Hairdresser* 54, no. 7 (July 1931): 48.

14. Robert N. Mayer, *The Conservative Movement: Guardians of the Marketplace* (Boston: Twayne Publishing, 1989), 18.

15. Norman I. Silber, *Test and Protest: The Influence of Consumers Union* (New York: Holmes & Meier, 1983), 28. A 1939 survey of Consumers Union's 85,000 members verified this assumption: 5 perent of the members earned less than $1,000 per year, while 13 percent earned more than $5,000 per year. The largest group of readers (most of whom were in the $1,000–$5,000 income bracket) self-identified as professionals: teachers, school administrators, and engineers in particular.

16. Colston Warne, *The Consumer Movement: Lectures* (Manhattan, KS: Family Economics Trust Press, 1993), 12.

17. Henry Harap, *The Education of the Consumer: A Study in the Curriculum Matter* (New York: The Macmillan Company, 1924).

18. Stuart Chase, *The Tragedy of Waste* (New York: The League for Industrial Democracy, 1925); four years later, he wrote *The Challenge of Waste* (New York: The Macmillan Company, 1929).

19. Stuart Chase and F. J. Schlink, *Your Money's Worth: A Study in the Waste of the Consumer's Dollar* (New York: Macmillan, 1927), 4.

20. Silber, *Test and Protest*, 18; an insert in *Consumers' Research Bulletin*, April 1933.

21. Warne, *Consumer Movement*, 25.

22. *Consumers' Research Bulletin, Confidential* 1, no. 12 (April 1931), 3. The source was "Koremlu: A Dangerous Depilatory Containing Thallium Acetate," *JAMA* 96, no. 8 (21 February 1931): 629–31

23. "Astringents," *Consumers' Research Bulletin (Not Confidential)*, October 1932, 11.

24. "Cream Rouges," *Consumers' Research Bulletin, Confidential* 3, no. 3 (November 1939): 4 (November 1936); "Hold Your Man with Hand Lotions: Analyses of Eight Well-Known Brands," *Consumers' Research Bulletin (Not Confidential)*, 2, no. 6 (April 1935):13; "Even 'Shampoos' Present Unsuspected Hazards," *Consumers' Research Bulletin, Confidential* III, no. 9 (May 1937): 8–9; and "Toilet Soaps," *Consumers' Research Bulletin, Confidential* IV, no. 3 (November 1937): 2–5.

25. "Pure Food Law Fails to Protect Consumers—Big Offenders Repeat Offenses with Impunity and Practically No Penalties," *Consumers' Research Bulletin, Confidential* 0.9 (March 1930), 2–3.

26. Sarah H. Newman, "Food Standards and Grades," in *Consumer Activists: They Made a Difference: A History of Consumer Action Related by Leaders in the Consumer Movement*, ed. Erma Angevine (Mt. Vernon, NY: Consumers Union Foundation, 1982), 128.

27. 46 Stat. 1019 (1930), 21 U.S.C. §10.

28. Newman, "Food Standards and Grades," 129.

29. 42 Stat. 1500 (1923), 21 U.S.C. §6. See S. F. Riepma, *The Story of Margarine* (Washington, DC: Public Affairs Press, 1970) for the other side of the Butter Standard Act. In addition to establishing different grades, or qualities, of butter, it also distinguished butter from its competitor, oleomargarine.

30. Harold N. Cole, "The Dermatoses Due to Cosmetics," *JAMA* 82, no. 24 (14 June 1924): 909.

31. Wolff Freudenthal, "Tobacco, Alcohol and Cosmetics in their Relation to the Upper Respiratory Tract," *Laryngoscope* 37 (March 1927): 230.

32. Gwen Kay, "'Marring the Fair Face of Nature:' Physicians Contemplate Cosmetics in the Inter-War Years," Northeastern Popular Culture Association Annual Meeting, 1996, Hamden, CT.

33. F. A. Diasio, "Clinical Observations on the Use of a Bismuth Compound as a Hair Dye," *Medical Journal and Record* (17 May 1933): 405.

34. It is surely not coincidental that a woman wrote a strong defense. "It seems a pity . . . that cosmetics should sometimes be condemned by the medical profession as wholly injurious . . . on what appear to be insufficient grounds." Alice Carleton, "The Uses and Dangers of Cosmetics," *British Medical Journal* (10 June 1933): 1001.

35. Cole, "The Dermatoses Due to Cosmetics," 1909.

36. William H. Goeckermann, "A Peculiar Discoloration of the Skin, Probably Resulting from Mercurial Compounds (Calomel) in Proprietary Face Creams," *JAMA* 84, no. 7 (14 February 1925): 506–7.

37. Hiram Miller and Laurence Taussig, "Cosmetics," *JAMA* 84, no. 26 (27 June 1925): 1999.

38. Lawrence K. McCafferty, "Hair Dyes and Their Toxic Effects," *Archives of Dermatology and Syphilology* (August 1926): 136–44.

39. J. E. Lane and M. J. Strauss, "Toilet Water Dermatitis, with Special Reference to 'Berlock' Dermatitis," *JAMA* 95, no. 10 (6 September 1930): 717–19.

40. Marion Sulzberger and Fred Wise, "The Contact or Patch Test in Dermatology: Its Uses, Advantages and Limitations," *Archives of Dermatology and Syphilology* (March 1931): 519–31; and Everett S. Lain, "Cosmetic Eruptions," *Southern Medical Journal* 25 (July 1932): 718–22.

41. Lester Hollander, "Dermatitis Produced by Cosmetics (La Gerardine)," *JAMA* 101, no. 4 (22 July 1933): 259.

42. Walter Lillie and Henry Parker, "Retrobulbar Neuritis Due to Thallium Poisoning," *JAMA* 98, no. 16 (16 April 1932): 1347–49.

43. Thomas P. Waring, "Another Case of Thallium Poisoning Following the Use of Koremlu Cream," *JAMA* 97, no. 10 (5 September 1931): 703.

44. Lain, "Cosmetic Eruptions," 722.

45. Miller and Taussig, "Cosmetics," 2001–2.

46. A regular contributor to *Hygeia*, Pusey wrote a definitive dermatology textbook and edited *The Archives of Dermatology and Syphilology* for almost twenty years, making it a world-class journal. William Allen Pusey, *The Care of Skin and Hair* (New York: D. Appleton Co., 1912), "Preface."

47. Some beauty guides touted cold creams in preference to soap. When soaps were first commercially produced in the late nineteenth century, they were extremely alkaline and harsh. As technology and chemistry improved, however,

so did soaps. By the 1920s, washing in hot, soapy water would not dry out the face, contrary to the theories advanced by some uninformed beauty columnists.

48. Most doctors who promoted or supported use of cosmetics were women. One curious and gendered difference occurred in popular (as opposed to medical) literature. Women physicians wrote books with the word "beauty" in the title; their male counterparts used "skin care" or "skin health" instead, even though the books were essentially the same.

49. "In Memoriam: Lulu Hunt Peters," *Medical Review of Reviews* 41, no. 8 (1935): 428–31.

50. Lulu Hunt Peters, *Diet and Health with Key to Calories* (Chicago: Reilly & Lee Co., 1918) and idem, *Diet for Children (and Adults) and the Kalorie Kids* (New York: Dodd, Mead, 1924).

51. Mary MacFadyen, *Beauty Plus: The Smart Woman's Key to Beauty, Health and Charm* (New York: Emerson Books, 1938), 13.

52. Helena Rubinstein, *The Art of Feminine Beauty* (New York: Horace Liveright, 1930), 235. For more on Rubinstein, see Patrick O'Higgins, *Madame: An Intimate Biography of Helena Rubinstein* (New York: Viking, 1971); Maxene Fabe, *Beauty Millionaire: The Life of Helena Rubinstein* (New York: Crowell, 1972); and her autobiography, *My Life for Beauty* (New York: Simon & Schuster, 1964).

53. Cole, "The Dermatoses Due to Cosmetics," 1911.

54. Unbeknownst to Downing, however, the "natural look" was achieved with cosmetics. John Godwin Downing, "Cosmetics—Past and Present," *JAMA* 102 (23 June 1934): 2088.

55. Of particular concern was the question of health insurance. See Jonathan Engel, *Doctors and Reformers: Discussion and Debate over Health Policy, 1925–1950* (Columbia: University of South Carolina Press, 2002); Beatrix Hoffman, *The Wages of Sickness: The Politics of Health Insurance in Progressive America* (Chapel Hill: University of North Carolina Press, 2001); and Ronald Numbers, *Almost Persuaded: American Physicians and Compulsory Health Insurance, 1912–1920* (Baltimore: Johns Hopkins University Press, 1978).

56. I developed this in "Facing Off: Dermatologists, Cosmetologists and the Skin of America's Women," presented at the 1999 American Association for the History of Medicine Meeting, New Brunswick, NJ. For more on the history of dermatology, see John Thorne Crissey and Lawrence Charles Parrish, *The Dermatology and Syphilology of the Nineteenth Century* (New York: Praeger Scientific, 1981) and Paul E. Bichet, *History of the American Dermatological Association in Commemoration of its 75th Anniversary* (New York: Froben Press, 1952).

57. "Numerous instances are reported in which cutting, burning, or otherwise tampering with such moles has resulted in the appearance of cancerous tumors and their rapid dissemination throughout the body, resulting in death. The ability to distinguish between such defects as are benign and such as are dangerous comes only with extensive study. Obviously, that knowledge is not to be acquired either by a year's apprenticeship in a beauty shop or by six months in a 'beauty college.'" Morris Fishbein, *The New Medical Follies: An Encyclopedia of Cultism and Quackery in these United States* (New York: Boni and Liveright, 1927), 87.

58. On licensure and exclusion of certain forms of medical practice, see Harry Coulter, *Divided Legacy: A History of the Schism in Medical Thought* (New York:

McGrath Publishing Co., 1975) and Paul Starr, *The Social Transformation of American Medicine* (New York: Basic Books, 1982), 102–12.

59. Miller and Taussig, "Cosmetics," 2001.

60. Dr. William C. Woodward, in discussion in Ibid., 2002.

61. The nine states with licensure requirements were Arkansas, Connecticut, Illinois, Louisiana, Missouri, New Mexico, Oregon, Utah, and Wisconsin. Legislation was pending in California, Texas, Oklahoma, Michigan, Iowa, Nebraska, and New Hampshire. Fishbein, *The New Medical Follies,* 69.

62. Woodward in Miller and Taussig, "Cosmetics," 2002.

63. The term "quasi-dermatologist" is Woodward's, by which he meant that cosmetologists would step near, if not over, the boundaries as established by law. An example of this evolving situation would be a customer who notices that her scalp itches; rather than consult a physician for relief of seborrhea, she mentions it as she is getting her hair cut, and the beautician gives her a salve, powder, or other preparation to relieve the itch.

64. Electrolysis was considered purely cosmetic rather than medical in its nature and value; the voltage necessary, and the delicate areas of skin meant that it was, or should be, administered with care. Woodward in Miller and Taussig, "Cosmetics," 2002.

65. Lawrence McCafferty and Serafino Genovese, "Cosmetics: Composition—Dermatoses—Treatment," *New York State Journal of Medicine* 28, no. 6 (March 15, 1928): 309.

66. *Newsletter #60,* 5, #2 Main Series, 1 January–19 February 1925, Newsletter Collection, J. Walter Thompson Archives, Hartmann Center for Sales, Advertising and Marketing History, Duke University, Durham, North Carolina (hereafter JWT Archives).

67. John Godwin Downing, "Physician and Cosmetics," *Drug and Cosmetic Industry* 35, no. 1 (July 1934): 27. Downing made similar claims in "Cosmetics—Past—Present," *JAMA* 102, no. 3 (June 1934): 2099.

68. "Procter & Gamble's Report," *Drug Trade Weekly* 6, no. 12 (September 30, 1922): 592. See also Oscar Schisgall, *Eyes on Tomorrow: The Evolution of Procter & Gamble* (Chicago: J. G. Ferguson Publishing Co., 1981).

69. "P&G Income," *Oil, Paint & Drug Reporter* 124, no. 18 (23 October 1933): 28B.

70. "Noxema Chemical Co. Income," *Oil, Paint & Drug Reporter* 123, no. 3 (16 January 1933): 32.

71. "Helena Rubinstein," *Drug and Cosmetic Industry* 32, no. 3 (March 1933): 254.

72. "Coty, Inc.," *Drug and Cosmetic Industry* 35, no. 6 (December 1934): 653.

73. Common allergens in cosmetics included orris root and rice powder (face powders), cochineal and aniline dyes (lip rouges), and perfumes (particularly lavender), often added to scent powders and other products.

74. Dr. Howard Fox, in discussion following presentation by Hiram Miller and Lawrence Taussig, "Cosmetics," *JAMA* 84, no. 26 (27 June 1925): 2001.

75. James Harvey Young, "Arthur Cramp, Quackery Foe," *Pharmacy History* 37, no. 4 (1995): 176–82.

76. *Nostrums and Quackery,* Chicago: American Medical Association, 1906 (vol. 1), 1921 (vol. 2), and 1936 (vol. 3). For more on the department, see Burrow, *AMA,* 110 and 255.

77. Dr. Kathryn Whitten, Fort Wayne, IN, to AMA, 28 March 1931; American Medical Association Historical Health Fraud and Alternative Medicine Collection (hereafter AMA Collection), box 167, folder 5 (cosmetics).

78. Arthur Cramp, AMA, to Miss Isobel Dupray, Los Angeles, 13 June 1932; AMA Collection, box 167, folder 5 (cosmetics).

79. Thomas Lewis, Arden Chemical Co., Inc., to My dear Doctor Cramp, 5 March 1928; AMA Collection, box 168, folder 3 (Eliz Arden).

80. Herman Goodman, "Cosmetic Dermatology: Steps in a New Direction," *American Medicine* 39, no. 1 (June 1933): 244.

81. James Harvey Young, "Food and Drug Regulations under the USDA, 1906–1940," *Agricultural History* 64, no. 2 (Spring 1990): 134–42; and idem, "Food and Drug Enforcers in the 1920s," *Business and Economic History* 21 (1992): 119–28.

82. See Gwen Kay, "Healthy Public Relations: The FDA's 1930s Legislative Campaign," *Bulletin of the History of Medicine* 75 (2001): 446–87; and Suzanne White Junod, "The Food and Drug Administration Says, 'Read the Label'" (presented at the 2002 meeting of the American Association for the History of Medicine, Kansas City, KS).

83. A. T. Retzlaff, "The Food Law in Kitchen Language," broadcast on the National Broadcasting Corporation on 27 May 1930. Radio talks, PR manuscripts (021.2); General correspondence, 1930, NACP 88.

84. "Uncle Sam at Your Service," broadcast October 15, 1934. "Uncle Sam at Your Service," PR manuscripts (021.2); General correspondence, 1934, NACP 88. Emphasis in original.

85. Bureau of Investigation, "Koremlu: A Dangerous Depilatory," *JAMA* 96, no. 8 (21 February 1931): 629–31.

86. In this experiment, eight- and eleven-year-old sisters were given repeated exposure to thallium acetate. J. H. Twiston Davies and M. C. Andrews, "A Case of Thallium Acetate Poisoning," *British Medical Journal* 1 (17 December 1927): 1139.

87. W. S. Duncan and E. H. Crosby, "A Case of Thallium Acetate Poisoning Following the Prolonged Use of a Depilatory Cream," *JAMA* 96, no. 22 (30 May 1931): 1866–68. Similar symptoms were listed in separate cases submitted by Sigmund Greenbaum and Jay Schamberg, appearing under the joint title, "Reports of Thallium Acetate Poisoning Following the Use of Koremlu," *JAMA* 96, no. 22 (30 May 1931): 1868.

88. Waring, "Another Case of Thallium Poisoning Following the Use of Koremlu Cream," 703.

89. Better Business Bureau, New York City, to FDA, 16 February 1931 and E. B. Buchanan, director Cleveland Health Department laboratories, to FDA, 30 March 1931. Cosmetics (583); General correspondence, 1931, NACP 88.

90. A small sample of letters sent to the FDA include Mrs. Baron, 30 April 1931; Dr. Bassett, health officer for Savannah, 18 June 1931; Shirley Wynne, New York City Public Health Commissioner, 14 July 1931; and G. W. Garrison, Arkansas State Health Officer, 1 September 1931. All in Cosmetics (583); General correspondence, 1931, NACP 88.

91. Current Comment, "Koremlu Fails," *JAMA* 99, no. 5 (30 July 1932): 394.

92. Sigmund Greenbaum, "Dermatoconjunctivitis due to LashLure, an Eyelash and Eyebrow Dye," *JAMA* 101, no. 5 (29 July 1933): 363–64.

93. S. B. Forbes and W. C. Blake, "Fatality Resulting from the Use of Lash-Lure on the Eyebrow and Eyelashes," *JAMA* 103, no. 19 (10 November 1934): 1442.

94. The letter, Hazel Fay Musser to President Roosevelt, 2 January 1934, was initially forwarded to the FDA, as per standard procedure. Proposed legislation (062); General correspondence 1934, NACP 88. The letter, attributed to Hazel Fay "Brown," appeared in Ruth DeForest Lamb, *American Chamber of Horrors: The Truth about Food and Drugs* (New York: Farrar & Rinehart, 1936).

95. Inecto published a salon owners' journal, *Beautician*, for some time. Despite claims of safety, Inecto injured its share of women, and some speculated it too might contain paraphenylenediamine. Ruth Lamb to Mrs. Musser, 18 January 1936; Food and Drug Act (G), Proposed legislation (062), General correspondence, 1936, NACP 88.

96. Letters focusing on the legislation's progress were written by Lamb on 29 May 1935 and 12 November 1935, after sessions of hearings; a "just friends" letter was sent far earlier, on 28 January 1935. All Ruth Lamb to Mrs. Musser; Food and Drug Act (G), Proposed legislation (062), General correspondence, 1935, NACP 88.

97. Ruth Lamb to Mrs. Musser, 20 May 1935; Food and Drug Act (G), Proposed legislation (062), General correspondence, 1935, NACP 88.

98. Mrs. Musser to Ruth Lamb, 30 March 1936; Food and Drug Act (G), Proposed legislation (062), General correspondence, 1936, NACP 88.

99. Clyde Harner, "Dermato-Ophthalmitis Due to the Eyelash Dye Lash-Lure"; Olivier Bourbon, "Severe Eye Symptoms Due to Dyeing the Eyelashes"; R. C. Jamieson, "Eyelash Dye (Lash-Lure) Dermatitis with Conjunctivitis"; and A. W. McCally et al., "Corneal Ulceration Following the Use of Lash-Lure," all in *JAMA* 101, no. 20 (11 November 1933): 1559–61.

100. Mr. C. R. Clark, Georgia state chemist, to FDA, 28 August 1933. Cosmetics (581.3); General correspondence, 1933, NACP 88.

101. "Cosmetics labeled with therapeutic claims subject to action under food and drug laws," 13 May 1932. Press notices, PR manuscripts (021.1); General correspondence 1932, NACP 88.

102. "Uncle Sam at Your Service" broadcast 11 July 1932. "Uncle Sam at Your Service," PR manuscripts (021.2); General correspondence 1932, NACP 88; and W. W. Vincent, "Current Features of Food and Drug Control," broadcast 26 May 1932. PR manuscripts (022); General Correspondence 1932, NACP 88.

103. "Campbell warns public against dangerous eyelash dye," 26 October 1933. Press releases, PR manuscripts (021.1); General correspondence 1933, NACP 88.

104. Although she does not mention the broadcast, it was likely "Uncle Sam at Your Service" aired 12 June 1933. "Uncle Sam at Your Service," PR manuscripts (021.2); General correspondence 1933, NACP 88.

105. Elsa Todd, New York, to FDA, 26 October 1933. Cosmetics (583); General correspondence 1933, NACP 88.

106. In James Harvey Young, *The Medical Messiahs: A Social History of Health Quackery in Twentieth-Century America* (Princeton, NJ: Princeton University Press, 1967); ch. 4, 6, and 7 discuss the USPS, FTC, and USDA respectively.

107. For a breezy overview of FTC enforcement and court decisions, see Ivan Preston, *The Great American Blowup: Puffery in Advertising and Selling*, rev. ed.

(Madison: University of Wisconsin Press, 1996), ch. 8–10.

108. "Marsay School of Beauty Culture;" Docketed case files 1915–1943, Docket #1504, General Records of the Federal Trade Commission; Record Group 122, National Archives Washington, DC (hereafter NA).

109. "Pond's Extract Company;" Docketed case files, 1915–1943, case #2019, NA 122. A similar event occurred with tobacco; Stephen Fox, *The Mirror Makers: A History of American Advertising and Its Creators* (New York: William Morrow and Co.1984), 115–16.

110. "Madame C. J. Walker;" Transcripts of hearings on fraud cases, 1913–1945, case #131, box #39; Office of the Solicitor; Office of the Postmaster General; Records of the Post Office, Record Group 28, NA. For more on the history of the company, see the Madam C. J. Walker Collection, Manuscripts and Archives, Indiana Historical Society. Several folders still under time seal may contain company legal records relevant to this case. On the company itself, see A'Lelia Bundles, *On Her Own Ground: The Life and Times of Madam C. J. Walker* (New York: Scribner, 2001); Julie Willett, *Permanent Waves: The Making of the American Beauty Shop* (New York: New York University Press, 2000), 13–14, 19, 20.

111. Cole, "The Dermatoses Due to Cosmetics," 1911.

Notes to Chapter 4

1. Arthur Kallet and F. J. Schlink, *100,000,000 Guinea Pigs: Dangers to Everyday Foods, Drugs, and Cosmetics* (New York: Vanguard Press, 1933).

2. Ibid., 205.

3. Ibid., 250.

4. Ibid., 298–99.

5. D. H. Walsh, Baltimore, to W. Wharton, Eastern District chief, 16 January 1933. PR manuscripts—100,000,000 Guinea Pigs (021.3), General correspondence, 1933, Record Group 88, National Archives College Park (hereafter NACP).

6. Earnest Lux to President Roosevelt, 2 April 1933; PR manuscripts—100,000,000 Guinea Pigs (021.3), General correspondence, 1933, NACP 88.

7. Mrs. E. H. Winters to Eleanor Roosevelt, 21 October 1933; PR manuscripts—100,000,000 Guinea Pigs (021.3), General correspondence, 1933, NACP 88.

8. H. Arthur Gilman to FDA, 10 April 1933, and Paul Dunbar to Gilman, 11 April 1933; PR manuscripts—100,000,000 Guinea Pigs (021.3), General correspondence, 1933, NACP 88.

9. This breakdown and assessment of who had sent them was in answer to a query specifically about postcards from V. H. Pelz, editor of *Food Field Reporter.* Presumably "professional" included home economists, teachers, engineers, public health officials, and the like. V. H. Pelz to Ruth Lamb, 11 December 1933, and Lamb to Pelz, 12 December 1933; PR manuscripts—100,000,000 Guinea Pigs (021.3), General correspondence, 1933, NACP 88.

10. M. C. Phillips, *Skin Deep: The Truth about Beauty Aids—Safe and Harmful* (New York: Vanguard Press, 1934).

11. Ibid., xi.

12. *Publishers' Weekly*, 9 September 1933; PR manuscripts—100,000,000 Guinea Pigs (021.3), General correspondence, 1933, NACP 88.

13. On the early days of the New Deal, see David Kennedy, *Freedom from Fear: The American People in Depression and War, 1929–1945* (New York: Oxford University Press, 1999), especially 104–287; Robert McElvaine, *The Great Depression: America 1929–1941* (New York: Times Books, 1993), especially 121–69; Michael Parrish, *Anxious Decades: American in Prosperity and Depression, 1920–1941* (New York: W. W. Norton,1992), especially 270–316; Anthony Badger, *The New Deal: The Depression Years, 1933–1941* (New York: Hill & Wang, 1989); Arthur M. Schlesinger, *The Age of Roosevelt: The Coming of the New Deal* (Boston: Houghton Mifflin, 1988); and William Leuchtenberg, *Franklin Delano Roosevelt and the New Deal: 1932–1940* (New York: Harper & Row, 1963).

14. This was a particularly delicate and difficult task, as Congress did not pass the AAA until after the planting and birthing season: to reduce crops and livestock immediately, fields were plowed under, and piglets, lambs, and calves were slaughtered.

15. For more on Rexford Tugwell, see Bernard Sternsher, *Rexford Tugwell and the New Deal* (New Brunswick, NJ: Rutgers University Press, 1964); Unofficial Observer (John Franklin Carter), *The New Dealers* (New York: The Literary Guild, 1934), 85–92; and the Rexford Tugwell Papers at the Franklin and Eleanor Roosevelt Library, Hyde Park, NY. For his early involvement with this law, see James Harvey Young, *Medical Messiahs: A Social History of Health Quackery in Twentieth-Century America* (Princeton, NJ: Princeton University Press, 1967), particularly ch. 8; Charles O. Jackson, *Food and Drug Legislation in the New Deal* (Princeton, NJ: Princeton University Press, 1970), particularly 3–48; and Philip J. Hilts, *Protecting America's Health: The FDA, Business and One Hundred Years of Regulation* (New York: Knopf, 2003), ch. 5.

16. The committee included Walter G. Campbell, FDA chief; Paul Dunbar, FDA assistant chief; C. W. Crawford, chief, FDA Office of Interstate Inspection; P. M. Cronin, J. B. O'Donnell, and J. F. Moore, USDA solicitors; F. P. Lee, Georgetown University Law School, formerly legislative counsel to the Senate; Milton Handler, Columbia University Law School, authority on trade regulatory problems; and David Cavers, Duke University Law School, expert on administrative law and governmental regulations of industry. Stephen Wilson, *Food and Drug Regulations* (Washington, DC: American Council on Public Affairs, 1942), 93.

17. For different perspectives on this early stage, see "The New Food, Drug, and Cosmetics Legislation" (Special Issue), *Law and Contemporary Problems* 6, no. 1 (Winter 1939), particularly David F. Cavers, "Forward" and idem, "The Food, Drug and Cosmetic Act of 1938: Its Legislative History and Its Substantive Provisions," 2–42.

18. Wilson, *Food and Drug Regulations*, 93–94. As late as 1936, when almost everyone referred to it as the Copeland bill, some members of the House persisted in referring to it as the Tugwell bill. 80 *Cong. Rec.* 10678 (1936).

19. Ole Salthe, "State Food, Drug and Cosmetic Legislation and its Administration," *Law and Contemporary Problems* 6, no. 1: 165–79; Cavers, "The Food, Drug, and Cosmetic Act of 1938," especially 10, and Vincent A. Kleinfeld, "Legislative History of the Federal Food, Drug, and Cosmetic Act," both in *Food Drug Cosmetic Law Quarterly* (hereafter *FDCLQ*) (December 1946): 536, 557–58; Ole Salthe, "A Legislative Monument to Senator Royal S. Copeland," *FDCLQ* (June 1947): 253–63; Suzanne White Junod, "Alternative Drugs: Homeopathy,

Royal Copeland, and Federal Drug Regulations," *Pharmacy in History* 42, nos. 1–2 (2000): 13–35; see also the Royal S. Copeland Collection, Michigan Historical Collections, Bentley Historical Library, University of Michigan.

20. Editorial, *Drug and Cosmetic Industry* 32, no. 4 (April 1933): 303. In the "Regulatory News" column, there was more: "A measure now being drafted, if enacted, will completely revise the food and drugs act to give the Federal Government control over the manufacture and sale of drugs, cosmetics and food. Dr. Rexford G. Tugwell, assistant Secretary of Agriculture, is reported to be preparing the bill which is expected to go to Congress with an accompanying message by President Roosevelt, within the near future." *Drug and Cosmetic Industry* 32, no. 4 (April 1933): 353.

21. On principle, *Drug and Cosmetic Industry* was opposed to the bill. Charles Wesley Dunn, counsel for the organization, had already given several senators his version of a food and drugs bill. "News," *Oil, Paint and Drug Reporter* 123, no. 17 (24 April 1933): 15, 24.

22. The article continued, "The next step will be for the lobbies of the food, drug, and cosmetic manufacturers and dealers, advertising agencies and newspaper and magazine publishers, to tear it to pieces with the help of and encouragement of those members of Congress who recognize that a legislator's first and best-rewarded duty is to protect the community interests of the big businessmen in his constituency." "Food and Drug Bill," *Consumers' Research Bulletin (General)* July 1933, 8.

23. Cavers discusses this problem, and the disproportionate impact of industry input in "Forward," *Law and Contemporary Prob* 6, no. 1 (Winter 1939): 1.

24. Gwen Kay, "Seeing the Fair the FDA Way: The 1933 Century of Progress Exposition," *Journal of Illinois History* 5, no. 3 (2002): 197–212.

25. Every part of the FDA's display in Chicago had previously been exhibited, and much of it had also appeared in *100,000,000 Guinea Pigs*. However, the attendant publicity of the World's Fair garnered far more attention, more quickly than had either previous fairs or CR publications.

26. For more on world fairs, see Robert W. Rydell, John Findling, and Kimberly Pelle, *Fair America: World's Fairs in the United States* (Washington, DC: Smithsonian Institution Press, 2000); Rydell, *World of Fairs: The Century-of-Progress Expositions* (Chicago: University of Chicago Press, 1993); and the Chicago Century of Progress Exposition Collection, Department of Special Collections, University of Illinois, Chicago Library (hereafter UIC).

27. For more information on FDA at fairs, see Gwen Kay, "Healthy Public Relations: The FDA's 1930s Legislative Campaign," *Bulletin of the History of Medicine* 75, no. 3 (Fall 2001): 446–87.

28. C. W. Wharburton, director of extension work, to Walter G. Campbell, FDA chief, 20 January 1932. Exhibits (043), General correspondence, 1932, NACP 88.

29. The complete list was only compiled in November 1932. "Federal Participation in A Century of Progress (The Chicago World's Fair Centennial Celebration)," U.S. Commissioners File, UIC.

30. Solon Barber, Information Services, to Paul Dunbar, and G. Linton, assistant chiefs, 27 October 1932, Exhibits (043), General correspondence, 1932, NACP 88.

31. The exhibit clearly had its origins in earlier displays and the ongoing FDA radio broadcasts, including twenty-five years of enforcing the Pure Food law, read-the-label campaigns, and fraudulently labeled items. Barber to Campbell, Dunbar and Linton, 21 October 1932, Exhibits (043), General correspondence, 1932, NACP 88.

32. Despite the exposition's many successes, though, it did not capture the American imagination the way the 1939 New York World's Fair did. See Rydell, *World of Fairs*, and David Gelertner, *The 1939 World's Fair* (New York: Basic Books, 1996).

33. The panels were described in a memorandum from G. P. Larrick to Chief, 8 September 1933, Exhibits (043), General correspondence, 1933, NACP 88; in a letter from Harry Garrett, Chicago Bureau chief, to Solon Barber, Washington, DC, 13 September 1933: ibid. Photographs of the exhibit are in the Ruth Lamb Atkinson Papers, Special Collections, Vassar College Libraries, Poughkeepsie, NY, and "Deficiencies in the 1906 Pure Food and Drugs Act," Food and Drug Act, Pamphlets (oversize), Eleanor Roosevelt Papers, Franklin and Eleanor Roosevelt Library, Hyde Park, NY.

34. In their interpretation, the problem lay not with products on the market, but with the FDA's lax enforcement methods. "News article," *Oil Paint and Drug Reporter* 124, no. 19 (30 October 1933): 47 discusses Tugwell's purported criticism of the exhibit; an editorial in *Drug Cosmetic Industry* 33, no. 5 (November 1933): 431 also has Tugwell taking the FDA to task for "failing to check the rank abuses."

35. In separate memoranda to Clarke, Central District chief; and Wharton and Vincent, Eastern and Western District chiefs, respectively, on 15 and 18 February 1933, Solon Barber described the physical layout of the exhibit, particularly in relation to other exhibits within the building. Exhibits (043), General correspondence, 1933, NACP 88.

36. "Uncle Sam at Your Service," aired 15 May 1933, PR manuscripts (021), General correspondence, 1933, NACP 88.

37. Corresponding clerk to Dr. Harry Krasnow, 7 September 1933; PR manuscripts (021.2), General correspondence, 1933, NACP 88.

38. On Eleanor Roosevelt's visit, see Kay, "Healthy Public Relations," 459–60. The Clippings Service for the FDA preserved at least six different accounts of Roosevelt's visit to FDA headquarters to look at the exhibit. Scrap books, book 2, box 1, Miscellaneous subject files, General Office of the Commissioner, 1905–38, NACP 88.

39. In addition to its "Legislative Column" and editorials, *Oil, Paint and Drug Reporter* followed the hearings minutely, often reprinting entire testimonies. On Campbell using "Chamber" exhibits at the first hearings, see "S 1944 Hearings," *Oil, Paint and Drug Reporter* 124, no. 26 (11 December 1933): 16+.

40. McNary also had a history of interest in the subject. The 1930 canner's bill, establishing rules for labels and contents of canned goods, bore his name.

41. "Hearings before a Subcommittee of the Committee on Commerce, United States Senate, 73rd Congress, 2d Session, on S 1944, A Bill to Prevent the Manufacture, Shipment, and Sale of Adulterated or Misbranded Food, Drugs, and Cosmetics," December 7, 1933 (hereafter S 1944), 1.

42. Ibid., 11.

43. Ibid.

44. Ibid.

45. Ibid., 13.

46. Ibid., 14.

47. Ibid., 16.

48. As previously noted, the drug and cosmetic industry trade journals duly recorded the appearance of the "chamber" panels. For more on Campbell's use of the "Chamber" exhibit during S 1944 hearings (7 December 1933), see 27, 34, 38–46, 288, 337, 371, and 379.

49. S 1944, 340.

50. Ibid., 344.

51. Ibid.

52. Ibid., 357.

53. Kallet and Schlink, *100,000,000 Guinea Pigs*. For more on these two men and this book, see Young, *Medical Messiahs*, 151–57. Kallet's testimony at S 1944, 355–56, immediately followed by Schlink, 356–57.

54. S 1944, 355.

55. Ibid., 54.

56. Ibid., 57. Emerson also submitted, for the record, statements of support from state chemists and public health officials in Alabama, Arizona, Delaware, Indiana, Iowa, Kentucky, Maine, Mississippi, North Carolina, Oklahoma, Oregon, South Dakota, Texas, Tennessee, West Virginia, Wisconsin, and Wyoming.

57. James Harvey Young, *The Toadstool Millionaires: A Social History of Patent Medicines in America before Federal Regulation* (Princeton, NJ: Princeton University Press, 1961), 214.

58. S 1944, 315.

59. "A Study and Digest of the Tugwell Bill," *Toilet Requisites* (January 1934): 18–20. Other articles include a piece on *Printer's Ink*, recounting Northam Warren's testimony in December 1933 before the Senate committee, 21 December 1933. Consumers' Research Collection, Tugwell Bill, Cosmetic Applications, box 353, folder 10; Special Collections, Rutgers University, New Brunswick, NJ (hereafter CR).

60. "A Study and Digest of the Tugwell Bill," *Toilet Requisites*, 20.

61. This news strike helps explain the paucity of newsprint on the hearings, and this bill, over the next five years. Stories that did appear were typically generated from news releases. "The *New York Times* only once gave front-page mention to this subject—and then only to report a disturbance in the Senate galleries." Wilson, *Food and Drug Regulations*, 100.

62. S 1944, 280. Schlotterer never addressed a more intriguing issue—Board of Trade support for the (short-lived) National Recovery Act.

63. Ibid., 281–88 included at least thirty-seven responses.

64. Ibid., 282.

65. Ibid., 289.

66. Ole Salthe had been director of the Bureau of Food and Drugs in the New York City Department of Public Health. In 1924, he left that position to serve as Copeland's technical advisor. Wilson, *Food and Drug Regulations*, 105; and David Cavers, "The Food , Drug and Cosmetic Act of 1938: Its Legislative History and Its Substantive Provisions" in *Law and Contemporary Problems* 6, no. 1 (Winter 1939): 8–9.

67. Wilson, *Food and Drug Regulations,* 102.

68. Cavers, "The Food, Drug and Cosmetic Act of 1938," 10.

69. "Hearings before the Committee on Commerce, United States Senate, 73d Congress, 2d session on S 2800, A Bill to Prevent the Manufacture, Shipment, and Sale of Adulterated or Misbranded Food, Drink, Drugs, and Cosmetics" (hereafter S 2800), 27 February 1934, 34.

70. Ibid., 35.

71. Ibid., 80.

72. Ibid., 81.

73. Ibid., 82. This group bears remarkable similarity to the core members of the WJCC. On the WJCC, see Nancy Cott, *The Grounding of Modern Feminism* (New Haven, CT: Yale University Press, 1987) and Jan Doolittle, "'Organized Women under Attack': The Women's Joint Congressional Committee and Its Legislative Campaigns for Mothers and Children, 1920–1930" (Ph.D. diss., Binghamton University, 2000).

74. S 2800, 167.

75. The final section of *Skin Deep* traced the state of the Copeland bill, and accosted the Senate for not passing a decent piece of consumer legislation.

76. Cavers, "The Food, Drug and Cosmetic Act of 1938," 10–11.

77. S 2800, 276. The telegram, an abbreviated version of a much longer letter, read, "Representatives of consumers for whose protection a food and drugs bill has been drawn are being refused a fair hearing by the Senate committee now holding hearings on the bill. Will you not use your influence to see that the obvious pro-commercial bias of the committee does not permit these hearings to act and a bill to go through without consumers being given full opportunity to state their criticism."

78. Wilson, *Food and Drug Regulations,* 109. For Kallet's version, see Copeland Bill (Government food and drug legislation), box 355, Consumers' Research, Special Collections, Rutgers University, New Brunswick, NJ.

79. S 2800, 230.

80. Cavers, "The Food, Drug and Cosmetic Act of 1938," 12.

81. S 2800, 511–72.

82. Ibid., 546–47.

83. Ibid., "Report of the Chambers of Commerce," 621.

84. Cavers, "The Food, Drug and Cosmetic Act of 1938," 12.

85. "Hearings Before a Subcommittee of the Committee on Commerce United States Senate, 74th Congress, 1st Session on S 5, A Bill to Prevent the Manufacture, Shipment, and Sale of Adulterated or Misbranded Food, Drink, Drugs and Cosmetics and to Regulate Traffic Therein" (hereafter S 5), 234.

86. Ibid., 64.

87. Elizabeth Eastman, representing the National Board of the YWCA, submitted briefs on behalf of the American Nurses' Association and the NWTUL; Alice Edwards, secretary of the AHEA, spoke on behalf of the Women's Homeopathic Medical Fraternity. Ibid., 41–43.

88. Ibid., 16.

89. Although neither Campbell nor the FDA publicity machine said a great deal about this bill, the agency position was unwavering. In a letter to Correspondent Clerk Crawford, Alice Edwards, AHEA secretary, thanked Campbell

for his support and included an updated list of the women's organizations supporting the bill. Alice Edwards to Crawford, 9 May 1935, in FDA Act (A),
Proposed legislation (062.1), General correspondence 1935, NACP 88.

90. S 5, 16f. Reasons for exclusion included soap never being considered a cosmetic, and not wanting to "tax cleanliness," which could negatively impact public health.

91. This aggregate is from testimony during S 5 hearings: pp. 35 (National
Congress of Parents and Teachers), 40 (AAUW), 41 (American Dietetic
Association and YWCA), 42 (Girls Friendly Society and American Nurses
Association), 43 (National Women's Trade Union League), and 150 (GFWC).

92. S 5, 34.

93. Ibid., 38.

94. Mrs. Alvin Barber spoke for the AAUW, S 5, 40–41; a brief was submitted
for the NWTUL by Miss Elizabeth Eastman, S 5, 43.

95. Ibid., 41.

96. 79 *Cong. Rec.* 4262 (1935).

97. Cavers, "The Food, Drug and Cosmetic Act of 1938," 13.

98. Charles Jackson, Food & Drug Legislation in the New Deal (Princeton:
Princeton University Press, 1970), 95.

99. S 2800, 109 and 231.

100. Cavers, "The Food, Drug and Cosmetic Act of 1938," 13–14.

101. In an earlier episode, Tugwell had reduced the tolerance for lead arsenate
on apples but because of protests, Secretary Wallace was forced to revert to the
old standard. The International Apple Association, based in Rochester, NY, had a
strong lobby and lots of sensational help on the measure, both because of their
perceived generosity (selling the oversupply on credit so unemployed men could
sell them and make a few cents), and because of the depth of commercial
orchards in Connecticut, Massachusetts, New York, Oregon, Pennsylvania, and
Washington.

102. 70 *Cong. Rec.* 8356 (1935).

103. Cavers, "The Food, Drug and Cosmetic Act of 1938," 16.

104. Ibid.

105. Young, *Medical Messiahs,* especially 41–66.

106. "Hearing before a Subcommittee on Interstate and Foreign Commerce,
House of Representatives, 74th Congress, 1st Session, on HR 6906, HR 8805, HR
8941 and S 5 to Regulate Foods, Drugs and Cosmetics" (hereafter HR 6906), 43.

107. HR 6906, 43. On this occasion, Campbell brought a "raspberry jelly" with
little fruit but much artificial coloring and sweetener.

108. Ibid., 95.

109. Ibid., 76.

110. Ibid., 84.

111. HR 6906, NCPT, 363, and NLWV, 369.

112. HR 6906, 370.

113. Ibid., 385.

114. HR 6906, Toilet Goods Association, (TGA) 476; NHCA, 550. In addition to
congressional testimony, the TGA and the NHCA discuss these issues at length in
their organization journals, the *Drug and Cosmetic Industry* and *American
Hairdresser* respectively.

115. Lamb, *American Chamber of Horrors*, 327.

116. Ibid., vii.

117. The list included Mrs. Alvin Barbar, AAUW; Miss Mary Lindsley and Miss Marie Mount, American Dietetic Association; Miss Alice Edwards and Mrs. Paul Howe, AHEA; Miss Clara Noyes, ANA; Miss Margaret C. Maule, Girls' Friendly Society; Dr. Julia M. Greene, Homeopathic Medical Fraternity; Dr. Louise Taylor Jones and Dr. Helen Kain, MWNA; Miss Elizabeth Eastman, National Board of the YWCA; Mrs. William T. Bannerman and Miss Ruth T. Bottomly, National Congress of Parents and Teachers; Mrs. Louis Ottenberg, NCJW; Mrs. Harris T. Baldwin, Miss Gwen Geach, Miss Florence Kirlin and Miss Edith Rockwood, NLWV; Miss Elisabeth Christman, NWTUL; Mrs. Harvey T. Wiley, District of Columbia FWC; and Miss Izora Scott, NWCTU

118. Editorial, *Drug and Cosmetic Industry* 38, no. 3 (March 1936): 309.

119. Ibid., 310.

120. "News of the Screen," *New York Times*, 19 November 1937. A December 23 letter from Lamb to William Tredt, Minneapolis station, confirmed 20th Century Fox as the studio. Both in Food and Drug Act (G), Proposed legislation (062), General correspondence, 1937, NACP 88.

121. 80 *Cong. Rec.* 10230–344 (1936).

122. Ibid., 10680 (1936).

123. Ibid., 10678 (1936). In point of fact, Tugwell had been uninvolved with the bill for several years. In 1934, he had gone to Puerto Rico to study the economy. In May 1935, he became head of the Resettlement Administration, charged with helping those dislocated because of the Dustbowl. Sternsher, *Rexford Tugwell and the New Deal*, 211–20.

124. 80 *Cong. Rec.* 10680 (1936).

125. 81 *Cong. Rec.* 1961 (1937).

126. Ibid., 2001–2001 (1937). See also Wilson, *Food and Drug Regulations*, 127–128.

127. Cavers, "The Food, Drug and Cosmetic Act of 1938," 18.

128. See HR 1613, 75th Cong., 1st sess. (1937) for the report; Representatives Chapman, Kenney, and Mapes argued that this provision was still inadequate to deter false advertising. Cavers, "The Food, Drug, and Cosmetic Act of 1938," 18.

129. The best accounts of this are James Harvey Young, "Sulfanilamide and Diethylene Glycol," in *Chemistry and Modern Society: Historical Essays in Honor of Aaron J. Ihde*, ed. John Parascandola and James C. Whorton (Washington, DC: American Chemical Society, 1983); Jackson, *Food and Drug Legislation in the New Deal*, especially ch. 7; Andrea Balis, "Sulfa Drugs and the 1938 Pure Food, Drug and Cosmetics Act," presented at Joint Atlantic Conference on the History of Biology, 1995, Cold Spring Harbor, NY; and Harry M. Marks, *The Progress of Experiment: Science and Therapeutic Reform in the United States, 1900–1990* (New York: Cambridge University Press, 1997), 79–82.

130. On what other companies were doing, see Dale E. Cooper, "Adequate Controls for New Drugs: Good Manufacturing Practice and the 1938 Federal Food, Drug and Cosmetic Act," *Pharmacy in History* 44, no. 1 (2002): 12–23; and Andrea Balis, "Miracle Medicine: The Impact of Sulfa Drugs on Medicine, the Pharmacy Industry, and Government Regulation in the U.S. in the 1930s" (Ph.D. diss., CUNY, 2000).

131. The FDA action was the subject of both the 1 November 1937 and 13 December 1937 broadcasts of "Housekeeper's Chat," "Uncle Sam at Your Service," PR manuscripts (021.2), General correspondence, 1937, NACP 88. The exact details, and effectiveness, of the FDA efforts were released in the "Report of the Secretary of Agriculture on Deaths due to Elixir of Sulfanilamide Massengill," 18 November 1937, PR manuscripts (021.1), General correspondence 1937, NACP 88.

132. See the "Report of the Secretary of Agriculture" for the exact details; see also Wilson, *Food and Drug Regulations,* 130–31.

133. All of the FDA efforts, including what they could not do, were documented in the "Report of the Secretary of Agriculture," S. Doc. 124, 75th Cong., 2d sess. (1937).

134. 83 *Cong. Rec.* 391–424 (1938).

135. Ibid., 6263 (1938).

136. "The Pure Food and Drug Bill (S 5) emphatically demands a veto. As the bill now stands it weakens the powers of the Food and Drug Administration so seriously as to make the Act almost useless—far worse than the existing Act. Your veto of this piece of buncombe will have the enthusiastic approval of all the intelligent consumers in the United States." Morley Ayearst, New York University, to President Roosevelt, 20 June 1938, Proposed legislation (062), General subject, 1938, NACP 88.

137. "Federal Food and Drug Bill Condemned," *JAMA* 110 (1938): 1492.

138. 83 *Cong. Rec.* 7771–7779, 7889–7903 (1938).

139. Ibid., 7903 (1938).

140. Ibid., 9088–9095 (1938).

141. Cavers, "The Food, Drug and Cosmetic Act of 1938," 21.

142. 83 *Cong. Rec.* 9101 (1938).

143. "The Act will stand as a legislative monument to the memory of the late Senator Royal S. Copeland of New York, who fought for a really effective measure throughout the five-year struggle over revision of the Act of 1906." PR manuscripts (021), General subject, 1938, NACP 88.

144. Quoted in Cavers, "The Food, Drug and Cosmetic Act of 1938," 42.

145. Campbell, quoted in ibid.

Notes to Chapter 5

1. Members of the Toilet Goods Association were warned in two separate bulletins, "Bull. No. 103" and "Bull. No. 110," about advertising claims which were no longer acceptable and cosmetic claims subject to caution; Cosmetics Toiletries and Fragrance Association (hereafter CTFA), Washington, DC.

2. For more on the FDA side of enforcement, see Suzanne White, "'The Class of '39:' Implementing the Food, Drug and Cosmetic Act," *Journal of the Association of Food and Drug Officials of the United States,* 52, no. 4 (1988): 10–25.

3. A 16 July 1938 press release, "Government seizes poisonous eyelash dye," was quickly followed by a 25 July release, "Government continues seizure of poisonous eyelash dye." The summary of the year's activity also highlighted this activity, as per the 6 December 1938 press notice, "Immediate action under new food and drug act, says annual report." "Housekeeper's Chat," highlighted FDA rapid response and enforcement of parts of the law in the 18 July broadcast, "The

New Food, Drug and Cosmetic Law" and the 5 September broadcast, "Dangerous eyelash and eyebrow dyes—LashLure and Magic-Di-Stik." In Press notices and "Uncle Sam at Your Service" files, respectively, PR manuscripts (021.1), General subject, 1938, Record Group 88, National Archives College Park (hereafter NACP).

4. "Editorial," *Drug and Cosmetic Industry* 42, no. 1 (January 1938): 29.

5. Arthur Kallet and F. J. Schlink, *100,000,000 Guinea Pigs: Dangers in Everyday Foods, Drugs, and Cosmetics* (New York: Vanguard Press, 1933), 92–96.

6. The basic procedure for enforcing the 1938 law was identical to that of the 1906 law. When products were found in violation of the law, the FDA issued a notice of judgment (NJ) against the company. An NJ contained a summary of the court action against the company and outlined what and how the company had broken the law. On occasion, an NJ might contain interviews with company personnel, etc., regarding this action. Also, the law stipulated that synopses of these cases be published. This mechanism provided a legal record and allowed for criminal prosecution (and fines) against companies by private parties.

7. "Under the new Food, Drug and Cosmetics Act," the notice continued, "the interstate shipment of dangerous cosmetics is immediately prohibited. The act, in most of its provisions, does not become effective until June 25, 1939." "Government seizes poisonous eyelash dye," 16 July 1938, Press notices; Press release manuscripts, General subject, 1938, NACP 88.

8. In fact, some of the first "official" comment on the new law emphasized public safety. Wallace declared the law "a great step forward in the protection of the American public." And, ever cognizant of earlier (perceived) agency failures, Wallace concluded by noting that "this means that the American public will be protected against dangerous cosmetics such as eyelash dyes that have been known to cause blindness." "Wallace Says New Food Law Big Improvement over Old," 27 June 1928; PR manuscripts (021.1), General subject, 1938, NACP 88.

9. "LashLure: A dangerous aniline hair dye," Bureau of Investigation column, *JAMA* 101, no. 13 (23 Septemberr 1933): 1017.

10. In the interview, which the FDA observer characterized as beginning "in a belligerent tone," Kolmitz claimed that the 1933 version of Lash Lure did not contain PPD. She also berated the FDA for the (negative) publicity over Mrs. Musser, and the discrepancy between her version of the 1933 interview and the FDA report of the inspector's visit. "Memo of Interview: Geo[rge] P. Larrick, Mr. Roy S. Pruitt, and Miss Charlotte Kolmitz," 24 January 1939, Cosmetics—deceptive and misleading (583.-20); General subject, 1939, NACP 88. Kolmitz was an enigma. She had chemists on staff: one had warned her of the dangers of using PPD. She also sent a sample to the FDA for testing, to check the dye lot. Without seeming to acknowledge (or realize) who she was, the reply she received was the standard "the FDA will test dye lots as per TGA recommendations." W. G. Campbell, chief, to Charlotte Kolmitz, Glamour Cosmetics, 1 December 1938; Cosmetics—deceptive and misleading (583-.20); General subject, 1938, NACP 88.

11. John Harvey, Western District chief, to "Western District comment," 16 August 1938; Accession #52 A89, Seizure #694D, RG88, FDA History Office, Rockville, MD (hereafter FDA History Office).

12. Accession #52 A89, Seizures 694D, RG88, FDA History Office.

13. Ibid.

14. Ibid.

15. Seizure records, submitted by Grant Morton, chief Los Angeles station. Accession #52 A89, Seizures 694D, RG88, FDA History Office.

16. Kolmitz-Dellar response, contained within Morton's report; Accession #52 A89, Seizures 694D, RG88, FDA History Office.

17. Dependable Cosmetics list, also within Morton's report; Accession #52 A89, Seizures 694D, RG88, FDA History Office.

18. Accession #52 A89, Seizures 694D, RG88, FDA History Office.

19. As late as April 1939, many in the cosmetic industry were preparing for June implementation. In the "Legal Angles" column, S. L. Mayham stated emphatically that the 25 June date was "going to remain." All the details were not yet worked out, "but that was true of the Wiley law. . . ." April 1939, *Drug and Cosmetic Industry* 44, no. 4 (April 1939): 457–58. In May, *Drug and Cosmetic Industry* editors argued against delay: "Enforcement of the old law was a constant development over the entire 32 years it was in effect." "Considering the Drug Act," *Drug and Cosmetic Industry* 44, no. 5 (May 1939): 562. In July, an editorial urged manufacturers to act as if the law were already place: "just because the enforcement date has been delayed, don't think that it won't be enforced as a law at some point." "Don't Delay Further" (Editorial), *Drug and Cosmetic Industry* 45, no. 1 (July 1939): 25.

20. A. E. Lowe, chief New York station to chief, Eastern District, 8 June 1939. Accession #52 A89, Seizure #60146D, RG88, FDA History Office.

21. Memorandum of interview with Mr. Bernard d'Escayrac conducted by Mr. A. E. Lowe, Accession #52 A89, Seizure #60146D, RG88, FDA History Office.

22. This cable was presented at a second interview with Mr. d'Escayrac, conducted by Mr. A. E. Lowe on 9 June 1939. Accession #52 A89, Seizure #60146D, RG88, FDA History Office.

23. Memorandum of interview with Mr. Bernard d'Escayrac by Mr. A. E. Lowe, 15 June 1939, Accession #52 A89, Seizure #60146D, RG88, FDA History Office.

24. A. E. Lowe, chief New York station to chief, Eastern District, 17 June 1939. Accession #52 A89, Seizure #60146D, RG88, FDA History Office.

25. Memorandum by Mr. Cummings, 17 June 1939, included as part of Lowe's letter to the chief, Eastern district, Accession #52 A89, Seizure #60146D, RG88, FDA History Office.

26. Cummings's memorandum details this conversation as well; Accession #52 A89, Seizure #60146D, RG88, FDA History Office.

27. A. E. Lowe to chief, Eastern District, 17 June 1939; Accession #52 A89, Seizure #60146D, RG88, FDA History Office.

28. "U.S. orders seizures of 40,000 lipsticks," *Baltimore Sun* 17 June 1939 (clipping part of Guerlain file, Accession #52 A89, Seizure #60146D, RG88, FDA History Office).

29. "40,000 lipsticks to be seized here as violating new U.S. drug law," *New York Times* 17 June 1939 (clippings part of Guerlain file; Accession #52 A89, Seizure #60146D, RG88, FDA History Office).

30. "Teeth of the law to clamp down Upon Poisonous Lipstick," *Washington Post* 22 June 1939; (Guerlain file; Accession #52 A89, Seizure #60146D, RG88, FDA History Office).

31. John Woods, Jr., food and drug inspector, to chief, New York station, 19 June 1939; Accession #52 A89, Seizure #60146D, RG88, FDA History Office.

32. L. L. Lusby, acting chief, New York station to chief, Eastern District, 19 June 1939; Accession #52 A89, Seizure #60146D, RG88, FDA History Office.

33. Memorandum report of John Woods, Jr., food and drug inspector, New York station, 1939; John Woods to chief, New York station, 22 June 1939; and G. C. Swan, acting chief, New York station to chief, Eastern District, 22 June 1939; Accession #52 A89, Seizure #60146D, RG88, FDA History Office.

34. Memorandum of interview with Mr. Louis G. Bernstein, attorney representing Guerlain; Mr. W. G. Campbell and Mr. Geo. P. Larrick, 22 June 1939; Accession #52 A89, Seizure #60146D, RG88, FDA History Office.

35. John Woods, Jr., food and drug inspector to chief, New York station, 20 June 1939; Accession #52 A89, Seizure #60146D, RG88, FDA History Office.

36. Ibid.

37. L. L. Lusby, acting chief New York station to chief, Eastern District, 27 June 1939; Accession #52 A89, Seizure #60146D, RG88, FDA History Office.

38. Memorandum of interview with Dr. Leonard Goldwater by Guy Swann, acting chief New York station, 26 June 1939; Accession #52 A89, Seizure #60146D, RG88, FDA History Office.

39. Memorandum of interview: Dr. Leonard Goldwater and Dr. Theodore Klumpp, drugs division, 13–14 July 1939; Accession #52 A89, Seizure #60146D, RG88, FDA History Office.

40. Memorandum of interview: Dr. A. O. Gettler, Ph.D., toxicologist for medical examiner's office, professor at New York University Medical School; and Dr. Robert Herwick, M.D. (New York station), 3 July 1939; Accession #52 A89, Seizure #60146D, RG88, FDA History Office.

41. A. E. Lowe, chief New York station to chief, Eastern District, 28 June 1939; Accession #52 A89, Seizure #60146D, RG88, FDA History Office.

42. Lowe had also noted—almost as a postscript—that two women wrote to the station asking for more information on Guerlain and the effects of cadmium and selenium. He concluded that they had been injured by the product. Further efforts to track them down and get injury reports were to no avail. A. E. Lowe, chief New York station to chief, Eastern District, 28 June 1939; Accession #52 A89, Seizure #60146D, RG88, FDA History Office.

43. Memorandum of interview: Dr. Lawrence Cotter (Mrs. Kelley's physician), and R. W. Weilerstein, medical section, 29 June 1939; Accession #52 A89, Seizure #60146D, RG88, FDA History Office. The language Dr. Cotter uses is remarkably similar to that in case reports of injuries caused by Koremlu and Lash Lure.

44. Notice of entry of decree, 22 August 1939; Accession #52 A89, Seizure #60146D, RG88, FDA History Office.

45. John Cain, food and drug inspector, New York station to chief, New York station, 6 October 1939. In a report, the inspector detailed the Guerlain seizures, tabulating the number of lipsticks removed from containers, and the appropriate catalog numbers. Accession #52 A89, Seizure #60146D, RG88, FDA History Office.

46. G. W. O'Keefe, assistant collector, U.S. Customs Service (Treasury Department) to Mr. Kentworthy, FDA, 9 March 1940. Customs requested the date(s) of lipstick seizure; date of exportation; how it was packed at the time of both seizure and deportation; the item number or quality number of the pieces of each item, and quantity. Accession #52 A89, Seizure #60146D, RG88, FDA History Office.

47. Rachel Palmer, Consumers Union, to Dr. Theodore Klumpp, chief, drugs division, 6 September 1939; and Theodore Klumpp to Mrs. Rachel Lynn Palmer, Consumers Union, 12 September 1939; Accession #52 A89, Seizure #60146D, RG88, FDA History Office.

48. Rachel Lynn Palmer, Consumers Union, to Dr. Theodore Klumpp, chief, drugs division, 29 September 1939; and Theodore Klumpp, M.D. chief, drugs division to Mrs. Rachel Lynn Palmer, Consumers Union, 14 October 1939; Accession #52 A89, Seizure #60146D, RG88, FDA History Office.

49. Ralph Watson, of Byerly, Watson and Simonds, to A. E. Lowe, chief, New York station, 7 April 1941; Accession #52 A89, Seizure #60146D, RG88, FDA History Office.

50. Lowe discussed the regulations of the Department of Agriculture concerning government employees and records in a civil suit, and assumed that Farm Security Administration (FSA, the new agency under which the FDA operated) regulations were similar. A. E. Lowe, chief, New York station, to chief, Eastern District, 26 March 1941; Accession #52 A89, Seizure #60146D, RG88, FDA History Office.

51. W. G. Campbell, commissioner of food and drugs, to Ralph Watson, Byerly, Watson and Simonds, 9 April 1941; Accession #52 A89, Seizure #60146D, RG88, FDA History Office.

52. "Beauty Boss of America Bald-Headed," (New Orleans) *Times Picayune,* 16 September 1938. News stories (021); General subject, 1938. NACP 88.

53. P. B. Dunbar to chiefs, Central and Western Divisions, 4 January 1939. Lash and brow dyes (583–620), General subject, 1939, NACP 88.

54. P. B. Dunbar to chief, Eastern District, 4 January 1939. Lash and brow dyes (583–620), General subject, 1939, NACP 88.

55. G. P. Larrick, acting chief to chief, Eastern District, 2 February 1939. 583–20 (lash and brow dyes), General subject, 1939, RG88, NARA.

56. P. B. Dunbar to chief, Eastern District, 23 January 1939 re: Roux Lash and Brow Dye, Lash and brow dyes (583–20), General subject, 1939, NACP 88.

57. W. S. Frisbie, chief, Division of State Cooperation to C. S. Ladd, state food commissioner and chemist, North Dakota, 31 March 1941. Lash and brow dyes (583–20), General subject, 1941, NACP 88.

58. In a four-day period, in May 1940, Acting FDA Chief George Larrick sent three missives regarding women injured by Roux Lash and Brow Tint. In each letter, he requested the name of the attending physician, hospital records, allergy test results, information on the beauty shops, and any other pertinent information. George Larrick to chief, Eastern District, 16 May 1940, re: Mrs. Hal Mott; George Larrick to chief, Eastern District, 16 May 1940 re: Miss Ellen Dalzell; and George Larrick, acting chief to chief, Eastern District, 20 May 1940 re: Miss Matilda McAvoy. Lash and brow dyes (583–620), General subject, 1940, NACP 88.

59. Larrick, Acting Food and Drug Commissioner, suspected that the U.S. attorney general was unwilling to press for trial. G. P. Larrick, acting food and drug commissioner, to J. A. Cummings, acting chief, New York station, 22 April 1941. 581.3–620 (lash and brow dyes; Roux). General subject, 1941, NACP 88.

60. This suggestion was made by George Larrick, acting commissioner of food and drugs to chief, Western District, 6 September 1941. Lash and brow dyes (581-.20), General subject, 1941, NACP 88.

61. Discussion about the role and extent of FDA "aid" was the subject of some internal discussion: P. B. Dunbar to General Counsel, n.d. (c. 13 September 1941); and W. G. Campbell, commissioner of food and drugs, to General Counsel, 20 September 1941. Lash and brow dyes (581-.20), General subject, 1941, NACP 88.

62. Memorandum of an interview with the Honorable Howard Coole, Representative, North Carolina, representing Miss Estelle Taylor; Battle, Levy, Fowler and Meaman attorney for Miss Estelle Taylor; Assistant Counsel, Federal Security Agency; Attorney, Federal Security Agency; and Dan Dahle, FDA inspector, 8 October 1941; and P. B. Dunbar, acting commissioner of food and drugs, confirming agency cooperation in a letter to chief, New York station, 9 October 1941. Lash and brow dyes (581-.20), General subject, 1941, NACP 88.

63. Dr. Dahle, acting chief of the cosmetics division, and either Dr. Weilerstein, in the drugs division, or Mr. McKinnon would be the FDA's witnesses. W. G. Campbell to chief, Eastern District, 28 October 1941. Lash and brow dyes (581-.20), General subject, 1941, NACP 88.

64. Dan Dahle, acting chief of the cosmetics division, to Mr. Milton Neaman of Battle, Levy, Fowler and Neaman, 16 October 1941. Lash and brow dyes (581-.20), General subject, 1941, NACP 88.

65. During the Taylor civil suit, Larrick required information on witnesses who testified for the claimant, possibly in hopes of gathering information to discredit them if or when they appeared during the government's trial. Geo[rge] P. Larrick, acting commissioner of food and drugs, to chief, Eastern District, 22 December 1941. The same day, he also asked the chief, Western District, for more information on the injury of a Mrs. Earl Harris, including whether she had certifications from demonstrators authorizing her to use Roux. Lash and brow dyes, Roux (581.3–20), General subject, 1941, NACP 88.

66. G. P. Larrick, acting commissioner of food and drugs, to chief, Eastern District, 22 December 1941. Lash and brow dyes, Roux (581.3–20), General subject, 1941, NACP 88.

67. In March 1938, the TGA assembled a panel, primarily of dermatologists and allergists, to aid in examining the colors submitted. The committee included Drs. Louis Schwartz, U.S. Public Health Service; Joseph Goodman, Boston; Herman Goodman, assistant director of Social Hygiene, Department of Health, New York City; and Marion Sulzberger, New York City. "Toilet Goods Association Bull. No. 86," 14 March 1938; CTFA.

68. "Notes of meeting between TGA, FDA representatives" (provided by TGA to FDA), 18 July 1938; Lash and brow dyes (583-.80), General subject, 1938, NACP 88.

69. The list of colors, and manufacturers, is detailed in H. O. Calvery, chief, Division of Pharmacology (FDA) to Mr. H. Gregory Thomas, TGA, 25 August 1938. Lash and brow dyes (583-.80), General subject, 1938, NACP 88.

70. The early attention to the list of coal tar dyes gives credence to this claim. By early December, the TGA issued a tentative list of certified coal tar colors, pending USDA approval. "Toilet Goods Association Bull. No. 122," 2 December 1938; CTFA.

71. W. G. Campbell to Wharton, 2 January 1940. General, cosmetics (021), General subject, 1940, NACP 88.

72. In June 1938, just after both bills were signed into law, the TGA issued a

bulletin addressing this subject. "Advertising claims embraced in the cautionary list set forth below should not be published or distributed unless approved by the Board of Standards of the TGA, or sufficiently corroborated by the advertiser." One list contained "cosmetic claims subject to caution," another a "list of advertising claims which are not acceptable." "Toilet Goods Association Bull. No. 110," CTFA.

73. J. G. Shibley, acting chief, Chicago office, to National Mineral Company, 10 May 1939; Cosmetics—deceptive and misleading packaging (580-.11), General subject, 1939, NACP 88.

74. W. G. Campbell, Commissioner of Food and Drugs to Chief, Central District, 8 July 1941. Nail polish (585.1-.14), General subject, 1941, NACP 88.

75. The initial complaint was detailed in Walter G. Campbell to chief, Central District, 10 April 1941. A subsequent interview with a representative for the distributors did not allay FDA fears; according to the memorandum of the interview, "the subject was evasive." Memorandum of interview: Mr. A. J. Petit of Petit, Olin and Overmyer, representing Associated Distributors, Inc., and Dr. H. Wales (FDA), 8 November 1941. Nails (585-.1), General subject, 1941, NACP 88.

76. "Actions under the new drug and cosmetic law provisions increase," 24 February 1949. Press notices (021), General subject, 1939, NACP 88.

77. Program No. 19, "Here's Your Answer" for the week beginning 11 July 1942 (written by Mr. Linton). Radio talks (021.2), General subject, 1942, NACP 88.

78. Theodore Klumpp, "Significance of the New Federal Food, Drug and Cosmetic Act," Wisconsin Medicine Journal 39 (November 1940): 974.

79. William Sawyer Eisenstadt, "Contact dermatitis due to nail polish," Minnesota Medicine 24 (March 1941): 180.

80. John P. Henry, "Nail polish dermatitis," Memphis Medicine Journal 15 (October 1940): 160.

81. Comments of Dr. J. F. Burgess, Montreal, Canada, following "Dermatitis Venenata due to nail lacquer," presented by Earl Osborne, James Jordan, and Paul Campbell at the 1941 annual meeting of the American Dermatological Association and printed in Archives of Dermatology and Syphilology 44 (October 1941): 612. Most likely, the company had changed their formula due to ingredient shortages.

82. Ralph Salsberg, "Correspondence: Dermatitis due to nail polish foundation," Archives of Dermatology and Syphilology 48 (October 1943): 419. Salsberg was aided by Vorac Corporation, which manufactured both plasticizers and the nail polish in question.

83. Harry Keil and Laird Van Dyck, "Dermatitis due to nail polish: A study of 26 cases with the chief allergenic component toluene sulfonamide formaldehyde resin with related substances," Archives of Dermatology and Syphilology 50 (July 1944): 43–44. A follow-up study, inspired by this, demonstrated that six of thirty women reacted to the toluene sulfonamide formaldehyde alone, and nine of the thirty reacted to the toluene sulfonamide formaldehyde with something else. William L. Dobes and Philip Nippert, "Correspondence: Contact eczema due to nail polish," Archives of Dermatology and Syphilology 50 (October 1944): 270.

84. Joseph Kalish, "Cosmetic stockings," Drug and Cosmetic Industry 51, no. 1 (July 1942): 44–45. A year earlier, Kalish had written convincingly about the need for a product like this ("Cosmetic stockings," Drug and Cosmetic Industry 49, no. 3

[September 1941]: 268–69+). "Clearly, I was accurate in my September assessment," he wrote in July 1942, "that manufacturers neglected this area, because
many questions have come into this office" (44).

85. As John Swann, FDA History Office, has pointed out, a concern regarding
leg makeup would have been the large surface area involved, compared to the
face, particularly if a toxic ingredient were used.

86. Twenty-seven percent admitted to using the product occasionally. The
most preferable method of application—91 percent—was a liquid product.
"Merchandising News and Packaging Notes: Leg Make-Up," *Drug and Cosmetic
Industry* 51, no. 6 (December 1942): 653. An added complication was that women
in some factory and manufacturing jobs wore pants, thus decreasing their opportunities to wear "stockings."

87. "Keeping Posted: Cosmetic Stocking Boom?" *Drug and Cosmetic Industry*
52, no. 3 (March 1943): 265.

88. "Merchandising News and Packaging Notes: Cosmetic Stockings," *Drug
and Cosmetic Industry* 52, no. 4 (April 1943): 397.

89. Margaret Church first suggested the multiple sales opportunities engen-
dered by leg makeup, including depilation and pedicures, in "There's a Profit in
Leg Make-Up," *American Hairdresser* 65, no. 17 (July 1942): 10–11. In the early
summer of 1943, *American Hairdresser* ran "Handmade Hosiery," *American
Hairdresser* 66, no. 6 (June 1943): 45, and published an article extolling the virtues
of this product in the journal it produced for salon customer, *Finesse* (also entitled
"Handmade Hosiery," *Finesse* [Summer 1943]).

90. The ingredient in question was a dye similar to the dye supplied in oleo-
margarine; that is, it is red when concentrated and yellow when diluted. Francis
A. Ellis, "Contact Dermatitis Due to 'Leg Makeup,'" *Archives of Dermatology &
Syphilology* 49 (March 1944): 197.

91. There were at least six additional articles between 1941 and 1945 on nail
polish dermatitis, accounting for about 100 cases of dermatitis.

92. Eugene Oswald, "Dermatitis Due to Hair Lacquer," *Archives of
Dermatology & Syphilology* 49 (February 1944): 136.

93. Stephan Epstein, "Contact Dermatitis Caused by Hair Lacquer Pads,"
JAMA 123, no. 7 (16 October 1943): 409.

94. Hazel Kozlay, "Home Beauty Services Can Be Checked (Editorial),"
American Hairdresser 66, no. 12 (December 1943): 27.

95. Alfred Hollander, "Allergic Dermatitis Caused by Hair Lacquer
Products," *Archives of Dermatology and Syphilology* 48 (October 1943): 656.

96. Louis Schwartz, "An Outbreak of Dermatitis from Hair Lacquer," *Public
Health Reports* 58, no. 12 (29 October 1943): 1624. Included in this case may have
been a letter from Drs. Leon Ginsburg and Francis Ellis, recounting their twenty-
four patients seen in September and October 1943, and discussed in "Hair
Lacquer Pad Dermatitis," *Archives of Dermatology and Syphilology* 49 (March 1944):
198. A week earlier, the offending product, Hubére's, had been determined in
four cases of hair lacquer dermatitis; John Wanamaker's and Strawbridge &
Clothier's stores removed it from their shelves after a local Philadelphia physician contacted them. Sigmund Greenbaum, "Correspondence: Hair Lacquer
Dermatitis," *JAMA* 123, no. 7 (16 October 1943): 436.

97. J. B. Howell, "Contact Dermatitis from Hair Lacquer," *JAMA* 123, no. 7 (16

October 1943): 408–9. The sudden outbreak was "comparable to the episode of resin in underwear dermatitis observed some two years ago." Howell scripted an addendum: ten more cases presented since he had submitted the paper two weeks earlier, nine following use of Hubére.

98. Thomas S. Saunders, "Contact Dermatitis from the Use of Lacquer on the Hair," *Northwest Medicine* 43 (January 1944): 19.

99. The 1941 Insulin Amendment required the FDA to test and certify the purity and potency of insulin. The 1945 Penicillin Amendment required the FDA to do the same for penicillin; this was later extended to include all antibiotics and was in effect until 1983 when it was deemed no longer necessary. On the regulation and monitoring of penicillin production, see Henry Welch, "The Government Certification Program for Penicillin," in *Antibiotics*, ed. George W. Irving and Horace T. Hendrick (Brooklyn: Chemical Publishing Company, 1949), 43–63, and David Adams, "Wartime Bureaucracy and Penicillin Allocation: The Committee on Chemotherapeutic and Other Agents, 1942–44," *Journal of the History of Medicine and Allied Sciences* 44, no. 2 (April 1989): 196–217. This is, however, only one of the many activities the FDA was involved in at this time.

100. *American Hairdresser* only began to address this issue in January 1945, with Hazel Kozlay's editorial, part of which was devoted to "Home Permanent Threat Must Be Eliminated" (*American Hairdresser* 68, no. 1: 34).

101. Allen H. Bunce, Francis T. Parker, and George T. Lewis, "Accidental death from absorption of heatless permanent wave solution," *JAMA* 116, no. 4 (5 May 1941): 1515.

102. Bunce et al., "Accidental death," 1517.

103. "Editorial: Uncontrolled publicity again plays havoc," *American Hairdresser* 64, no. 5 (May 1941): 31.

104. This phrase appeared, for instance, in notices of judgment against Madam Marva Hair Coloring (Accession #52 A89, seizure #46330-D, Notice of Judgment #14, box #71, RG88, FDA History Office), and Mary Luckie Lash & Brow Dye (Accession #52 A89, seizure #15987, Notice of Judgment #5, box #25, RG88, FDA History Office), in which a woman was permanently injured "but does not compare to that of PPD."

105. The Bureau of Investigation ran "Stipulations: Agreements between the Federal Trade Commission and Promoters of Various Products" two of five weeks in September; see *JAMA* 126, no. 3 (16 September 1944): 189, and *JAMA* 126, no. 5 (30 September 1944): 318.

Notes to Epilogue

1. See Philip J. Hilts, *Protecting America's Health: The FDA, Business, and One Hundred Years of Regulation* (New York: Knopf, 2003).

2. The laws set safety limits on pesticide residues on agricultural commodities, and required chemical companies to establish the safety and efficacy of new food and color additives respectively. The Food and Color Additives Amendments contained a Delaney Proviso, prohibiting approval of additives shown to cause cancer in human or laboratory animals.

3. The Kefauver-Harris Act was designed to ensure drug efficacy and greater

safety. Towards that end, manufacturers were required to prove effectiveness before placing a product on the market. On thalidomide in particular, see Richard McFadyen, "Thalidomide in America: A brush with tragedy," *Clio Medica* 11, no. 2 (1976): 79–93. On drug regulations before and after 1962, see John Swann, "Sure Cure: Policy on Drug Efficacy before 1962," in *The Inside Story of Medicines: A Symposium,* ed. Gregory Higby and Elaine Stroud (Madison, WI: American Institute for the History of Pharmacy, 1997), 223–61; Louis Lasagna, "Congress, the FDA, and New Drug Development Before and After 1962," *Perspectives in Biology and Medicine* 32, no. 3 (Spring 1989): 322–43; and Lester Hollister, "The FDA Ten Years after the Kefauver-Harris Amendments," *Perspectives in Biology and Medicine* 17, no. 2 (Winter 1974): 243–49.

4. Vitamins as a regulated product have been a hot topic for twenty-five years. The 1976 Vitamins and Minerals Amendment, also known as the Proxmire Amendment, prevented the FDA from either establishing standards to limit the potency of vitamins and minerals in foods, or regulating vitamins and minerals as drugs. The 1990 Nutrition Labeling and Education Act required all packaged food to bear nutrition labels; claims for health foods needed to be consistent with those established by Health and Human Services. The 1994 Dietary Supplement and Health Education Act established specific labeling requirements and defined "dietary supplements" and "diet ingredients" as food (and hence subject to FDA oversight).

5. Rima Apple, *Vitamania: Vitamins in American Culture* (New Brunswick, NJ: Rutgers University Press, 1996), especially 159–78.

6. As Cynthia Russet has elegantly expressed it, the feminists of the 1920s and 1930s were fighting for the right to wear cosmetics free of injury, while the feminists of the 1960s and 1970s were fighting for the right to not wear cosmetics at all.

7. "The Act will stand as a legislative monument to the memory of the late Senator Royal S. Copeland of New York, who fought for a really effective measure throughout the five-year struggle over revision of the Act of 1906." PR manuscripts, Press notices, General subject, 1938, NACP 88. On Wiley, see the Alice Lakey papers in FDA correspondence, General subject, 1933, NACP 88; see also a reprint of a speech he gave, published in the GFWC's official organ, "The passage of the bill was due the women's federated clubs of the country. Trust them to put over the goalline every time." *Federation Bulletin* (December 1911), 133.

works cited

Archival Sources

American Institute for the History of Pharmacy, Legislation, Cosmetics and Journal Collections.

American Medical Association Historical Health Fraud and Alternative Medicine Collection.

Cosmetic, Toiletries and Fragrance Association, Library and *Bulletin* collection, Washington, DC.

Duke University Special Collections, Hartmann Center for Sales, Advertising and Marketing History, J. Walter Thompson Archives.

Franklin and Eleanor Roosevelt Library, files of Eleanor Roosevelt, Rexford Tugwell, Presidential Personal Files, Presidential Office Files.

Food and Drug Administration, History Office.

General Federation of Women's Clubs, Washington, DC, Manuscripts and Archives Collections.

Hagley Museum and Center for Business History, Avon Collection.

Indiana Historical Society, Madam C. J. Walker Papers.

Library of Congress, Anna Kelton Wiley Papers.

Michigan Historical Society, Royal S. Copeland Papers.

National Archives, College Park and Washington, DC.: Records of the U.S. Department of Agriculture (Record Group 16); Food and Drug Administration (Record Group 88); U.S. Post Office (Record Group 122); Federal Trade Commission (Record Group 25).

National Cosmetology Association, Museum of Cosmetology, Arts and Sciences journals and oral history collections, Chicago, IL.

Rutgers University, Special Collections, Consumers' Research.

Smith College, Sophia Smith Collection, League of Women Voters Records.

Vassar College, Special Collections, Ruth Lamb Askinson Papers.

Secondary Sources

Accum, Frederick. *A Treatise on the Adulteration of Food* (Philadelphia: 1820).

Adams, Samuel Hopkins. *The Great American Fraud*. New York: P. F. Collier & Son, 1907.

Allen, Frederick. *Only Yesterday: An Informal History of the Nineteen-Twenties*. New York: Harper & Brothers Publishers, 1931.

Andersen, Kristi. *After Suffrage: Women in Partisan and Elected Political Before the New Deal*. Chicago: University of Chicago Press, 1995.

Anderson, Oscar. *The Health of the Nation: Harvey W. Wiley and the Fight for Pure Food*. Chicago: University of Chicago Press, 1958.

Angeloglou, Magee. *A History of Make-up*. New York: Macmillan, 1970.

Apple, Rima. *Vitamania: Vitamins in American Culture*. New Brunswick: Rutgers University Press, 1996.

Askinson, George W. *Perfumes and Cosmetics, Their Preparation and Manufacture*. New York, Norman W. Healey Publishing Co., 1915.

Ayer, Harriet Hubbard. *Harriet Hubbard Ayer's Book of Health and Beauty*. New York: King-Richardson, 1902.

Ayer, Margaret Hubbard, and Taves, Isabella. *The Three Lives of Harriet Hubbard Ayer*. Philadelphia: J. B. Lippincott Company, 1957.

Badger, Anthony J. *The New Deal: The Depression Years, 1933–1941*. New York: Hill and Wang, 1989.

Bailey, Beth. *From Front Porch to Back Seat: Courtship in Twentieth-Century America*. Baltimore: Johns Hopkins University Press, 1988.

Balis, Andrea. "Miracle Medicine: The Impact of Sulfa Drugs on Medicine, the Pharmacy Industry, and Government Regulation in the U.S. in the 1930s." Ph.D. diss., CUNY, 2000.

Banner, Lois. *American Beauty*. Chicago: University of Chicago Press, 1983.

Basten, Fred, with Robert Salvatore and Paul Kaufman. *Max Factor's Hollywood: Glamour, Movies, and Make-up*. New York: General Publishing Group, 1995.

Beard, Mary Ritter. *America through Women's Eyes*. New York: The Macmillan Company, 1933.

———. *Woman as Force in History: A Study in Tradition and Realities*. New York: The Macmillan Company, 1946.

Benson, Elizabeth. *The Younger Generation, With an Introduction by Frank Crowninshield*. New York: Greenberg Publisher, 1927.

Benson, Susan Porter. *Counter Cultures: Saleswomen, Managers, and Customers in American Department Stores, 1890–1940*. Urbana: University of Illinois Press.

Berle, Adolf. *America's Recovery Program*. London: Oxford University Press, 1934.

Bichet, Paul E. *History of the American Dermatological Association in Commemoration of Its 75th Anniversary*. New York: Froben Press, 1952.

Blackwelder, Julia Kirk. *Now Hiring: The Feminization of Work in the United States, 1900–1995*. College Station: Texas A&M University Press, 1997.

Blair, Karen. *The Clubwoman as Feminist: True Womanhood Redefined, 1858–1914*. New York: Holmes & Meier Publishers, 1980

Blake, Mabelle Babcock. *The Education of the Modern Girl*. Boston and New York: Houghton Mifflin Company, 1929.

Blaszczyk, Regina. *Imagining Consumers: Design and Innovation from Wedgewood to Corning*. Baltimore: Johns Hopkins University Press, 2000.

Bordin, Ruth. *Woman and Temperance: The Quest for Power and Liberty, 1873–1900*. Philadelphia: Temple University Press, 1983.

Borus, Daniel (Ed.). *These United States: Portraits of America from the 1920s*. Ithaca: Cornell University Press, 1992.

Breckinridge, Sophonisba P. *Women in the Twentieth Century: A Study of Their Political, Social and Economic Activities*. New York: McGraw-Hill Book Company, Inc., 1933.

Brinkley, Alan. *Voices of Protest: Huey Long, Father Coughlin, and the Great Depression*. New York: Knopf, 1982.

Brown, Dorothy M. *American Women in the 1920s: Setting a Course*. Boston: Twayne Publishers, 1987.

Brumberg, Joan Jacobs. *Fasting Girls: The Emergence of Anorexia Nervosa as a Modern Disease*. Cambridge, MA: Harvard University Press, 1985.

———. *The Body Project: An Intimate History of American Girls*. New York: Vintage Books, 1997.

Buchanan, Anne. *The Lady Means Business: How to Reach the Top in the Business World*. New York: Simon & Schuster, 1942.

Bundles, A'Lelia. *On Her Own Ground: The Life and Times of Madam C. J. Walker*. New York: Scribner, 2001.

Burrow, James G. *AMA: Voice of American Medicine*. Baltimore: Johns Hopkins University Press, 1963.

———. *Organized Medicine in the Progressive Era: The Move Toward Monopoly*. Baltimore: Johns Hopkins University Press, 1977.

Census, U.S. Department of the Bureau of the. *Historical Statistics of the United States, Colonial Times to 1970, Bicentennial Edition, Part 1*. Washington, DC: 1975.

Chafe, William. *The American Woman: Her Changing Social, Economic, and Political Roles, 1920–1970*. New York & London: Oxford University Press, 1972.

———. *The Paradox of Change: American Women in the Twentieth Century*. New York & London: Oxford University Press, 1991.

Chase, Stuart. *The Tragedy of Waste*. New York: The League for Industrial Democracy, 1925.

———. *The Challenge of Waste*. New York: The Macmillan Company, 1929.

Chase, Stuart, and Schlink, Frederick. *Your Money's Worth: The Waste of the Consumer Dollar*. New York: The Macmillan Company, 1927.

Chilson, Francis. *Modern Cosmetics: The Formulation and Production of Cosmetics, Together with a Discussion of Modern Production and Packaging Methods and Equipment*. New York: Drug and Cosmetic Industry, 1934.

Cohen, Lizbeth. *Making a New Deal: Industrial Workers in Chicago, 1919–1934*. New York: Cambridge University Press, 1990.

Congressional Record. 58th Cong., 3d sess. 1905.

———. 59th Cong., 1st and 2d sess. 1906.

———. 74th Cong., 1st sess. 1935.

———. 74th Cong., 2d sess. 1936.

———. 75th Cong, 1st sess. 1937.

———. 75th Cong., 2d sess. 1938.

Connelly, Mark. *The Response to Prostitution in the Progressive Era*. Chapel Hill: University of North Carolina Press, 1980.

Cooley, Arnold J. *The Toilet and Cosmetic Arts in Ancient and Modern Times*. Philadelphia: Lindsay & Blakiston, 1866.

Cott, Nancy. *The Grounding of Modern Feminism*. New Haven: Yale University Press, 1987.

Coulter, Harris. *Science and Ethics in American Medicine, 1800 to 1914*. Richmond, CA: North Atlantic Books, 1982.

Courtenay, Florence. *Physical Beauty: How to Develop and Preserve It*. New York: Social Culture Publications, 1922.

Cowan, Ruth Schwartz. *More Work for Mother: The Ironies of Household Technology from the Open Hearth to the Microwave*. New York: Basic Books, 1983.

Cramp, Arthur. *Nostrums and Quackery*. Chicago: American Medical Association, 1911, 1913, and 1935.

Crissey, John Thorne, and Parish, Lawrence Charles. *The Dermatology and Syphilology of the Nineteenth Century*. New York: Praeger Scientific, 1981.

Croly, Jane Cunningham. *The History of the Woman's Club Movement in America*. Washington, DC: General Federation of Women's Clubs, 1898.

Damon-Moore, Helen. *Magazines for the Millions: Gender and Commerce in the "Ladies' Home Journal" and the "Saturday Evening Post," 1880–1910*. Albany: SUNY Press, 1994.

Davis, Marjorie. *A Woman's Place Is at the Typewriter: Office Work and Office Workers, 1870–1980*. Philadelphia: Temple University Press, 1982.

Davis, Maxine. *The Lost Generation: A Portrait of American Youth Today*. New York: The Macmillan Company, 1936.

Deets, Picket. *Enemies of Youth*. Washington, DC: The Capital Book Company, 1925.

D'Emilio, John, and Freedman, Estelle. *Intimate Matters: A History of Sexuality in America*. New York: Harper & Row, 1988.

Diner, Steven. *A Very Different Age: Americans of the Progressive Era*. New York: Hill & Wang, 1998.

Doolittle, Jan. "'Organized and Under Attack': The Women's Joint Congressional Committee and Its Legislative Campaigns for Mothers and Children, 1920–1930." Ph.D. diss., Binghamton University, 2000.

Douglas, Ann. *The Feminization of American Culture*. New York: Knopf, 1977.

———. *Terrible Honesty: Mongrel Manhattan in the 1920s*. New York: Knopf, 1995.

Douglas, Mary. *Purity and Danger: An Analysis of Concepts of Pollution and Taboo*. London: Routledge & Kegan Paul, 1966.

Due, Tananarive. *The Black Rose*. New York: One World (Ballantine Books), 2000.

Duffy, John. *The Sanitarians: A History of American Public Health*. Urbana: University of Illinois Press, 1990.

Dumenil, Lynn. *Modern Temper: American Culture and Society in the 1920s*. New York: Hill and Wang, 1995.

Ehrenreich, Barbara, and English, Deirdre. *For Her Own Good: 150 Years of the Experts' Advice to Women*. Garden City, NY: Anchor Press, 1978.

Engel, Jonathan. *Doctors and Reformers: Discussion and Debate over Health Policy, 1925–1950*. Charleston: University of South Carolina Press, 2002.

Ettling, John. *The Germ of Laziness: Rockefeller Philanthropy and Public Health in the New South*. Cambridge: Harvard University Press, 1981.

Ewen, Stuart. *Captains of Consciousness: Advertising and the Social Roots of the Consumer Culture*. New York: McGraw-Hill, 1976.

Fabe, Maxene. *Beauty Millionaire: The Life of Helena Rubinstein*. New York: Thomas Y. Crowell, 1972.

Fass, Paula. *The Damned and the Beautiful: American Youth in the 1920s*. New York: Oxford University Press, 1977.

Filene, Catherine (Ed.). *Careers for Women: New Ideas, New Methods, New Opportunities—To Fit a New World*. New York: Houghton Mifflin Company, 1920.

Filler, Louis. *The Muckrakers*. Stanford: Stanford University Press, 1968.

Fishbein, Morris. *The New Medical Follies: An Encyclopedia of Cultism and Quackery in These United States*. New York: Boni and Liveright, 1927.

———. *History of the American Medical Association, 1847–1947*. Philadelphia & London: W. B. Saunders Co., 1947.

Fisher, Dorothy Canfield. *Our Young Folks*. New York: Harcourt Brace & Company, 1943.

Fox, Richard Wightman, and Lears, T. J. Jackson (Eds.). *The Culture of Consumption: Critical Essays in American History, 1880–1980*. New York: Pantheon Press, 1983.

———. *The Power of Culture: Critical Essays in American History*. Chicago: University of Chicago Press, 1993.

Fox, Stephen R. *The Mirror-Makers: A History of American Advertising and Its Creators*. New York: Morrow, 1984.

Frankel, Noralee, and Dye, Nancy S. (Eds.). *Gender, Class, Race and Reform in the Progressive Era*. Lexington: University of Kentucky Press, 1991.

Furrman, Frida Kerner. *Facing the Mirror: Older Women and Beauty Shop Culture*. New York & London: Routledge, 1997.

Fye, Bruce. *American Cardiology: The History of a Specialty and Its College*. Baltimore: Johns Hopkins University Press, 1996.

Garceau, Oliver. *The Political Life of the AMA*. Hamden, CT: Archon Books, 1941.

Garvey, Ellen Gruber. *The Adman in the Parlor: Magazines and the Gendering of Consumer Culture, 1880s to 1910s*. New York: Oxford University Press, 1996.

Gavenas, Mary Lisa. *Color Stories: Behind the Scenes of America's Billion-Dollar Beauty Industry*. New York: Simon & Schuster, 2002.

Gelertner, David. *The 1939 World's Fair*. New York: Basic Books, 1996.

Ginzberg, Lori. *Women and the Work of Benevolence: Morality, Politics and Class in the Nineteenth-Century United States*. New Haven, CT: Yale University Press, 1990.

Goodman, Herman. *Your Hair: Its Health, Beauty and Growth*. Garden City, New York: Halcyon House, 1943.

Goodwin, Lorine Swainston. *The Pure Food, Drink, and Drug Crusaders, 1879–1914*. Jefferson, NC: McFarland & Company, Inc., Publishers, 1999.

Gottseman, Ronald. Introduction to *The Jungle*, by Upton Sinclair. New York: Penguin Classics, 1985.

Grier, Katherine G. *Culture and Comfort: Parlor-making and Middle-Class Identity, 1850–1935*. Washington, DC: Smithsonian Institution Press, 1997.

Gunn, Fenja. *Artificial Face*. New York: 1971.

Haber, Samuel. *The Quest for Authority and Honor in the American Professions, 1750–1900*. Chicago: University of Chicago Press, 1991.

Haiken, Beth. *Venus Envy: A History of Cosmetic Surgery*. Baltimore: Johns Hopkins University Press, 1997.

Halpern, Sydney. *American Pediatrics and Social Dynamics of Profession, 1880–1980*. Berkeley: University of California Press, 1988.

Halttunen, Karen. *Confidence Men and Painted Ladies: A Study of Middle-Class Culture in America, 1830–1870.* New Haven: Yale University Press, 1982.

Harap, Henry. *The Education of the Consumer: A Study in the Curriculum Matter.* New York: The Macmillan Company, 1924.

Harrigan, Johanne. "The Making of a Contender: The Political Awakening of the American Medical Association and Its Impact on the Sheppard-Towner Act." M.A. thesis, Oswego State University, 2003.

Harris, Alice Kessler. *Women Have Always Worked: An Historical Overview.* Old Westbury: Feminist Press, 1981.

———. *Out to Work: A History of America's Wage-Earning Women.* New York: Oxford University Press, 1982.

Harris, Barbara. *Beyond Her Sphere: Women and the Professions in American History.* Westport, CT: Greenwood Press, 1978.

Harvey, Ellen Gruber. *The Adman in the Parlor: Magazines and the Gendering of Consumer Culture, 1880s to 1910s.* New York: Oxford University Press, 1996.

Hayes, Samuel P. *Conservatism and the Gospel of Efficiency: The Progressive Conservation Movement, 1890–1920.* Cambridge, MA: Harvard University Press, 1959.

Henderson, Gerald. *The Federal Trade Commission: A Study in Administrative Law and Practice.* New Haven, CT: Yale University Press, 1924.

Hickok, Lorena. *One-Third of a Nation: Lorena Hickok Reports on the Great Depression.* Urbana: University of Illinois Press, 1981.

Hill, Joseph. *Women in Gainful Occupations, 1870 to 1920.* Washington, DC: U.S. Bureau of the Census, 1929.

Hillis, Marjorie. *Live Alone and Like It: A Guide for the Extra Woman.* New York: The Bobbs-Merrill Company, 1936.

Hilts, Philip J. *Protecting America's Health: The FDA, Business, and One Hundred Years of Regulation.* New York: Alfred A. Knopf, 2003.

Hine, Darlene Clark. *Black Women in White: Racial Conflict and Cooperation in Nursing, 1890–1950.* Bloomington: Indiana University Press, 1989.

Hobson, Barbara. *Uneasy Virtue: The Politics of Prostitution and the American Reform Tradition.* New York: Basic Books, 1987.

Hoffman, Beatrix. *The Wages of Sickness: The Politics of Health Insurance in Progressive America.* Chapel Hill: University of North Carolina Press, 2001.

Hofstadter, Richard. *The Age of Reform: From Bryan to F.D.R.* New York: Vintage, 1955.

———. *The Progressive Movement, 1900–1915.* Englewood Cliffs, NJ: Prentice Hall, 1963.

Holt, W. Stull. *The Federal Trade Commission: Its History, Activities and Organizations.* New York: D. Appleton and Company, 1922.

Horowitz, Helen Lefkowitz. *Campus Life: Undergraduate Cultures from the End of the Eighteenth Century to the Present.* New York: Alfred A. Knopf, 1987.

Houde, Mary Jean. *Reaching Out: A Story of the General Federation of Women's Clubs.* Chicago: The Mobium Press, 1989.

Hoy, Suellen. *Chasing Dirt: The American Pursuit of Cleanliness.* New York: Oxford University Press, 1995.

Humphrey, Mrs. *Beauty Adorned.* London: T. Fisher Unwin, 1901.

Irwin, Inez Hayes. *Angels and Amazons: A Hundred Years of American Women.*

Garden City, NY: Doubleday, Doran & Company, Inc., 1934.

Jackson, Charles. *Food and Drug Legislation in the New Deal.* Princeton: Princeton University Press, 1970.

Joseph, Max. *A Short Handbook on Cosmetics,* authorized English translation. New York: E. B. Treat & Co., 1910.

Kallet, Arthur, and Schlink, F. J. *100,000,000 Guinea Pigs: Dangers in Everyday Foods, Drugs, and Cosmetics.* New York: The Vanguard Press, 1933.

Kennedy, David. *Freedom from Fear: The American People in Depression and War, 1920–1945.* New York: Oxford University Press, 1993.

Kleinfeld, Sonny. *Staying at the Top: The Life of a CEO.* New York: New American Library 1986.

Kolko, Gabriel. *The Triumph of Conservatism: A Reinterpretation of American History, 1900–1916.* New York: Free Press of Glencoe, 1963.

Krutch, Joseph Wood. *The Modern Temper: A Study and a Confession.* New York: Harcourt, Brace & Company, 1929.

Kurian, Georg (Ed.). *The Historical Guide to American Government.* New York: Oxford University Press, 1998.

Kwolek-Folland, Angel. *Incorporating Women: A History of Women and Business in the United States.* New York: Twayne Publishers, 1998.

Ladd-Taylor, Molly. *Mother-Work: Women, Child Welfare and the State, 1890–1930.* Urbana: University of Illinois Press, 1994.

Laird, Pamela. *Advertising Progress: American Business and the Rise of Consumer Marketing.* Baltimore: Johns Hopkins University Press, 1998.

Lake Placid Conferences on Home Economics: Proceedings (Essex County, New York: Lake Placid Club, n.d. [c. 1910]).

Lamb, Ruth deForest. *American Chamber of Horrors: The Truth about Food and Drugs.* New York: Farrar and Rinehart, 1936.

Leach, William. *Land of Desire: From the Department Store to the Department of Commerce, The Rise of America's Commercial Culture.* New York: Pantheon Books, 1993.

Lears, T. J. Jackson. *No Place of Grace: Antimodernism and the Transformation of American Culture, 1880–1920.* New York: Pantheon Books, 1981.

———. *Fables of Abundance: A Cultural History of Advertising in America.* New York: Basic Books, 1994.

Leavitt, Judith Walzer. *The Healthiest City: Milwaukee and the Politics of Health.* Princeton: Princeton University Press, 1982.

Leavitt, Sarah. *From Catherine Beecher to Martha Stewart: A Cultural History of Domestic Advice.* Chapel Hill: University of North Carolina Press, 2002.

Leuchtenburg, William E. *The Perils of Prosperity, 1914–32.* Chicago: University of Chicago Press, 1958.

———. *Franklin D. Roosevelt and the New Deal: 1932–1940.* New York: Harper & Row, 1963.

Levin, Oscar L. *Save Your Hair!* New York: Greenberg Publishers, Inc., 1926.

Levine, Lawrence. *Highbrow/Lowbrow: The Emergence of Cultural Hierarchy in America.* Cambridge: Harvard University Press, 1988.

Lewis, Alfred Allan, and Woodworth, Constance. *Miss Elizabeth Arden.* New York: Coward, McCAnn & Geoghegan, Inc., 1972.

Lindenmeyer, Kriste. *A Right to Childhood: The U.S. Children's Bureau and Child*

Welfare, 1912–1946. Urbana: University of Illinois Press, 1997.

Lindsey, Benjamin, and Evans, Wainwright. *The Revolt of Modern Youth*. New York: Boni & Liveright, 1925.

Link, Arthur S. *Woodrow Wilson and the Progressive Era, 1910–1917*. New York: Harper Torchbooks, 1954.

Lynd, Robert, and Lynd, Helen Merrell. *Middletown: A Study in Modern American Culture*. New York: Harcourt Brace Jovanovich, 1929.

MacDonald, Fred. *Don't Touch That Dial! Radio Programming in American Life, 1920–1960*. Chicago: Nelson-Hall, 1979.

MacFadden, Bernard. *Hair Culture: Rational Methods for Growing the Hair and for Developing Its Strength and Beauty*. New York: MacFadden Publications, Inc., 1924.

MacFadyen, Mary. *Beauty Plus—The Smart Woman's Key to Beauty, Health and Charm*. New York: Emerson Books, Inc., 1938.

Manko, Katina Lee. "'Ding, Dong! Avon Calling!' Gender, Business and Door-to-Door Selling, 1890–1955." Ph.D. diss., University of Delaware, 2001.

Marchand, Roland. *Advertising the American Dream: Making Way for Modernity, 1920–1940*. Berkeley: University of California Press, 1985.

Marino, Marianne, *Max Factor: The Man Who Changed the Face of the World*. Tale Weaver, 1989.

Marks, Harry. *The Progress of Experiment: Science and Therapeutic Reform in the United States, 1900–1990*. New York: Cambridge University Press, 1997.

Matthews, Glenna. *The Rise of the Public Woman: Woman's Power and Woman's Place in the United States, 1630–1970*. New York: Oxford University Press, 1992.

Mattson, Kevin. *Creating a Democratic Public: The Struggle for Urban Participatory Democracy during the Progressive Era*. University Park: Pennsylvania State University Press, 1998.

May, Henry. *The End of American Innocence: A Study of the First Years of Our Own Time, 1912–1917*. New York: Columbia University Press, 1957.

Mayer, Robert N. *The Conservative Movement: Guardians of the Marketplace*. Boston: Twayne Publishing, 1989.

McDonough, Everett G. *Truth about Cosmetics*. New York: Drug and Cosmetic Industry, 1937.

McElvaine, Robert. *The Great Depression: America, 1929–1941*. New York: Times Books, 1993.

Meckel, Richard. *"Save the Babies": American Public Health Reform and the Prevention of Infant Mortality, 1850–1929*. Baltimore: Johns Hopkins University Press, 1990.

Meyerowitz, Joanna J. *Women Adrift: Independent Wage Earners in Chicago, 1880–1930*. Chicago: University of Chicago Press, 1988.

Moats, Alice Leone. *No Nice Girl Swears*. New York: Knopf, 1936.

Modern Brides: Mechanical Technology in the Workplace. New York: Cooper-Hewitt, 1994.

Mohr, James. *Doctors and the Law: Medical Jurisprudence in Nineteenth-Century America*. New York: Oxford University Press, 1993.

Moley, Raymond. *After Seven Years*. New York: Harper & Brothers, 1939.

———. *The First New Deal*. New York: Harcourt, Brace & World, 1966.

Morris, Edmund. *Theodore Rex*. New York: Random House, 2001.

Mowry. *Theodore Roosevelt and the Progressive Movement*. Madison: University of Wisconsin Press, 1946.

Muller, Richard. *Hair: Its Nature, Growth and Most Common Affections, with Hygienic Rules for Its Preservation*. New York: William R. Jenkins Company, 1913.

Munro, Leaf. *Listen Little Girl: Before You Come to New York*. New York: Frederick A. Stokes Company, 1938.

Namorato, Michael. *Rexford G. Tugwell: A Biography*. New York: Praeger, 1988.

Namorato, Michael (Ed.). *The Diary of Rexford G. Tugwell: The New Deal: 1932–1935*. New York: Greenwood Press, 1992.

Norris, James. *Advertising and the Transformation of American Society, 1865–1920*. New York: Greenwood Press, 1990.

Nostrums and Quackery. Chicago: American Medical Association, 1906 (vol. 1), 1921 (vol. 2), and 1936 (vol. 3).

Numbers, Ronald. *Almost Persuaded: American Physicians and Compulsory Health Insurance, 1912–1920*. Baltimore: Johns Hopkins University Press, 1978.

O'Higgins, Patrick. *Madame: An Intimate Biography of Helena Rubinstein*. New York: The Viking Press, 1971.

O'Neill, William. *The Progressive Years: America Comes of Age*. New York: Dodd, Mead, 1975.

Okun, Mitchell. *Fair Play in the Market Place: The First Battle for Pure Food and Drugs*. DeKalb: Northern Illinois University Press, 1986.

Olney, Martha M. *Buy Now, Pay Later: Advertising, Credit and Consumer Durables in the 1920s*. Chapel Hill: University of North Carolina Press, 1991.

Peiss, Kathy. *Cheap Amusements: Working Women and Leisure in Turn-of-the-Century New York*. Philadelphia: Temple University Press, 1986.

———. *Hope in a Jar: The Making of America's Beauty Culture*. New York: Metropolitan Books, 1998.

Peters, Lulu Hunt. *Diet and Health, with Key to the Calories*. Chicago: The Reilly and Lee Co., 1918.

———. *Diet for Children (and Adults) and the Kalorie Kids*. New York: Dodd, Mead, 1924.

Phillips, M. C. *Skin Deep: The Truth about Beauty Aids—Safe and Harmful*. New York: The Vanguard Press, 1934.

Pivar, David. *Purity and Hygiene: Women, Prostitution and the "American Plan," 1900–1930*. Westport, CT: Greenwood Press, 2002.

Poucher, William. *Perfumes, Cosmetics and Soaps*. London: Chapman & Hall, 1930.

Preston, Ivan. *The Great American Blowup: Puffery in Advertising and Selling*, rev. ed. Madison: University of Wisconsin Press, 1996.

Putnam, Nina Wilcox. *Tomorrow We Diet*. New York: George H. Doran Company, 1922.

Pusey, William Allen. *The Care of Skin and Hair*. New York: D. Appleton Company, 1912.

Radway, Janice. *A Feeling for the Book: The Book-of-the-Month Club, Literary Taste, and Middle-Class Desire*. Chapel Hill: University of North Carolina Press, 1992.

Reverby, Susan. *Ordered to Care: The Dilemma of American Nursing, 1850–1945*. New York: Cambridge University Press, 1987.

Reverby, Susan, and Rosner, David. *Health Care in America: Essays in Social History*. Philadelphia: Temple University Press, 1979.

Riepma, S. F. *The Story of Margarine.* Washington, DC: Public Affairs Press, 1970.

Robinson, Gwendolyn. "Class, Race, and Gender: A Transcultural Theoretical and Sociohistorical Analysis of Cosmetic Institutions and Practices to 1920." Ph.D. diss., University of Illinois at Chicago, 1984.

Rooks, Noliwe M. *Hair Raising: Beauty, Culture, and African American Women.* New Brunswick: Rutgers University Press, 1996.

Rosen, Elliot. *Hoover, Roosevelt and the Brains Trust: From Depression to New Deal.* New York: Columbia University Press, 1972.

Rosen, George. *The Specialization of Medicine, with Particular Reference to Ophthalmology.* New York: Froben Press, 1944.

Rosen, Ruth. *The Lost Sisterhood: Prostitution in America, 1900–1918.* Baltimore: The Johns Hopkins University Press, 1983.

Rosenberg, Charles. *Explaining Epidemics and Other Studies in the History of Medicine.* Cambridge: Cambridge University Press, 1992.

Rosenberg, Rosalind. *Beyond Separate Spheres: Intellectual Roots of Modern Feminism.* New Haven: Yale University Press, 1982.

———. *Divided Lives: American Women in the Twentieth Century.* New York: Hill and Wang, 1992.

Rosensweig, Roy. *Eight Hours for What We Will: Workers and Leisure in an Industrial City, 1870–1920.* Cambridge: Cambridge University Press, 1983.

Rossiter, Margaret. *Women Scientists in America: Struggles and Strategies to 1940.* Baltimore: The Johns Hopkins University Press, 1982.

Rothstein, William. *American Physicians in the Nineteenth Century: From Sects to Science.* Baltimore: Johns Hopkins University, 1972.

Rubin, Joan Shelley. *The Making of Middlebrow Culture.* Chapel Hill: University of North Carolina Press, 1992.

Rubenstein, Helena. *The Art of Feminine Beauty.* New York: Horace Liveright, Inc., 1930.

———. *My Life for Beauty.* New York: Simon & Schuster, 1964.

Ryan, Mary. *Women in Public Life: Between Banners and Ballots, 1825–1880.* Baltimore: Johns Hopkins University Press, 1990.

Rydell, Robert W. *World of Fairs: The Century-of-Progress Expositions.* Chicago: University of Chicago Press, 1993.

Rydell, Robert, et al. *Fair America: World's Fairs in the United States.* Washington, DC: Smithsonian Institution Press, 2000.

Sagarin, Edward. *Cosmetics: Science and Technology.* New York: Interscience Publishers, Inc., 1957.

Sammons, Romeyn. *Cosmetology Jurisprudence: A Treatise and Manual on the Legal Liabilities, Duties and Constitutional Rights of Beauty Culture Operators, Cosmeticians and Barbers, and of Manufacturers and Dealers in Appliance, Cosmetics, Drugs, etc.* Los Angeles: Parker & Baird Company, 1938.

Scanlon, Jennifer. *Inarticulate Longings: The* Ladies' Home Journal, *Gender and the Promises of Consumer Culture.* New York & London: Routledge, 1995.

Scharf, Lois. *To Work and to Wed: Female Employment, Feminism, and the Great Depression.* Westport: Greenwood Press, 1980.

Scharf, Lois, and Jensen, Joan M (Eds.). *Decades of Discontent: The Women's Movement, 1920–1940.* Boston: Northeastern University Press, 1987.

Scharff, Virginia. *Taking the Wheel: Women and the Coming of the Motor Age*. New York: Free Press, 1991.

Schisgall, Oscar. *Eyes on Tomorrow: The Evolution of Procter & Gamble*. Chicago: J. G. Ferguson Publishing Co., 1981.

Schlesinger, Arthur M., Jr. *Learning How to Behave: A Historical Study of American Etiquette Books*. New York: The Macmillan Company, 1946.

———. *The Coming of the New Deal: The Age of Roosevelt*. New York: Houghton Mifflin Company, 1958.

———. *The Politics of Upheaval: The Age of Roosevelt*. New York: Houghton Mifflin Company, 1960.

Schlink, Frederick. *Eat, Drink, and Be Wary*. New York: The Vanguard Press, 1935.

Scott, Anne Firor. *Natural Allies: Women's Associations in American History*. Urbana: University of Illinois Press, 1991.

Scranton, Philip (Ed.). *Beauty and Business: Commerce, Gender, and Culture in Modern America*. New York and London: Routledge, 2001.

Silber, Norman I. *Test and Protest: The Influence of Consumers' Union*. New York: Holmes & Meier, 1983.

Sinclair, Upton. *The Jungle*. Ronald Gottesman, ed. New York: Penguin Classics, 1985.

Sklar, Katherine Kish. *Florence Kelley and the Nation's Work: The Rise of Women's Political Culture, 1830–1900*. New Haven, CT: Yale University Press, 1995.

Slosson, Preston. *The Great Crusade and After, 1914–1928*. New York: The Macmillan Company, 1931.

Stage, Sarah. *Female Complaints: Lydia Pinkham and the Business of Women's Medicine*. New York: W. W. Norton, 1979.

Stage, Sarah, and Vincenti, Virginia (Eds.). *Rethinking Home Economics: Women and the History of a Profession*. Ithaca, NY: Cornell University Press, 1997.

Starr, Paul. *Social Transformation of American Medicine*. New York: Basic Books, 1982.

Sternsher, Bernard. *Rexford Tugwell and the New Deal*. New York: Knopf, 1964.

Stevens, Rosemary. *American Medicine and the Public Interest*. Berkeley: University of California Press, 1998.

Strasser, Susan. *Never Done: A History of American Housework*. New York: Pantheon, 1982.

———. *Satisfaction Guaranteed: The Making of America's Mass Market*. Washington, DC: Smithsonian Institution Press, 1995.

Sullivan, Mark. *Our Times: The United States, 1900–1925*. New York: Charles Scribner's Sons, 1925–1935.

———. *The Education of an American*. New York: Doubleday, 1938.

Taylor, Molly Ladd. *Raising a Baby the Government Way: Mothers' Letters to the Children's Bureau, 1915–1932*. New Brunswick: Rutgers University Press, 1986.

Temin, Peter. *The Great Depression*. Cambridge, MA: National Bureau of Economic Research, 1994.

Tentler, Leslie. *Wage-Earning Women: Industrial Work and Family Life in the United States, 1900–1930*. New York: Oxford University Press, 1979.

Terkel, Studs. *Hard Times: An Oral History of the Great Depression*. New York: Avon Books, 1970.

Thompson Company, J. Walter. *Population and Its Distribution.* New York: McGraw-Hill, 1952.

Tobey, James. *The Children's Bureau: Its History, Activities and Organization.* Baltimore: Johns Hopkins University Press, 1925.

Tobias, Andrew. *Fire and Ice: The Story of Charles Revson.* New York: Warner Books, 1975.

Todd, Jan. *Physical Culture and the Body Beautiful: Purposive Exercise in the Lives of American Women, 1800–1870.* Macon, GA: Mercer University Press, 1998.

Tomes, Nancy. *The Gospel of Germs: Men, Women, and the Microbe in American Life.* Cambridge: Harvard University Press, 1998.

Trachtenberg, Alan. *The Incorporation of America: Culture and Society in the Gilded Age.* New York: Hill and Wang, 1982.

Tugwell, Rexford. *The Brains Trust.* New York: Viking Press, 1968.

Unofficial Observer [James Franklin Carter]. *The New Dealers.* New York: The Literary Guild, 1934. U.S. Agriculture Department. Bureau of Chemistry. *Bulletin #84: Influence of Food Preservatives and Artificial Colors on Digestion and Health.* Washington, DC: 1904–8.

U.S. Agriculture Department. Division of Chemistry. *Bulletin #13: Food and Food Adulterants.* Washington, DC: 1887–1902.

Vail, Gilbert. *A History of Cosmetics in America.* New York: Toilet Goods Association, 1947.

Verbrugge, Martha. *Able-Bodied Womanhood: Personal Health and Social Change in Nineteenth-Century Boston.* New York: Oxford University Press, 1986.

Vinikas, Vincent. *Soft Soap, Hard Sell: American Hygiene in an Age of Advertisement.* Ames: Iowa State University Press, 1992.

Wade, Louise Carroll. *Chicago's Pride: The Stockyards, Packingtown, and Environs in the Nineteenth Century.* Urbana: University of Illinois Press, 1987.

Walsh, Margaret. *The Rise of the Midwestern Packing Industry.* Lexington: University Press of Kentucky, 1982.

Ware, Susan. *American Women in the 1930s: Holding Their Own.* Boston: Twayne Publishers, 1982.

Warne, Colston. *The Consumer Movement: Lectures.* Manhattan, KS: Family Economics Trust Press, 1993.

Warner, John Harley. *The Therapeutic Perspective: Medical Practice, Knowledge, and Identity in America, 1820–1885.* Cambridge: Harvard University Press, 1986.

Watkins, T. H. *The Great Depression: America in the 1930s.* Boston: Little, Brown, 1993.

Weber, Gustavus. *The Food, Drug and Insecticide Administration: Its History, Activities, and Organization.* Baltimore: Johns Hopkins University, 1928.

Weinberg, Arthur, and Lila Weinberg. *The Muckrakers: The Era in Journalism That Moved America to Reform—The Most Significant Articles of 1901–1912.* New York: Simon & Schuster, 1961.

Weiner, Lynn. *From Working Girl to Working Mother: The Female Labor Force in the United States.* Chapel Hill: University of North Carolina Press, 1985.

Wells, Mildred White. *Unity in Diversity: The History of the General Federation of Women's Clubs.* Washington: General Federation of Women's Clubs, 1953, 1975.

Westin, Jeanne. *Making Do: How Women Survived the 1930s.* Chicago: Follett, 1976.

Wiebe, Robert. *The Search for Order, 1877–1920*. New York: Hill & Wang, 1967.

Wiley, Harvey. *An Autobiography*. Indianapolis: The Bobbs-Merrill company, 1930.

———. *The History of a Crime against the Food Law*. New York: Arno Press reprint, 1976.

Willet, Julie A. *Permanent Waves: The Making of the American Beauty Shop*. New York: New York University Press, 2000.

Wilson, Stephen. *Food and Drug Regulations*. Washington, DC: American Council on Public Affairs, 1942.

Wolfe, Margaret Ripley. *Lucius Polk Brown and Progressive Food and Drug Control: Tennessee and New York City, 1908–1920*. Lawrence: Regents Press of Kansas, 1978.

Wood, Mary I. *The History of the General Federation of Women's Clubs for the First Twenty-Two Years of Its Organization*. New York: History Department of the GFWC, 1912.

Woodbury, William. *Beauty Culture: A Practical Handbook on the Care of the Person Designed for Both Professional and Private Use*. New York: G. W. Dillingham Company, 1910.

Woodward, Helen. *The Lady Persuaders*. New York: Ivan Obolensky, Inc., 1960.

Worcester, Donald. *The Dust Bowl: The Southern Plains in the 1930s*. New York: Oxford University Press, 1979.

Yeager, Mary. *Competition and Regulation: The Development of Oligopoly in the Meat Packing Industry*. Greenwich, CT: Jai Press, 1981.

Young, James Harvey. *The Toadstool Millionaires: A Social History of Patent Medicines in America before Federal Regulations*. Princeton: Princeton University Press, 1961.

———. *Medical Messiahs: A Social History of Health Quackery in Twentieth-Century America*. Princeton: Princeton University Press, 1967.

———, chair of the symposium. *The Early Years of Food and Drug Control*. Madison: American Institute for the History of Pharmacy, 1982.

Young, James Harvey. *Pure Food: Securing the Federal Food and Drugs Act of 1906*. Princeton: Princeton University Press, 1989.

———. *American Health Quackery: Collected Essays*. Princeton: Princeton University Press, 1992.

Zimmerman, Jonathan. *Distilling Democracy: Alcohol Education in America's Public Schools, 1880–1925*. Lawrence: University Press of Kansas, 1999.

index

WOMEN, GENDER, AND HEALTH
Susan L. Smith and Nancy Tomes, Series Editors

This series focuses on the history of women and health, but also includes studies that address gender and masculinity. Works in the series examine the history of sickness, health, and healing in relation to health workers, activists, and patients. They also explore the ways in which issues of gender, race, ethnicity, and health have reflected and shaped beliefs, values, and power dynamics in society.

Beyond the Reproductive Body: The Politics of Women's Health and Work in Early Victorian England
MARJORIE LEVINE-CLARK

Handling the Sick: The Women of St. Luke's and the Nature of Nursing, 1892–1937
TOM OLSON AND EILEEN WALSH

Any Friend of the Movement: Networking for Birth Control, 1920–1940
JIMMY ELAINE WILKINSON MEYER

Reproductive Health, Reproductive Rights: Reformers and the Politics of Maternal Welfare, 1917–1940
ROBYN L. ROSEN

Sexual Borderlands: Constructing an American Sexual Past
EDITED BY KATHLEEN KENNEDY AND SHARON ULLMAN

Don't Kill Your Baby: Public Health and the Decline of Breastfeeding in the Nineteenth and Twentieth Centuries
JACQUELINE H. WOLF

A Social History of Wet Nursing in America: From Breast to Bottle
JANET GOLDEN

Motherhood in Bondage
MARGARET SANGER

Women in Labor: Mothers, Medicine, and Occupational Health in the United States, 1890–1980
ALLISON L. HEPLER

Bodies of Technology: Women's Involvement with Reproductive Medicine
EDITED BY ANN R. SAETNAN, NELLY OUDSHOORN, AND MARTA KIREJCZYK